Haile Selassie

Haile Selassie

His Rise, His Fall

~

Haggai Erlich

LYNNE
RIENNER
PUBLISHERS

BOULDER
LONDON

Published in the United States of America in 2019 by
Lynne Rienner Publishers, Inc.
1800 30th Street, Boulder, Colorado 80301
www.rienner.com

and in the United Kingdom by
Lynne Rienner Publishers, Inc.
Gray's Inn House, 127 Clerkenwell Road, London EC1 5DB

Library of Congress Cataloging-in-Publication Data
Names: Erlich, Haggai, author.
Title: Haile Selassie : his rise, his fall / Haggai Erlich.
Description: Boulder, Colorado : Lynne Rienner Publishers, 2018. |
   Includes bibliographical references and index.
Identifiers: LCCN 2018026431 (print) | LCCN 2018030584 (ebook) |
   ISBN 9781626377639 (ebook) | ISBN 9781626377547 (hardcover : alk. paper)
Subjects: LCSH: Haile Selassie I, Emperor of Ethiopia, 1892–1975. |
   Ethiopia—Kings and rulers—Biography.
Classification: LCC DT387.7 (ebook) | LCC DT387.7 .E75 2018 (print) |
   DDC 963/.06092 [B] —dc23
LC record available at https://lccn.loc.gov/2018026431

British Cataloguing in Publication Data
A Cataloguing in Publication record for this book
is available from the British Library.

Printed and bound in the United States of America

 The paper used in this publication meets the requirements
of the American National Standard for Permanence of
Paper for Printed Library Materials Z39.48-1992.

5 4 3 2 1

Contents

~

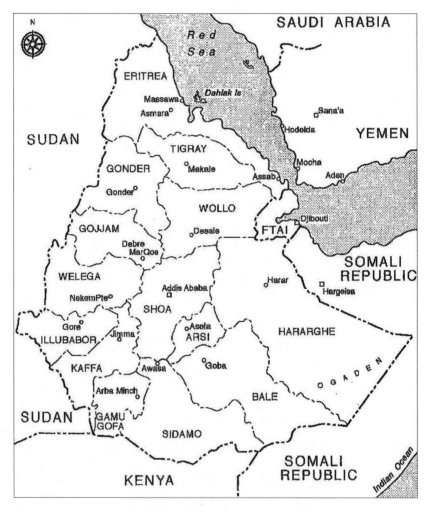

Map of Ethiopia in the 1960s

Preface

~

Who was Haile Selassie? What was the secret of his survival, and why did his life end in a brutal murder? In this book I attempt to reconstruct the life and times of Ethiopia's last emperor—one of the political icons of modern world history, and a man who believed in his own legend without noticing when it began to fade away.

Writing the book was a special experience for me. I have studied Ethiopia for more than fifty years, and I am still attracted to its uniqueness, to its biblical roots, and to its own way of coping with modern developments. As a young student, I first saw Haile Selassie in March 1972, when he came to open an exhibition in Addis Ababa. He was approaching the age of eighty, radiating intense dignity. Even an old socialist and kibbutz member, the Israeli minister of agriculture, bowed to him, as if it were the only natural thing to do. I elbowed my way to bow as well, in a vain hope to catch his eye. A few days later I encountered him again. I was waiting for the elevator in the Addis Ababa Hilton's lobby when two bodyguards arrived and pushed me aside. He entered, not bothering to nod a thank you. A third encounter nearly happened twenty years later, in February 1992, when sitting in my Tel Aviv University office I received a telephone call from Addis Ababa University. Could I come to Addis in two days? The supposed hidden grave of Haile Selassie had been located, and some historians were being invited to attend its opening. I said that I would try, but then found no credible way to explain such a request to the guardians of my university's research fund.

Much later still, in October 2016, attending a conference at Addis Ababa University, I visited Trinity Cathedral. There, in the east wing, stands the tombstone of Haile Selassie. I was about to finish the manuscript for this book, and I silently apologized to the emperor. The manuscript was not a salute to a larger-than-life figure but a balanced, scholarly story—as it should be—of Haile Selassie and of Ethiopia in his time.

* * *

My thanks go to the Israeli Academy for Science and Humanities (research grant 491/14); to my talented and resourceful research assistants, Roy Bar-Sadeh, Dekel Klein, and Or Pitusi; to Chaya Benyamin and Michelle Asakawa, who edited my English; to my publisher, Lynne Rienner, with whom I've worked for more than three decades; and to all my colleagues and students whom I forced time and again to hear the story of Haile Selassie. And, to my beloved wife, Yochi, my partner in all.

Ethiopian Names and Titles

Ethiopians have no family names. They are identified by their first name, often adding to it their father's name. A certain Makonnen Haile is the son of Haile Mangahsa whose father was Mangahsa Walda-Mariam, a son of Walda-Mariam Abebe. The full name of our hero, prior to his coronation as emperor, was Tafari Makonnen. Nobody will call him Mr. (*Ato*) Makonnen; Makonnen was his father. The same goes for all other Ethiopians—we shall mention them by their "first name" and often with their rank or title preceding it, sometimes with their father's name after it. Tafari Makonnen was promoted to the rank of a *ras*, and therefore he was known as Ras Tafari (or Ras Tafari Makonnen).

Until the 1974 revolution, and from early medieval times, there existed in Ethiopia a hierarchy of political and religious functions and titles. Following is a short list of them:

- *Abuna*: head of the church.
- *Atse*: emperor, king of kings.
- *Dajjazmach*: (commander of the door) a high rank of nobility, a general, a regional governor.

- *Echage*: head of the monks.
- *Fitawrari*: (commander of the front guard) a rank just below *Dajjazmach*.
- *Janhoy*: an appellation for the emperor.
- *Lij*: prince.
- *Negus*: king.
- *Negusa nagast*: king of kings, emperor.
- *Ras*: (head) the highest rank below a *negus*, a duke.
- *Wayzaro*: lady.

Haile Selassie in his prime, mid-1950s.

1

A Political Icon

~

Haile Selassie: His Rise, His Fall is a biography of one of the mysterious icons of the twentieth century, who reigned absolutely more years than any other ruler in our time.[1] The main argument follows Haile Selassie's greatest skill—how to read global situations and use them to ensure Ethiopian independence as well as his own personal advantage at home. The survival of Ethiopia, its territorial integrity, and its opportunity to advance in the world were all dependent on Haile Selassie, especially on his masterful ability to play the external-internal game. The following chapters tell and analyze the multifaceted story of modern Ethiopia at home and in world affairs, while examining Haile Selassie as a human being, flesh and blood.

Haile Selassie was born Tafari Makonnen, the son of Ras Makonnen, a relative of Emperor Menelik II (1889–1913). Ras Makonnen had been involved in nearly all affairs of the then thriving Christian Ethiopian empire: the victory over Western imperialism (culminating in the March 1896 battle of Adwa against the Italians), territorial expansion at the expense of local Muslims, and the cementing of Ethiopian independence. Young Tafari grew up in the town of Harar, his renowned father's citadel. His mother died soon after his birth, and his father was usually absent before dying when Tafari was fourteen years old.

Fragile in body but iron willed, young Tafari found himself swimming in a sea of palace intrigues in the capital of Addis Ababa.

If his father had been a loyal number two in the kingdom, Tafari sought to outdo his legacy. He would prove most manipulative at political combinations at home and in international affairs. He managed to exploit World War I to dispose of Menelik's official heir and assume the title *ras* (literally, "head") and successor of the new empress, Zawditu (1916–1930). In the 1920s Ras Tafari was tasked with confronting the old guard of Menelik's generation—older, experienced warlords, proud and self-assured—who strove to preserve Ethiopia's conservative feudal system. Ras Tafari opened Ethiopia to the West and joined the League of Nations in 1923. He gradually built a new layer of "Young Ethiopians," better educated and loyal to him. By the end of the decade, he was the only man left standing. With the sudden and mysterious death of the empress in 1930, Tafari was crowned Haile Selassie I. He was also proclaimed, as were all previous emperors, a descendant of King Solomon and Queen of Sheba. Like them, he became the "Lion of Judah."

Haile Selassie I was a power-hungry ruler. He saw centralization of his control as a way to ensure independence in facing foreign ambitions—mainly Italian. However, provincial rivalries, jealousies, and intrigues encouraged Mussolini's aggression and ultimately contributed to the breakout of the Second Italo-Ethiopian War and Ethiopia's consequent defeat. In 1936 the proud Lion of Judah became a humiliated refugee. He traversed years in exile, nearly forgotten in a little English town. Nevertheless, he managed to snatch a moment of glory away from that misery. His speech at the League of Nations, warning of what was to be expected from appeasing aggressive dictators, earned him a place in world history. In 1940, when Italy entered World War II on the side of Germany, the British called upon the exiled king to organize guerrilla fighters inside Ethiopia. The emperor returned and quickly rebuilt his power. As the Italians had destroyed the old provincial nobility, he became the undisputed ruler.

The following years saw Haile Selassie at his best as a reformer. He introduced innovations in the service of his own power: modern bureaucracy, renewed armed forces, new education system, and a parliamentarian constitution (1955) that defined his full power in Christian Ethiopian concepts. He also managed to release Ethiopia from Britain's sphere of influence and strengthened his country's connections to the United States. These steps helped him win the international diplomatic battle for Eritrea and gradually annex the ex-Italian colony to his empire. Subjugating the Eritreans to his absolutism and abolishing the rights they had obtained under the colonialists would prove counterproductive to stabilizing his rule.

Meanwhile, Haile Selassie toured the globe, enjoying his prestige as a symbol of the antifascist struggle. However, this time, winds of change started blowing into his biblical kingdom. Pan-Arabism energized young Muslims in Eritrea, and students returning from the West could hardly accept their political status as obedient subjects. In December 1960 his most trusted security men revolted, and he barely managed to survive. Haile Selassie considered it a revolt of ungrateful children, and it, along with a chain of disasters in his close family, marked the beginning of old age, loneliness, and conservatism. During his remaining years in power, the emperor did little to change the system and face Ethiopia's growing challenges—its backward economy, feudal politics, resentful minorities, and corrupted elite. Paradoxically, he developed education at all levels, as if preparing a new, modern generation to take over after him. In foreign affairs he still proved able to march with the times, changing his orientation from the Western powers to Africa. The emancipating continent adopted Haile Selassie as a father figure. In 1963 the Organization of African Unity (OAU) was established in Addis Ababa as a permanent headquarters. The emperor continued to enjoy his international standing—thriving on receptions and honors—while gradually sinking into old age and allowing no meaningful progress in his own kingdom.

The Lion of Judah, in a way, lived indeed like a descendant of King Solomon. According to Jewish tradition, King Solomon wrote three of the Bible's books. He is said to have composed the scroll Song of Solomon when he was young, a book full of poetic energy. In middle age he wrote the Book of Proverbs, full of wisdom. As an old man, he wrote Ecclesiastes: "The words of the Preacher, the son of David, king in Jerusalem. Vanity of Vanities, says the Preacher, Vanity of Vanities, All is vanity. What advantage does man have in all his work which he does under the sun?"[2]

This book considers the life of Haile Selassie in three parts: Chapters 2 through 4 describe his early life; his midlife is covered in Chapters 5 through 9; and Chapters 10 through 12 recount his enduring hunger for power in contrast with his deterioration, culminating in his brutal murder and humiliating end in a hidden grave.

Following his death, Haile Selassie remained a unique icon. He was, and still is, even identified with a religion. In the 1920s, black people in the Americas were redefining their self-awareness. One of their prominent leaders, Marcus Garvey, had been quoted saying

"Look to Africa, when a black king shall be crowned, for the day of deliverance is at hand." After Tafari was crowned in 1930, the Rastafarian movement began.[3] For millions of followers, Tafari's ascension to the crown was the realization of Garvey's prophecy. Thus, an international movement was born upon a triple foundation: the expectation of redemption to all blacks; a set of spiritual, biblically based Christian-Ethiopian beliefs; and the concept of Haile Selassie as a messiah, the reborn son of God. Haile Selassie, the Rastafarians believe, would redeem the blacks and return them all to Africa, the mother of humankind.

The Rastafari movement spread thanks to the world-famous singer Bob Marley and to the magic of reggae music, as well as through the bold cultural power of Rasta hair. Young people from all over the world, from all backgrounds and colors, identified with the urge for spiritual freedom expressed through Rastafari, and with the iconic image of its messiah, Haile Selassie. In 1968 the Jamaican-born Marley and his group transformed the famous song "Crying in the Chapel," a purifying Christian hymn (with over fifty different versions, including one by Elvis Presley), into: "Haile Selassie is the Chapel. . . . That man is the Angel, Our God, the King of Kings."[4]

While the myths and iconography of Haile Selassie merit study, we shall study Haile Selassie as just a man: as a king who derived power from the religious culture of Ethiopia, but who was ultimately an earthly politician, and a meaningful historical figure with all dimensions of strength and weakness.

Among Ethiopians Haile Selassie remained a controversial figure. No discussion of their modern past can avoid him. As the years pass, Ethiopia changes rapidly. New forces, emerging ethnic and religious groups, new regimes, and new challenges provide ever-renewed perspectives. We shall confine ourselves here to just a sample. After *Time* magazine published in 2011 a list of "Top 25 Political Icons"— including Haile Selassie,[5] dozens of responses were published on the Tadias Online Magazine, including the following:[6]

ANTONIO: His Majesty did a lot for Africa and for Ethiopia. Though he was not perfect and made mistakes, we should honor him and other African leaders for the good that they accomplished. My hope is that Ethiopia and other African countries do not forget their past in an ever increasingly global community. Always remember who you are and pass it on to the next generation.

TERU LEB: We need to appreciate what we had and what we have instead of always complaining and complaining and complaining. Let us appreciate him for the good he did. The bad has been elaborated for too long already.

ABDISA: He was the most outstanding leader in the modern history of Ethiopia. . . . After him the great people of Ethiopia are leaderless.

TSEHAI: Atse Haile Selassie did a lot for Ethiopia. He definitely could have done more. Let us not forget Ethiopia had nothing when he came to power. It was dark age. It is unfortunate that his life ended up with a tragedy.

YELMA SELESHI: The 1974 revolution swept away the monarchy and the ruthless faux-capitalist system that had reduced the masses to tenants whose fate was controlled by an archaic ruling class. . . . But in many ways history has been kind to the emperor because of the manner and dignity in which he shouldered the unprovoked and brutal attack on his people by a madman named Benito Mussolini. His speech before the League of Nations, proudly and intentionally delivered in Amharic, was as timeless as it was prophetic. I am no fan of Haile Selassie but listening to that speech still gives me chills. We must give credit where it is due.

DEGITU: The longevity of his rule itself makes characterization of his era very difficult. He had both progressive and stagnant periods during his reign. After all is said and done though, his positive contributions far outweigh his negatives. Of course he could have done much better than he did. . . . His impact on the self-esteem and pride and identity of Ethiopians and Africans is immeasurable. . . . And look what we did to him and his loved ones. We insulted him, we disgraced him, and finally we murdered him in cold blood and threw his body in an unmarked grave. . . . We the merciless, we the vengeful, we do not have the most elementary form of decency to name a single establishment after him in the capital or anywhere else. A person who impacted the country and the world so positively in all conceivable spheres of our life is a nobody among us Ethiopians.

MUNIT: Haile Selassie was in power for over 6 decades. . . .
No human being should be allowed to rule more than 10
years. That's even way too much.

Haile Selassie remained an enigmatic curiosity, not only for Ethiopians. Opinions polarize, as shown in the following three examples.
The Italian journalist Oriana Fallaci, famous for her blunt language, wrote after interviewing him in 1972, as he approached his
eightieth birthday:

> Among today's Italians, when discussing Haile Selassie, the sense of
> guilt and shame is such that they react by seeing only his positive traits:
> the merits of his past actions. His portrayals always brim with excessive
> respect, unwarranted admiration and delusion. They go on and on about
> his priestly composure, his regal dignity, his great intelligence. . . . They
> never dare tell us if he was something more, or less, than a victim. For
> example, that he was an old man hardened in principles which were
> centuries out of date; that he was the absolute ruler of a nation which
> has never heard the words *rights* and *democracy* . . . oppressed by
> hunger, disease, ignorance and the squalor of a feudal regime which
> even we [in Europe] did not experience during the darkest years of the
> Medieval period. . . . He [Haile Selassie] never had the time, nor the
> means, to live through the age when one learns to distinguish between
> right and wrong. Raised among plots, intrigues and cruelty, he learned
> to survive through cynicism and all his life was focused on the struggle
> to conquer power and to hold onto it. He achieved this without any scru-
> ples, often turning to methods which would have shocked the Borgias
> and Machiavelli put together.[7]

The Polish journalist Ryszard Kapuscinski did more than anyone else to engrave the memory of Haile Selassie in negative terms.
His best seller *The Emperor,* published in 1978, portrayed him as a
caricature of a demonic, old, and senile ruler. It is doubtful if Kapuscinski really studied relevant history and if he based his descrip-
tions on authentic evidences.[8] He accused the emperor of robbing
the poor: "The Emperor himself amassed the greatest riches. . . . He
and his people took millions from the state treasury amid cemeteries
full of people who had died of hunger, cemeteries visible from the
windows of the royal palace."[9]
Kapuscinski further wrote that Haile Selassie

> ruled a country that knew only the cruelest methods of fighting for
> power (or keeping it), in which free elections were replaced by poison
> and the dagger, discussions by shooting and gallows. He was a prod-
> uct of this tradition, and he himself fell back upon it. Yet at the same

time he understood that there was an impossibility in it, that it was out of touch with the new world. But he could not change the system that kept him in power, and for him power came first.[10]

Kapuscinski came from a communist dictatorship that he apparently wanted to ridicule. He hardly understood Ethiopia—neither the country's religious-political culture nor its African and Eastern sensibilities.[11] Surely Kapuscinski did not study Haile Selassie prior to the emperor's last years. We are therefore better off relying upon the words of Nelson Mandela, an equally iconic African figure, who first met with Haile Selassie in 1962. Mandela wrote in his memoirs:

Ethiopia has always held a special place in my imagination, and the prospect of visiting Ethiopia attracted me more than a trip to France, England and America combined. I felt I would be visiting my own genesis, unearthing the roots of what made me African. Meeting the Emperor himself would be like shaking hands with history.[12]

All studies of twentieth-century Ethiopia in one way or another deal with Haile Selassie. The history I present is derived from a rich collection of literature, books, and articles produced by my predecessors and my colleagues—none was indifferent in presenting his/her perspectives—as well as my own archival research. I do not claim to do justice to Haile Selassie's multidimensional and long history. My only aim has been to understand one of the complex and enigmatic personalities who sculpted today's Ethiopia, and in doing so, became one of the iconic symbols of the twentieth century.[13]

Notes

1. Japanese emperor Hirohito ruled longer, from 1926 to 1989, but he was hardly the political absolutist Haile Selassie was.
2. Ecclesiastes 1:2.
3. For example: M. G. Smith, Roy Augier, and Rex Nettleford, *The Rastafari Movement in Kingston, Jamaica* (Kingston: University College of the West Indies, 1960), p. 5.
4. For the lyrics and more see the "YouTube Guide" at the end of this book.
5. Here is the list: Mohandas Gandhi, Alexander the Great, Mao Zedong, Winston Churchill, Genghis Khan, Nelson Mandela, Abraham Lincoln, Adolf Hitler, Ernesto "Che" Guevara, Ronald Reagan, Cleopatra, Franklin Roosevelt, the Dalai Lama, Queen Victoria, Benito Mussolini, Akbar the Great (who established the Mogul Dynasty in the sixteenth century), Vladimir Lenin, Margaret Thatcher, Simón Bolívar ("Liberator of South America"), Qin Shi Huang (the emperor of China from 259 BCE to 210 BCE), Kim Il-Sung (North Korea's dictator, 1948–1994), Charles de Gaulle, Louis XIV, Haile Selassie, and sharing last place, King Richard the Lionheart

and Saladin. See http://content.time.com/time/specials/packages/article/0,28804 ,2046285_2045996_2045928,00.html.
6. http://www.tadias.com/02/06/2011/what-do-ronald-regan-and-haile-selassie -have-in-common.
7. Oriana Fallaci in June 1972, quoted in *Intervista con la Storia*, 6th ed. (Milan: Rizzoli, 1981), pp. 509, 519.
8. See a discussion of the Polish journalist in Asfa-Wossen Asserate, *King of Kings: The Triumph and Tragedy of Emperor Haile Selassie I of Ethiopia* (London: Haus Publishing, 2015), pp. 206–208.
9. Ryszard Kapuscinski, *The Emperor: Downfall of an Autocrat* (New York: Vingate Books, 1983), p. 160.
10. Ibid., pp. 101–102.
11. See Harold Marcus, "Prejudice and Ignorance in Reviewing Books About Africa: The Strange Case of Ryszard Kapuscinski's *The Emperor*," *History of Africa*, Vol. 17, (1990), pp. 373–378.
12. Nelson Mandela, *A Long Walk to Freedom: The Autobiography of Nelson Mandela* (Boston: Little, Brown, 1994), p. 255.
13. Here is a partial list of books written on Haile Selassie (some by more scholars, some by interested observers). The majority cover a certain period or issues, though some are closer to a full biography. A truly authoritative biography of Haile Selassie would necessitate a volume of thousands of pages. Asfa Yilma (Princess), *Haile Selassie, Emperor of Ethiopia* (London: S. Low, Marston, 1936); Asfa-Wossen Asserate, *King of Kings: The Triumph and Tragedy of Emperor Haile Selassie I of Ethiopia* (London: Haus Publishing, 2015); Brian Buckner-El, *Haile Selassie, the Conquering Lion of the Tribe of Judah* (iBooks, Lulu.com, 2011); Christopher Clapham, *Haile Selassie's Government* (London: Longman's, 1969); Angelo Del Boca, *The Negus: The Life and Death of the Last King of Kings* (Addis Ababa: Arada Books, 2012); Haile Selassie, *Selected Speeches of His Imperial Majesty Haile Selassie First, 1918 to 1967* (Addis Ababa: 1967); Paul Henze, *Layers of Time: A History of Ethiopia* (London: Hurst, 2000), chapters 7–8; Indrias Getachew, *Beyond the Throne: The Enduring Legacy of Emperor Haile Selassie I* (Addis Ababa: Shama Books, 2002); Ryszard Kapuscinski, *The Emperor: Downfall of an Autocrat* (New York: Vingate Books, 1983); Hans Wilhelm Lockot, *The Mission: The Life, Reign, and Character of Haile Selassie I* (London: Hurst, 1989); Harold Marcus, *Haile Selassie I: The Formative Years, 1892–1936* (Berkeley: University of California Press, 1987); Harold Marcus, ed., *My Life and Ethiopia's Progress: Haile Sellassie I, King of Ethiopia*, Volume 2, (East Lansing: Michigan State University Press, 1994); Anthony Mockler, *Haile Selassie's War* (New York: Random House, 1984); Leonard Mosley, *Haile Selassie: The Conquering Lion* (London: Weidenfeld and Nicolson, 1964); Anjahli Parnell, *The Biography of Empress Menen Asfaw: The Mother of the Ethiopian Nation* (Kealakekua, HI: Roots Publishing, 2011); Zewde Reta, *Tafari Makonnen razmu yasultan guzu* (Addis Ababa: Shama Books, 2005); Zewde Reta, *Yaqadamawi Haile Selassie Mengest* (Addis Ababa: Delhi, 2012); Christine Sandford, *Ethiopia Under Haile Selassie* (London: J. M Dent, 1946); Christine Sandford, *The Lion of Judah Hath Prevailed* (London: J. M. Dent, 1955); Haile Selassie, *Selected Speeches of Haile Selassie* (New York, 2000); Seyoum Haregot, *The Bureaucratic Empire: Serving Emperor Haile Selassie* (Trenton, NJ: Red Sea Press, 2013); David Talbot, *Haile Selassie I, Silver Jubilee* (The Hague: Van Stockum and Zomm, 1955); Theodore M. Vestal, *The Lion of Judah in the New World* (Santa Barbara, CA: Praeger, 2011); Edward Ullendorff, ed. and trans., *The Autobiography of Emperor Haile Sellassie I: 1892–1937* (New York: Oxford University Press, 1976).

2

In Father's Shadow

~

Tafari Makonnen was born on July 23, 1892. His father, Ras Makonnen Walda-Mikael, was a person of great importance.[1] But any discussion of Haile Selassie should begin with his mother. Yeshimabet Ali was not a member of the imperial leading elite.[2] *Yeshimabet* is a name with a great promise, meaning "mother of a thousand." But Yeshimabet Ali would not fulfill the name's promise. Nine times she became pregnant, and eight times she gave birth , but none of the babies survived their first year. Tafari was her tenth child and the only one to thrive into adulthood. While pregnant with him, the town of Harar, where her husband governed, was under plague. So, she relocated to a poor little town nearby[3] to give birth more safely. The exhausted mother died nineteen months after Tafari's birth, in March 1894. "All this I heard, of course, much later," Haile Selassie wrote in his memoires, "from those in charge of my upbringing."[4]

The baby was baptized in Harar and was named Tafari, meaning "he who is feared and respected." A baptismal name was also declared: Haile Selassie, a name that connotes the power of the trinity in the classical language of Ge`ez. By order of Ras Makonnen, baby Tafari was to be raised by his niece, Mazlekia Haile Selassie. Four months after she began nursing Tafari, she gave birth to her own son, Imru Haile Selassie. Imru and Tafari grew together as brothers, as close as twins. "Our upbringing," the emperor wrote, "was like that of the sons of ordinary people, and there was no undue softness

9

about it as was the case with princes of that period." Imru remembered their childhood somewhat differently. In his own autobiography, he wrote that they enjoyed a beautiful house and a team of servants ready to attend to their wishes.[5]

Imru and Tafari spent the entirety of their childhood together. Later they had their differences, but as old men they renewed their bond. Young Tafari also had an older biological brother, Yilma Makonnen. He was born to a woman whom his father, Makonnen, did not marry, and whom Ras Makonnen left when he met Yeshimabet. Tafari's brother was seventeen years his senior and would have only a short role in Ethiopian history.

The Admired Father

Ras Makonnen was a most important figure in Emperor Menelik's Ethiopia, arguably second only to the emperor himself.[6] He was born in 1852 to a daughter of Sahla-Selassie, king of Shoa, the central region of the country. Shoa dominated Ethiopia in its medieval golden age, and its royal house remained autonomous in later periods. The grandfather of Makonnen was the grandfather of Menelik, who became king of Shoa in 1865. The kingdom, a center for Amharic speakers, came under the sovereignty of Emperor Yohannes IV (1872–1889), a strongman from Tigray, Ethiopia's northern region, which is inhabited by Tigrinya speakers. However, in the last quarter of the nineteenth century, history favored the Shoans. It is important to mention it here, for the issue of Tigray is central in our story of Haile Selassie.

The land of the Tigrinya speakers was the arena in which Ethiopia fought for its independence in the last quarter of the nineteenth century. Major battles against the invading Egyptians (1875 to 1884), the Sudanese Jihadi fighters of the Mahdiyya Movement (1885 to 1889), and the Italian imperialists (1887 to 1896) were fought mainly on Tigray soil. Tigray and Tigrayans paid most of the price for these costly Ethiopian victories. The region was devastated and impoverished, its population nearly decimated. Emperor Yohannes himself was killed in battle in March 1889, and a good half of the northern region fell to the Italians. In January 1890, this half of Tigray became the Italian colony of Eritrea.

All along that period Shoa prospered. Protected from aggressive invaders by Tigray, the Shoans easily expanded southward, doubling the kingdom's size and much more. King Menelik of Shoa, while still nominally a vassal of Emperor Yohannes, traded with the Italians and bought huge quantities of arms. In 1886 he established his new capital of Addis Ababa, which thrived on taxes and commerce from the newly annexed southern territories. By the time Emperor Yohannes was killed, Menelik's power had far surpassed the emperor's. In November 1889, Menelik was declared the new emperor, and he ruled Ethiopia safely until his death in 1913. Makonnen Walda-Mikael was Menelik's right hand from the beginning, and he remained so for years. He and his generation in Ethiopia knew only victories. Makonnen was personally involved in practically all dimensions of this great success of the rising Christian-Ethiopian African empire.

Harar

In January 1887 the armies of Menelik captured the walled city of Harar. It was the ancient capital of Islam in the Horn of Africa and a center of a vast region inhabited mostly by Somali and Oromo peoples. The victory and occupation closed a circle. Harar had been the headquarters of the Islamic holy warrior Ahmad Gragn, who conquered and devastated Christian Ethiopia in the sixteenth century (1529–1543). The memory of that humiliation, the only time Ethiopia had been defeated and occupied by Muslims, was engraved as a trauma in Christian minds. Moreover, Harar was a commercial junction, and the region was a source of considerable income. Menelik gave the task of transforming Harar into a contributing part of his expanding empire to his cousin Makonnen. He also promoted him to *dajjazmach* (commander of the door) and three years later, in April 1890, to *ras* ("head"). Ras Makonnen was quick to prove himself. Harar, both the town and the region, prospered. Makonnen and his administrators were able to maintain there a large army, second perhaps only to Shoa's. From then on, he who controlled Harar was well positioned to compete for the whole empire.

Ras Makonnen was a devout Christian, but he also knew how to communicate with Muslims. In Harar he built new churches, tolerated ancient and new mosques, and cultivated a local community of traders. He appointed a "president of the Muslims," *rais al-muslimin*. In 1904 an envoy of the Ottoman sultan Abd al-Hamid II visited Harar. In a book he published later he dedicated a long description to the prosperous Muslims of Harar, to their religious freedom, and to their gratitude to Makonnen. Praise for the enlightened Makonnen stood out against the Ottoman envoy's disappointment at the situation in Addis Ababa. The Muslims in the capital, he lamented, had not even one mosque, nor were they allowed to have a cemetery.[7]

Victorious Ethiopia

The Ethiopia of Menelik (and of his predecessors) had no separation between military and administrative positions. Ras Makonnen excelled in both spheres. Preparing in 1895 for a showdown with the Italians, Menelik entrusted Makonnen with general command. Makonnen oversaw the assembly of an all-Ethiopian army, organizing its supplies and arms, and directing its positions in the field. The dramatic victory in the battle of Adwa, in early March 1896, had many fathers. Ras Makonnen's role in the victory was not ignored, especially not after Ethiopian historiography came under the control of his son.[8] This is not to say the credit given to Makonnen was undeserved. Ethiopian victory was primarily logistic, a result of the African empire's ability to recruit some quarter of a million fighters and discipline, arm, feed, and lead them. The Italians made mistakes at Adwa, but ultimately the Ethiopians' victory was owing to their organization, which was notably a product of the talents of Ras Makonnen and his leadership.

After the victory of Adwa, Makonnen was tasked with its consolidation. In early 1897 a British diplomatic mission came to Addis Ababa. Britain, France, Italy, Germany, Austria, and other European nations, as well as the Ottomans, recognized Ethiopia's new boundaries. The matter of Ethiopia's border with British Somaliland was entrusted to Makonnen, and Menelik asked the British to travel with him to Harar. In June 1897 Makonnen came to an agreement with the British on the border—a border that is more or less intact today (with minor changes). The agreement ensured Ethiopian sovereignty over vast Somali-inhabited territory, most notably the desert of Ogaden, which includes Harar. The designation remained problematic. The Somalis never gave up the claim to Ogaden. The border line itself, also with Italian Somalia, was not clearly demarcated, a matter that will be of significance later in our story.

Meanwhile, as the British were in the process of conquering Sudan, Menelik developed a dialogue with its ruler, the Kahlifa Abdallah. The latter agreed that lest the British destroy him, parts of Sudan should be transferred to Ethiopia. Accordingly, in 1898 Menelik sent Ras Makonnen to annex the region of Beni Shangul. Thus, today's western border of Ethiopia was demarcated.[9]

After dealing with these affairs in the south, east, and west, Ras Makonnen was sent to deal with the north—the region of Tigray. Here the problem was far more challenging. The Tigrayans never really came to terms with Shoan domination. In September 1898, following a rebellion led by a son of Emperor Yohannes, Ras Makonnen led a large army to Tigray. In February 1899 the rebellion's leader surrendered and was sent to Addis Ababa to spend the rest of his days in prison. Makonnen himself was assigned to govern Tigray and stationed his headquarters in Yohannes's castle in Makale. He stayed in Tigray till early 1900, the first and last Shoan governor of the proud Tigray. Makonnen left behind a new order that assured that the Tigrayans would remain captive to their endless local rivalries, divided and indirectly ruled from Addis Ababa. (This would be the case until 1991).[10]

When Makonnen was in Tigray, a new challenge to his government in Harar emerged. The Somali *sayyid* Muhammad bin Abdallah Hasan had returned from Mecca and claimed leadership over his people. The British called him "the Mad Mullah [*mawla*]" and for convenience's sake, we shall call him by this nickname, the mawla. He will be a part of our story during the next two decades. The Somali mawla preached a holy war against all infidels, mainly the British and the Ethiopians. Combining Islamic militancy with local popular culture, the mawla, a poet and a cunning warrior, would go down as the father of Somali nationalism. The majority of the Somalis who followed him were from the Ogaden clans, those who dwelt in areas raided by Makonnen's men. The mawla, for his part, naturally set his eyes on Harar and tried to capture the holy town. When Ras Makonnen returned to Harar later in 1890, he began cooperating with the British in Somaliland against the mawla. Their combined military missions to isolate and catch him in the big desert nevertheless failed, and the mawla would live to become a part of young Tafari's story.[11]

Jerusalem and Europe

Ras Makonnen was a God-fearing and devout Christian. A Ge'ez biography written by his priest attests to this in biblical phrases.[12]

Haile Selassie testified: "I observed my father striving to fulfill to the best of his ability, the Christian ordinances enjoined, by giving his money to the poor in trouble and to the church, and by praying at every convenient hour."[13] Like all Christian Ethiopians, Ras Makonnen never forgot Jerusalem. In order to deepen Ethiopian hold in the city of Solomon (the Ethiopian share in the holy city was until then only the ancient monastery of Deir al-Sultan), Makonnen conducted negotiations with the Ottomans. In 1890 he traveled to Istanbul and received from Sultan Abd al-Hamid II authorization to own property in Jerusalem. Makonnen, together with Menelik's wife, Taytu, was the living spirit behind the new Ethiopian enterprise of purchasing and building in Jerusalem. He no doubt instilled this affection for Jerusalem in his son.

Tafari did not fail to observe his father's other activities in foreign affairs. "He had to carry out and to conclude the whole business of relations with foreign countries which [are] nowadays [1930s] undertaken by Ministers of Foreign Affairs."[14] At the end of 1889 Makonnen went to Rome to finalize a treaty Menelik had signed with the Italians earlier that May. In Italy, Ras Makonnen arranged for arms shipments to Ethiopia. From Rome he went for a short visit to Paris. In 1902 Makonnen sailed to London to represent Ethiopia at the coronation of King Edward II. Being the first senior Ethiopian to be seen and officially received in European capitals, Makonnen laid the foundation of modern Ethiopian foreign relations. His personality, his manners, and his dignity left quite an impression on the West.

Father's Legacy

Tafari was fourteen years old when Ras Makonnen died. Even in these brief years he never really enjoyed long periods of a fatherly presence. "Many were the months," he later wrote, "which my father had to spend traveling to Addis Ababa, and on military expeditions to other provinces of Ethiopia—more in fact than he was able to remain in his governorate of Harar. He also went to foreign countries as envoy of the government."[15] Tafari never really enjoyed motherly love, and it is doubtful if his busy father could accommodate him with some tenderness. The following excerpt from Haile Selassie's memoirs may shed light on his formative experience as the son of the great Makonnen:

As the love that existed between my father and myself was altogether special, I can feel it up to the present. He always used to praise me for the work which I was doing and for being obedient. His officers and his men used to love me respectfully because they observed with admiration the affection which my father had for me.[16]

Tafari's yearning for his father's approval, we may understand, ignited enormous ambition in him. Ras Makonnen prepared his son to follow in his footsteps, and Tafari shouldered the task, accumulating abilities. As he testified, the image of his father always went with him, moving him to achieve, to excel, to gain more power, to forge new paths. He witnessed how his father maneuvered using both tactics of intimidation and generosity, benevolence and cruelty.[17] Tafari, like all young sons, admired his father but also aspired to outdo him. He would not be an obedient, useful number two. He would be number one. The one and only.

Reprinted from Mahtma Selassie Walda-Masqal, Zikr Neger (Addis Ababa: Berhanena Selam, 1947).

Ras Makonnen and his son Tafari, probably 1903.

Makonnen's legacy to his son had another dimension—education. When Tafari was three and a half years old, his father went to oversee the anti-Italian military campaign. He returned to Harar after a whole year of absence. When he left, he handed Tafari to the local Catholic mission, and when he returned, he further saw to his son's education. Makonnen was among few in his generation who did not despise Europeans. In spite of the Adwa victory, Makonnen understood that there was much to learn from Westerners. Haile Selassie later wrote: "Since my father had seen European civilization, having been to Europe twice, and since he was convinced of the value of education, through conversing with some of the foreigners who had come to Ethiopia, he strongly desired that I shall learn from them a foreign language."[18] Ras Makonnen asked the French doctor Joseph Vitalien and the priest Andre Jarosseau to teach Tafari. (Jarosseau remained his friend for the next three decades.[19]) He also arranged for an Ethiopian Capuchin monk, Abba Samuel Wolde Kahin, to teach both Tafari and Imru French and other subjects.[20] Haile Selassie wrote that as a child he was entirely immersed in learning. His learning included also traditional Ethiopian studies: the language of Ge`ez, fundamentals of Ethiopian Christianity, the Ethiopian calendar, scriptures and history of holy men, Ethiopia's Hebraic cultural origins, prayers, the Psalms of David, and Ethiopia's historical connection to the Bible and Jerusalem.

Tafari mastered French and in later years learned English and some Italian. This combination of traditional Ethiopian and Western education was unique at that time. Indeed, the life of Haile Selassie would be that of a religious king and a modern nationalist. He was both a religious conservative and an admirer of Western ways, and he lived long enough to change emphases in accordance with changing situations and interests. "For the rest of his life," wrote his biographer Angelo Del Boca, "he would try to reconcile Ethiopian provincialism with European modernity, without ever turning his back on his traditions, however crude they might be, just as he remained faithful to his religion."[21]

As was noted earlier, Tafari spent his childhood with Imru. Because he hardly had the chance to experience the presence of other children, he and Imru developed a special brotherly connection that would persist until their last days. Of the two, Tafari was doubtless the smarter, and by far more talented. His advantages over Imru were perhaps enough to instill in Tafari a sense of intellectual superiority that never left—surely, not least when it came to other

Ethiopians. Meanwhile, as a boy, he remained polite and well mannered. In January 1905 a German diplomatic mission to Menelik's court visited Harar. A member of the mission, Professor Felix Rosen, reflected on his meeting the twelve-year-old prince: "Tafari is delicate and slight for his age," he reported. "His features are pure Semitic, while his skin is fair; in Abyssinia, both of these traits are a sign of noble blood. . . . His bearing was measured and dignified and yet at the same time charmingly childlike. The conversation was confined to civilities and compliments."[22]

In November 1905, when Tafari was just over the age of thirteen, Ras Makonnen, amid a traditional ceremony, pronounced his son a dajjazmach (any rank holder could enact one rank beneath his). Makonnen gathered his men and declared: "All of you are my servants whom I have raised up and whom I love. Therefore, I entrust to you, with God, my son Tafari. His fate is in the hands of the Creator, but I commend him to you lest you should bare him ill will."[23]

Dajjazmach Tafari indeed inherited the loyalty of Ras Makonnen's soldiers. Now he was mature, his own man. He later wrote:

> As has been observed in the preface of this book, I decided to write a record of my work beginning at the age of thirteen; everything I had done prior to that was under the direction and guidance of my tutor. From the age of thirteen onwards, although my physical strength may not have been great, my spiritual and intellectual powers began to increase gradually and thus had the entrance gate of this world opened. And this was the time at which I started to act on my own will . . . to climb the ladder of introduction to the world."[24]

Notes

1. This chapter is based also on Harold Marcus, *Life and Times of Menelik II, Ethiopia 1844–1913* (New York: Oxford University Press, 1975), pp. 226–227; and Harold Marcus, *Haile Selassie I: The Formative Years, 1892–1936* (Berkeley: University of California Press, 1987), "Beginnings, 1892–1906," pp. 1–6.

2. Her father was dajjazmach Ali Abba Jifar, a local ruler from the region of Wallo, who belonged to the Oromo people—not to the Amhara elite. He was a Muslim who converted to Christianity. Yeshimabet's mother belonged to the Gurage people, also lower on the ethnic ladder of that time.

3. The name of the place was Egersa Goro, where Haile Selassie later built a church.

4. Edward Ullendorff, (ed. and trans.), *The Autobiography of Emperor Haile Sellassie I, 1892–1937* (New York: Oxford University Press, 1976), p. 15; this source is hereafter cited as *HSAB*. See the chapter titled "The Story of My Childhood up to My Appointment as a Dejazmach (1892–1906)," pp. 13–19.

5. Ras Imru Haile Selassie, *Kayahut mastawsau* (Addis Ababa: Addis Ababa University Press, 2010 [2002 Ethiopian calendar]), pp. 1–2.

6. See Tim Carmichael, "Ras Makonnen," in Siegbert Uhlig et al. (ed.*), Encyclopaedia Aethiopica* Vol. 3 (Wiesbaden: Harrassowitz Verlag, 2007), pp. 686–687; this source is hereafter cited as *EAE*.

7. On the visit of Sadiq al-Azm, on his book *Rihlat al-habasha* (1905), and his praise for Makonnen, see H. Erlich, *Ethiopia and the Middle East* (Boulder: Lynne Rienner Publishers, 1994), pp. 76–82.

8. See Pierre Petrides, *Le Heros d'Adoua: Ras Makonnen, Prince d'Ethiopie* (Paris: E. Plon, 1963).

9. See the chapter "Menelik and the Sudanese Khalifa: Concepts of Pragmatism," in H. Erlich, *Islam and Christianity in the Horn of Africa*, (Boulder: Lynne Rienner Publishers, 2010), pp 30–36. Beni Shangul became important recently as the region where the Great Ethiopian Renaissance Dam on the Blue Nile is being built.

10. On Tigray and Shoa in that period see more in H. Erlich, *Ethiopia and Eritrea, Ras Alula, 1875–1897*, (East Lansing: Michigan State University Press, 1982).

11. On Makonnen and the mawla, see Erlich, *Islam and Christianity*, "The Christian Conqueror and the Sayyid's Jihad," pp. 44–51, 61–62.

12. Gra-geta Hayla-Giorgis, *Zenahu Lele'ul Ras Mekwennin*, a Ge`ez language history of Ras Makonnen with a preface by Blatta Welde-Qirqos, 1965. A 97-page English translation was prepared for the late professor Richard Caulk and is available at the Institute of Ethiopian Studies (hereafter cited as *IES)*, Addis Ababa University.

13. *HSAB*, p. 19.

14. *HSAB*, p. 17.

15. *HSAB*, p. 15.

16. *HSAB*, p. 19.

17. *HSAB*, pp. 21–22.

18. *HSAB*, p. 17.

19. See Tim Carmichael, "The Lion of Judah's Pen: Introducing a Collection of Ras Täfäri Mäkwännen/Emperor Haylä Sellassé's 'Personal' Correspondence," *International Journal of Ethiopian Studies*, Vol. 4, No. 1/2 (Spring/Fall 2009), pp. 55–83.

20. Imru Haile Selassie, *Kayahut mastawsau*, pp. 3–4.

21. Angelo Del Boca, *The Negus: The Life and Death of the Last King of Kings* [an English edition of his 1995 book *Il Negus, Vita e morte dell'ultimo re dei re*] (Addis Ababa: Arada Books, 2012), p. 49.

22. See Asfa-Wossen Asserate, *King of Kings: The Triumph and Tragedy of Emperor Haile Selassie I of Ethiopia* (London: Haus Publishing, 2015), [hereafter Asfa-Wossen*, King of Kings*] p. 9.

23. *HSAB*, p. 20.

24. *HSAB*, p. 19.

3

The Road to Power

~

In January 1906 Ras Makonnen set out from Harar to Addis Ababa. In route, he contracted typhus or, according to other accounts, dysentery. Makonnen was rushed to Qulubi, a Christian holy place, where he passed away on March 21, 1906. In his final hours he wrote to Menelik asking him to care for Tafari.

The town of Harar mourned—church bells rang, cannons fired. Tafari, though stunned, made preparations to be proclaimed Harar's governor.[1] It was too hasty. He was immediately summoned to Addis Ababa to Menelik's palace. The Ethiopians mourn forty days, and Tafari was told that only after the mourning period would the emperor make new appointments.

Addis Ababa was a revelation for Tafari. It was already a town of some fifty thousand inhabitants, with new buildings and foreign embassies in huge compounds. It held a sizable community of diplomats and traders: Western Europeans, Indians, Greeks, and Armenians. The town had been developing as a political and commercial center for the past two decades, prospering from Ethiopia's newly annexed regions. Members of the Shoan elite ruled the provinces and built palaces in Addis Ababa. They often traveled between their estates in the periphery and the capital. They represented a new, proud elite of self-assured conquerors, sporting decorated traditional dresses, riding warhorses, and carrying rifles. They were supremely confident in their superiority over Europeans, as well as over members of other groups in the Ethiopian empire.

19

The "Shoan Establishment" constituted the renewal of an old feudal system. The majority of its members stayed in power throughout the two decades that followed. Among the leading personalities were defense minister *Fitawrari* Habta-Giorgis Dinagde; the head of the church and Menelik's close adviser *Abuna* Matewos; and Ras Michael, formerly *Imam* Muhammad Ali, a Muslim who had converted to Christianity in 1878 and married Menelik's daughter. None of these elites or their colleagues took young Tafari seriously, surely not at that stage. The same was true of Taytu, the wife of Menelik, an outspoken woman who enjoyed her enormous power in court.

The year Tafari came to Addis Ababa, 1906, also marked his first mention in British diplomatic correspondence. Mr. G. Clerk of the legation wrote

> Dejaz Tafari is the younger son of Ras Makunnan and was always destined to be his heir. Queen Taytu has upset that plan, and the boy has now been brought to Addis Ababa to be educated. He is 14-years-old, with very fine Jewish features, and extremely intelligent. The great majority of his father's old officers are devoted to him, and if he is allowed to grow up [namely, if he would not be destroyed by the older manipulators in town] a great effort will undoubtedly be made to establish him as Ras of Harar.[2]

It was a good assessment, but it did not materialize quickly. The forty days of mourning were long enough to enable Taytu to manipulate her husband. According to Tafari, she had other plans for Harar. Her niece was married to Yilma Makonnen, Tafari's older brother. When the mourning period closed on May 9, 1906, Emperor Menelik declared Yilma governor of Harar. He ordered Tafari to transfer the soldiers of Makkonen, whom Tafari had brought to the capital, to his brother. Menelik appointed Tafari to a region near Addis Ababa but allowed him to stay in the capital.[3]

Earlier, in March, during the tenth-anniversary festivities honoring the victory of Adwa, some European diplomats tried to persuade Menelik to open a modern school in Addis Ababa. Many of the conservatives and the priests opposed the measure, but Abuna Matewos's advice prevailed: instead of hosting European teachers at the new school, invite Egyptian Copts. Consequently, as of late 1906 and throughout 1907, some ten Egyptian schoolmasters laid the foundations of the first modern school in Ethiopia, aptly named Menelik II.[4]

In his memoirs, Haile Selassie wrote that the emperor neglected to include him in the school's first class of students. Offended, young Tafari approached Menelik and declared his desire to study over administering a region. Menelik agreed. Since Tafari and Imru had already learned French (in Harar), a special class was opened just for them. At the Menelik II school, Tafari met for the first time Egyptians who were not Coptic clergymen but modern professionals. In the future, he would consider Egypt not only as a source of patriarchal authority but also as a model of modernization. For Tafari, Egypt was both a gateway to Europe and a part of it.

Menelik's Heir—Lij Iyasu

In October 1907 Yilma Makonnen, Tafari's older brother and governor of Harar, died of pneumonia. However, Tafari's hope to inherit Harar was frustrated once again, when in April 1908 Menelik appointed him to administer the large southern region of Sidamo. This time Tafari had to leave the capital. He took comfort at the fact that the emperor ordered three thousand of Makonnen's former guards from Harar to join him. "Since my appointment to the governorship of Sidamo," he wrote later, "I began to pronounce judgement while sitting in Court on Wednesdays and Fridays."[5] Tafari was fifteen years old but already a big man, a *tiliq saw*, at least in his own eyes.

Meanwhile, things went on simmering in Addis Ababa. Emperor Menelik had contracted syphilis back in 1904 and had slowly begun to lose his faculties. In June 1908 he suffered a stroke. Three days later, on June 11, Menelik decreed that his grandson, *Lij* (a court title given to a young member of the reigning royal house) Iyasu Michael, would succeed him. Iyasu was only thirteen years old, so it was also declared that until Iyasu reached maturity, Ras Tessama Nadaw, one of Shoa's leading men, would head a regency council.

Iyasu, Menelik's only male descendant, was the son of Ras Michael, the ambitious and opportunistic leader of the Oromo people in the region of Wallo, a commander of tens of thousands of horsemen. Michael made timely transitions—first from Islam to Christianity, and then from Yohannes to Menelik, whose daughter (named Shoaragga) he married. Taytu did not like the idea of Iyasu as next emperor. She preferred Zawditu, a daughter of Menelik's (not hers), whom she was sure she could control. As Menelik decayed, manipulations in court intensified. In January 1909 the emperor suffered yet another stroke, which practically paralyzed him. Menelik would have only occasional episodes of lucidity before his death in December

Reprinted from *Tsahafe Te'zaz Gabra-Selassie, Tarik Zaman Dagmawi Menelik (Addis Ababa: Berhanena Selam, 1967).*

Tafari and Emperor Menelik, probably 1906.

1913. Taytu, for her part, never concealed who was now the lady in power. She acted bluntly, expanding the circle of her enemies, notably the regent Tessama Nadaw, who remained fiercely loyal to the will of Menelik.

In April 1909 Tafari returned from Sidamo to Addis Ababa, where he was immediately plunged into the sea of jealousies and rivalries. He skillfully gained the trust of Taytu as well as her enemies. He also managed to befriend Lij Iyasu. The designated heir of Menelik was now fourteen years old, physically strong, and full of life. While Tafari read books or conversed in rear chambers with senior dignitaries, Iyasu went riding or visited the capital's brothels. While Tafari radiated Christian piety, Iyasu mingled with Muslim traders in the *mercato*, the huge market of Addis Ababa. Something, however, did unite them. They used to meet in Menelik's palace, where they played an Ethiopian version of billiards. They also organized public horse races.[6]

On October 28, 1909, Menelik suffered yet another stroke. Once the chance that the emperor would recuperate and back his wife faded, Taytu's enemies grew bolder. On March 21, 1910, they stripped the queen of any power. Ras Tessama summoned the regency council and made Iyasu and Tafari vow to remain united. Tafari promised he would never undermine Iyasu, and Iyasu promised to protect Tafari. As a part of the deal, Tafari was appointed governor of Harar. In a genius move, before leaving Addis Ababa he went to bid farewell to Taytu.[7]

Back in Harar

On May 12, 1910, Dajjazmach Tafari returned to Harar. The whole town gathered at the gate. Tafari was nearly eighteen and had grown a beard to look older. His expression was already royal and somewhat gloomy. Facing the cheerful crowd, Tafari released a few smiles, which to the delight of all were reminiscent of Makonnen's. From the gate, Tafari and the crowd proceeded to the central square and to the church built by the new governor's late father. The masses prayed and celebrated until dawn. And the city of Harar rejoiced and was glad.[8]

For Tafari, Harar was not only a source of power and wealth but also a model for what he would do one day for the whole empire. The town and surrounding region had been devastated by the previous governors' overtaxation. Tafari ordered a survey, by which he learned that only seventy thousand inhabitants could continue to pay without totally impoverishing their families. He therefore quickly returned to his father's reforms and improved them. Tafari divided the region into twelve districts, putting each under a trusted adviser. He cut the taxes in half and supported all soldiers from his budget, thereby ceasing their habit of living among the peasants and robbing them. Harar soon recuperated.[9] The Somali-inhabited desert hinterlands, however, remained open to his soldiers' raids. At the same time, the vulnerable Somalis were also raided by the mawla. When the latter tried to negotiate with Tafari, he was turned down.

A Friend for Life

Tafari, who trusted no one, did find love. On August 3, 1911, he married *wayzaro* Mennen Asfaw, his soulmate until her death in 1962. As

Haile Selassie later wrote,[10] what seemed at the beginning as a good arrangement proved a real bond.

Mennen was a granddaughter of Ras Michael, a niece of Lij Iyasu. She was said to be a beautiful young lady, a year and four months older than Tafari. He saw her first in Iyasu's palace, already a mother of four, a divorcee of a certain member of the nobility and a widow of another. The marriage of Tafari and Mennen was fruitful. They had six children: Princess Tananya-Warq was born on January 12, 1912; Prince Asfa-Wossen on July 27, 1916; Princess Tsahay on July 25, 1917; Princess Zanaba-Warq on October 13, 1919; Prince Makonnen on October 16, 1923; and Prince Sahla-Selassie on February 27, 1931.

Mennen gave Tafari all he needed in private life. She was a great comfort to Tafari, who was bereft of motherly love as a child. She gave him a big family, a safe shelter for his lonely soul, an expression of his paternalistic personality. Above all, she gave him friendship and a sense of confidence he had in nobody else (Haile Selassie once confided he did not trust even his own dog). "He seems to lead a sad life" a British minister wrote, "trusting no one."[11] Mennen, no doubt, was the person closest to Haile Selassie, perhaps his only friend.

In the context of 1911, the marriage meant also cementing Tafari's deal with Lij Iyasu. The regent Ras Tessama died in April. Iyasu, now sixteen, refused to accept another patron and declared himself head of the regency council. Bold and independent, Iyasu would not be a puppet of the system built by his grandfather. He began roving in the country, avoiding and ignoring the "big men" of Addis Ababa. Some historians interpret these journeys as in line with an old tradition of a roving emperor. Other historians see Iyasu as a revolutionary who tried to rid Ethiopia of a conservative, Amhara-centrist group of exploiters, who aimed to build and head a more pluralist system. The discussion of Iyasu still continues today.[12] In any case, the future of Iyasu at that time, and of Ethiopia, and of the rest of the world, was to be determined in the Great War (World War I), which waited at the gates. As for Tafari, he invested in fortifying his citadel in Harar and in sending tributes to Iyasu emphasizing and reemphasizing his loyalty.

Iyasu and the Gamble on Islam

Iyasu went on strengthening his network of loyalties.[13] By the end of 1914 most of the ministers were his men, with the notable exception of the defense minister, Fitawrari Habta-Giorgis. Many of those given the brush-off by Iyasu held deep-seated resentments. Habta-Giorgis, for example, never forgot that Iyasu had once publicly ordered him to dismount his horse and salute him on foot.[14]

At the same time, the Somali mawla grew confident in the desert of Ogaden. In early 1912 he offered Tafari an alliance against the British and against the other Europeans in the Horn of Africa. Tafari sent the mawla's envoys away and intensified his raids on the Somalis. He and the British consul in Harar, Major J. H. Dodds, saw eye to eye the danger of the mawla and of militant Islam—their threat to Harar and to the whole of Ethiopia. While Iyasu continued to build a coalition of forces outside the Shoan establishment, Tafari realized that his future depended on the survival of this very establishment. And on cooperation with the British, the Italians, and the French.

When Menelik died in December 1913, Iyasu avoided officially crowning himself. As the son of an ex-Muslim striving to rule Ethiopia, he may not have wanted the traditional coronation ceremony, which was entirely Christian. On May 31, 1914, Iyasu declared his father, Michael, a *negus*, a king, clearly indicating that Iyasu himself was a king of kings, an emperor. At the same time, Iyasu strengthened his ties with the Ottoman consul in Addis Ababa, Mazhar Bey, and through him, with the government of "the Young Turks" in Istanbul. When World War I broke out in the Middle East, in November 1914, the Ottomans declared an Islamic holy war against the Allies. Iyasu, it seemed, made his choice, but he had to be cautious, for the risks were high. He had effectively abandoned the moderate, apolitical Islam of his father's region of Wallo and instead drew closer to what was radiating from Ottoman propaganda. More concretely, he now set his eyes on Harar, the ancient Islamic capital of the holy warrior Ahmad Gragn. He was on his way to collision with Tafari, cooperation with the Somali mawla, and a substantial gamble on Ottoman victory.

In early December 1914, immediately after the Ottoman declaration of jihad became known, Iyasu made his move. He unilaterally appointed the *rais al-muslimin*, head of the Muslims of Harar, Abdallah Sadiq, as Tafari's deputy, without the latter's knowledge or acquiescence. The British were not slow to interpret this as a step toward turning Ethiopia into an Ottoman ally.[15] In February 1915 Iyasu came to Harar and started gathering information against Tafari. He spent three hours praying in the central mosque.[16] Imru Haile Selassie mentioned in his memoirs that he told Iyasu he was losing the support of the Christians, to which Iyasu answered that Christianity was too complicated while Islam was simple and clear. According to Imru, Iyasu added that he was sure the Ottomans would win the war.[17] Tafari was determined not to give up. Amid political turmoil, Tafari had a brush with death. On June 7, 1915, he went sailing with nine other people on Lake Haramaya, not far from Harar. Suddenly, the boat began leaking, then sinking. His old teacher, Abba Samuel, who could swim, managed after a long struggle to bring Tafari ashore. Tafari was exhausted and had nearly died. Seven others drowned, and in the commotion, nobody noticed that Abba Samuel also collapsed and died.[18] In his memoirs, Haile Selassie failed to note his salvation by Abba Samuel, mentioning him only among the dead.[19]

Back in Harar, Tafari absorbed more of Iyasu's blows. Tafari poured his heart out before the British consul. Iyasu, said Tafari, was a reckless person who would destroy Ethiopia. The "Head of the Muslims" in Harar, the British reported, served as a middleman between Iyasu and the mawla. He was authorized by Iyasu to impose in Harar "a reign of intrigue," further undermining Tafari by organizing a local police force that the British described as "a collection of undesirable Arabs."[20]

Iyasu himself left Addis Ababa in June 1915 and did not return before April 1916. In the following months, leaflets that were strongly pro-Ottoman, anti-British, and anti-Christian were dispersed around the country, especially in Harar. The leaflets were not signed, but they were most likely produced by the Ottomans and circulated with Iyasu's permission. They blamed the British for planning the conquest of Arabia in order to also destroy the Kaaba.[21] A satanic intention to destroy the holy Islamic shrine at the end of the days was traditionally attributed by radical Muslims to Christian Ethiopians.[22] Mazhar Bey was in contact with Istanbul on the one hand and with Iyasu on the other. He also liaised between Iyasu and the mawla. In April 1916 Tafari was summoned by Iyasu to Addis Ababa. Resentfully, he left Harar.

The Deposition of Iyasu

If in April 1916 there was still some point in gambling the future of Ethiopia on Ottoman victory, it quickly became irrational. On June 5 the British-inspired Arab Revolt broke out in Mecca, and the Ottomans had thereby lost the Asian shore of the Red Sea. Mazhar

Bey in Addis Ababa could now receive communications from Istanbul only indirectly via Europe. Yet he still continued to let Iyasu believe that the Ottomans would be victorious. On August 14 Iyasu crossed a point of no return. He removed Tafari from the government of Harar and undertook it himself.[23] In Iyasu's vision, we may presume, Harar was to be the capital of a new Ethiopian empire in the Horn of Africa, backed by Istanbul and including the Somali followers of the mawla. Iyasu now sent camel caravans to his Somali friend loaded with arms and a German technician. He also proposed marriage to one of the mawla's daughters. In Harar, preparations were made for the wedding.[24]

In early September Iyasu came to Harar. He ordered all arms be collected and proclaimed that the force of *rais al-muslimin* Abdallah Sadiq was the only official police. The interpreter of the British consul was handcuffed and sent to Addis Ababa.[25] Iyasu declared that he was a descendent of Prophet Muhammad and traveled to Dire Dawa, where he surveyed a parade of fighters dressed like Muslim holy warriors. An Ethiopian flag embroidered with the Islamic testimony that there was no God but Allah was waved there. Iyasu then traveled to Jijiga to meet with the mawla's envoys. He swore on the Koran that he was a Muslim and prayed with the crowd. In his speech he said he was instructed by the Ottoman sultan to liberate the Red Sea coast down to Berbera—a mission he promised to soon fulfill.[26]

Iyasu's vision was a dangerous illusion. Provoking the Allies at that time in this arena was unadvisable. Even less wise was the attempt to turn Harar again into a capital of militant Islam. Harar had been the capital of the sixteenth-century holy warrior Ahmad Gragn, who destroyed Ethiopia and left a traumatic memory for its Christians. The leading members of Menelik's generation were still the dominant, powerful elite of Ethiopia. Neither were the British, French, and Italian ministers in Addis Ababa slow to react.[27] On September 12, 1916, they filed a complaint to the Ethiopian foreign ministry on Iyasu's conduct.

On September 27, 1916, a public ceremony was held in the capital. Abuna Matewos, who back in May 1909 had sworn to Menelik he would protect Iyasu, tried to speak but was hushed angrily by the top leaders and the *echage*, the head of the monks. All was prepared in advance. Iyasu was deposed; Zawditu, Menelik's daughter, was proclaimed empress; and Tafari was promoted to ras and declared Zawditu's heir apparent. This statement was made:

The Christian faith, which our fathers had hitherto carefully retained by fighting for their faith with the Muslims and by shedding their blood, Lij Iyasu exchanged for the Muslim religion and aroused commotion in our midst; in order to exterminate us by mutual fighting he has converted to Islam and, therefore, we shall henceforth not submit to him; we shall not place a Muslim king on the throne of a Christian king; we have ample proof of his conversion to Islam.

Ten such proofs were read to the public.[28] A few days later, units of the Ethiopian army entered Harar and slaughtered some four hundred Somalis who were unfortunate to camp there.[29]

The rest of Iyasu's story is not of our direct interest. On October 27, 1916, the final confrontation took place between the Shoan camp and that of Iyasu. It was the greatest battle on Ethiopian soil since Adwa in 1896. Negus Michael, Iyasu's father, led some eighty thousand fighters to the battlefield at Segale (about 43 miles north of Addis Ababa). Habta-Giorgis, the defense minister, confronted him with forces numbering one hundred and twenty thousand soldiers. At the end of the day Negus Michael surrendered.[30] Iyasu, leading six thousand soldiers, was late to arrive at Segale. He fled and managed to hide in the Afar Desert until he was captured and imprisoned in 1921.[31] He spent the next years in jail. In 1932 Iyasu escaped, but he was apprehended and put in a cage near Harar. In November 1935, when Benito Mussolini threatened he would return the glory of Islam to Ethiopia, Haile Selassie saw to the strangling of Iyasu in this cage.

The End of the Somali Mawla

The deposition of Lij Iyasu proved a blessing for the Somali mawla. With Ethiopia under Christian hegemony and the British in control of the Red Sea, the isolated Muhammad bin Abdallah Hasan was too weak to be considered a going concern. London had decided not to bother chasing him. Only in October 1919, long after the end of the war, did the British decide to neutralize the mawla using new aircraft capable of finding him and his followers in the desert and bombing them.

In February 1920 the mawla escaped to an Ethiopian territory. Local Somalis from among his many enemies kept harassing him. Only some one hundred followers stayed on with the mawla, who was now sick and hungry, in the desert. When Tafari's men from Harar spotted him, they kept their distance and awaited their ruler's instructions. Tafari ordered them not to harm the mawla or to offer any help. The mawla became so desperate for aid that he argued that in fact he was an Ethiopian, claiming he was a son of Ras Michael (the father of Iyasu),[32] namely, of Imam Muhammad Ali who had converted to Christianity. It must have been a pitiful moment for the Islamic warrior, identifying himself with a Muslim who had committed the ultimate sin of adopting Christianity. But even this act of submission did not move Tafari. He was not ready to play the role of the *najashi*, the Ethiopian medieval Christian king who gave shelter to the pioneers of Islam.[33] Instead, he prescribed a slow death for the mawla, now an abandoned and helpless refugee in the deserts of Harar. Tafari's men would not allow any water or food to be supplied to the mawla and his remaining followers. Sun stricken, spitting blood, half mad, the man who will be remembered as the father of modern Somali identity died in December 1920. A modest stone marks his resting place.[34]

Notes

1. Marcus, *The Formative Years*, p. 7.
2. British Archives, FO [Foreign Office] 371/192, "General Report on Abyssinia for the Year 1906." Sent April 10, 1907.
3. *HSAB*, pp. 25–26.
4. See Haggai Erlich, "The Egyptian Teachers of Ethiopia," in Walter Raunig and Asfa-Wossen Asserate, *Athiopien zwischen Orient und Okzident* (Munster: LIT Verlag, 2004), pp. 117–138; Fasil Teshome, "The History of Menelik II School, 1907–1962," BA thesis, Addis Ababa University, College of Social Sciences, June 1986, available in the Institute of Ethiopian Studies, AAU.
5. *HSAB*, pp. 28–29.
6. Asfa-Wossen, *King of Kings*, p. xix; Imru Haile Selassie, *Kayahut mastawsau*, pp. 30–32.
7. *HSAB*, pp. 31–35.
8. See more in Marcus, *Formative Years,* "Beginnings, 1892–1916," pp. 1–21.
9. *HSAB*, pp. 36–41.
10. *HSAB*, p. 42.
11. FO 371/9993 Annual Report 1923, Russel to MacDonald, 16.2.1924.
12. See Eloi Ficquet and Wolbert Smidt (eds.), *The Life and Times of Lij Iyasu of Ethiopia: New Insights* (Munster: LIT Verlag, 2014).
13. The following paragraphs are based on Erlich, *Islam and Christianity*, "Radicalism, War, and Pragmatism: Ethiopia and the Somalis, 1899–1920," pp. 43–92.
14. Asfa-Wossen, *King of Kings*, pp. 22–23.
15. British Archives, CO [Colonial Office] 535/36, Archer to CO, 19.12.1914.
16. British Archives, FO 371/2228, Thesiger to Grey, 7 and 31 March 1915.
17. Imru Haile Selassie, *Kayahut mastawsau*, p. 38.
18. Marcus, *The Formative Years*, p. 16.
19. *HSAB*, pp. 42–43.

20. FO 371/2595, Dodds to Thesiger, 14.2.1916.

21. Archive of the Italian Foreign Ministry, Africa Italiana, (herafter cited as ASMAI) 65/11 Memorandum della Legazione Britanica in Addis Abeba, July–August 1916.

22. See Erlich, *Islam and Christianity*, pp. 55, 79, 129, 135–136, 170–172.

23. FO 371/ 2595, Thesiger to Grey, 23.8. 1916; *HSAB*, pp. 44–46.

24. ASMAI 65/11, Cerrina to Colonie, 17.8.1916.

25. ASMAI, 65/11, Colli to MAE and to Colonie, 4.9. 1916.

26. ASMAI, Colli to MAE, 11.91916; FO 371/2595 Thesiger to Grey, 14.9.1916.

27. ASMAI 65/11, Colli to MAE and to Colonie, 4.9.1916.

28. *HSAB*, pp. 48–50; the quotation is from p. 48.

29. Douglas Jardine, *Mad Mullah of Somalilnad* (London: H. Jenkins, 1923), p. 246, wrongly described the massacre as predating the deposition of Iyasu.

30. Marcus, *The Formative Years*, pp. 21–24.

31. Ibid., pp. 47–48.

32. Jardine, *Mad Mullah*, p. 303.

33. See Erlich, *Ethiopia and the Middle East*, pp. 43–92.

34. Mohamed Omar, *History of Somalia, 1827–1977* (New Delhi: Somali Publications, 2001), pp. 474–475, quoting Claud Russell's report, a copy in the National Archives of India, Foreign and Political Department, External, File 740, 1–7, 1923.

4

The Crown

~

In early February 1917 Addis Ababa prepared for a big day. The spaces between the palaces and the foreign embassies were cleaned. Clusters of shabby huts built from eucalyptus branches and dried mud were wiped away. The capital gussied up for the coronation of Zawditu, Menelik's daughter. In the months since the previous September, the political climate had calmed. The Shoan establishment celebrated its victory, and Iyasu's men dispersed. Negus Michael, Iyasu's father, was paraded in chains, carrying a stone on his neck. He prostrated himself before Zawditu, begging for his life. As was prearranged, she gestured a pardon. The stone and chains were removed, and Michael walked away. Iyasu's end, as mentioned, would come in 1935, but even in jail, Menelik's heir cast a shadow. The big men of Addis Ababa never forgot their debt to his grandfather, the great emperor.

Two very different men headed the coronation festivities: Habta-Giorgis and Tafari. The latter was only twenty-four years old, a tender-looking but sophisticated politician. He managed to avoid colliding with the members of the old guard and positioned himself before the European powers' representatives as the hope of the country: a young man ready to learn from the West. "Ras Tafari certainly means well and undoubtedly intends to try and reform his country," reported British Minister W. Thesiger in November 1916, "but it remains to be seen whether he has sufficient strength of character to accomplish his ends. . . . [It is important] that he will understand that we are prepared to help him."[1] The notion that Tafari was too soft persisted over the next decade. Three months later, Thesiger wrote: "Ras Tafari is evidently doubtful of his capacity to deal with the situation, and from hints which he has thrown out, it looks as though he were contemplating the possibility of being reduced to ask eventually for the establishment of a British protectorate over the whole country."[2]

Seven years later, in February 1924, Thesiger's successor, Claud Russel, reported

> Ras Tafari has developed a little since I have known him, but, on the whole, I cannot say that I entertain a better opinion of him. . . . He is ignorant, vain and childish, but it is impossible not to be attracted by his good manners, and his unfailing amiability. . . . I believe he is honestly desirous of improving the state of his country, but he totally lacks method and application. . . . It is difficult to forecast his future. . . . I think he will only keep his place so long as it does not suit a few powerful men to combine and oust him. . . . He lacks the bulk and stature which impress the Abyssinian. Also, he is reputed for being close-fisted. Worse still, he is wanting in effectiveness and in that ill-defined quality which is best described as "ascendancy." He is too humane, and too gentle, for the task before him. One feels he is not the man to wade through slaughter to a throne. . . . If I were to hazard a prophecy, I should say that the hopes of those will be disappointed who believe that the reign of Tafari will mark an epoch in the history of Abyssinia."[3]

The British minister was, it appears, quite a minor prophet. His underestimation of Tafari smacked of paternalism, and among the British, he was far from alone in this. In the not too distant future, Britain itself would pay for this patronizing attitude toward Haile Selassie and toward Ethiopia at large.

The Old Guard

Tafari's partner in organizing Zawditu's coronation ceremony was the strongest man of Menelik's generation. War Minister Habta-Giorgis, of Oromo origin, was an admired military commander who had participated in the Battle of Adwa. He became prime minister in 1909 and was the head of the group that sidelined Taytu and deposed Iyasu. Born in 1851, he was sixty-six years old at Zawditu's coronation, and he stood as both a symbol and guardian of Ethiopia's traditional might. With him were other members of the aging elite who were more or less the age group of Ras Makonnen, some thirty years senior to Tafari. Among them was the warlord Dajjazmach Balcha Safu; Ras Walda-Giorgis; Ras Hailu Tekla-Haimanot, the hereditary governor of Gojjam; and Ras Kassa Hailu, a grandson of Menelik's brother and one of the late emperor's closest associates. They, and others, had palaces in the capital and armies in their provinces.

Ras Kassa Hailu was the one who knew Tafari best, and gambled on him. (His son Ras Asrate Kassa would indeed become Haile Selassie's trusted man to their end.) The rest of the men at the top were far from admiring the young prince, the ambitious son of Ras Makonnen. Among those who were overtly reserved in their affection were the *echage* Walda-Giorgis and the *abuna* ("metropolitan") Matewos, the head of the church. The abuna, like all his predecessors since the fourth century, was an Egyptian monk sent as the Bishop of Ethiopia. Matewos was born in 1842 and was sent to Menelik's court in 1881. In Ethiopia he developed full loyalty to the emperor and never ceased interfering in politics. He was a tough conservative, an opponent of any innovation, and unfriendly to European foreigners. In 1917 Matewos was seventy-five years old but still active in politics. Only in 1922 would the aging abuna's influence weaken and present less of a problem to Ras Tafari.

We have no direct evidence of the meeting in which these men decided to elect Tafari as heir to Zawditu. The natural candidate should have been Ras Kassa Hailu. By hereditary rights he had a better claim, and he was experienced and even known in the West (Kassa had represented Ethiopia at the 1911 coronation of George V in England). But Habta-Giorgis feared that Kassa would be too powerful, and Kassa himself thought that Tafari would be a good compromise, because he did not radiate strength. Habta-Giorgis was later quoted: "We sat down and chose him as emperor, but when we stood up and tried to be rid of him we found it could not be done."[4] Historian Harold Marcus put it this way: "In fact so wily was Tafari that none remarked on his wiliness."[5]

First Empress Since the Queen of Sheba

The coronation events lasted a few days.[6] The people of Addis Ababa drank and dined, and the streets were decorated with pictures of Zawditu and Tafari. Prayers were held in public, with the main ceremony in the central cathedral of Qedus [Saint] Giorgis. Priests danced and sang the Psalms of David. The members of the imperial nobility marched to the cathedral. There, on David's throne, sat Zawditu, with the abuna to her right and the *echage* to her left. Ras Tafari sat near the abuna, a golden crown on his head. The rest of the dignitaries sat around them. Facing them sat representatives of foreign states—the British, French, and Italians on one side, and the Germans, Austrians, and Ottomans on the other. When a sign was given, the abuna anointed Zawditu and proclaimed her the new empress of Ethiopia.

At forty-one years of age, Zawditu became Ethiopia's first empress since the Queen of Sheba. And yet, no happiness could be detected in her eyes, not even in these holy moments. "Her Majesty," wrote the British minister, "is as far as can be judged, a woman of small intelligence and no education. It is probable that she has little knowledge or comprehension of current internal questions, and none of foreign affairs."[7]

Zawditu was destined to spend her days in boredom. From early childhood she had been used as a tool by her father, Menelik. In 1882, at the age of six, she was married to Emperor Yohannes's son, who was then twelve years old (he died six years later). Another unhappy marriage followed and ended quickly. Later, her stepmother, Taytu, married her to Ras Gugsa Wale, Taytu's nephew. This time, it was said, Zawditu was not unhappy, though the couple had no children. In any case, the union did not last long. The same coalition of elites that had decided on Tafari as Zawditu's heir decided also to separate her from Ras Gugsa Wale. The great men of Shoa thought that as husband of the empress, Gugsa Wale would become too powerful. Zawditu was forced to bid him farewell, and he was sent to govern the far-off region of Bagemdir (Gondar). Ras Gugsa Wale was not allowed to return to the capital, but in that northern province, he waited for his turn to step on the central stage. Haile Selassie chose not to elaborate on the matter in his memoires: "When Queen Zawditu sat on the throne, she being without son and heir, I was chosen, by the will of God and by the wish of the people, as Crown Prince and Regent Plenipotentiary of the Ethiopian realm."[8]

A Prince and a Modernizer

Tafari saw himself as a crown prince "by the will of God and by the wish of the people." He must have felt intellectually superior and destined to rule. In hindsight he knew well what he was facing and how to reach his goal and become emperor. Menelik had become an absolute monarch because he built a new system. He conquered new territories and defeated foreign enemies, thereby weaving a new set of loyalties: a contingent of victorious warlords who outlived him. Iyasu tried to build a counter coalition of periphery groups and Muslims. Tafari had a third choice. He patiently began to build a new cohort of "young Ethiopians" who would eventually replace the Adwa generation.[9] The key for developing this group was through modern education via Europe. Tafari himself felt comfortable with Europeans. He had been a student of missionaries and had learned French. Now, as a crown prince, he also learned English. He had English lessons every morning at six o'clock; by 1923 he finished *Reader Four,* a teaching book prepared for students in India.[10] One of his physicians, a French doctor, wrote that when Tafari spoke with his courtiers he looked bored, even angry. "On the other hand, especially when he is dealing with Europeans, his eyes know how to be soft, caressing, affable—even sincere."[11] Tafari's plan to derive power from modernization required time and patience: opening to the West gradually, initiating reforms at home, and affording advanced education to his young loyalists.

An elite army unit, *mahal safari,* which had served as the imperial bodyguard already in the days of Menelik, was positioned in the capital.[12] This unit would later form the basis of Haile Selassie's bodyguard, *kebur zabanya;* however, at that time the guard was loyal to Habta-Giorgis. At least twice, in early 1918 and May 1919, Tafari tried to bribe the guards' commanders and failed. Tafari was determined to attend the opening of the Paris Peace Conference in early 1919. Leaders from all over the world gathered in the French capital to decide the future of the world. But Habta-Giorgis vetoed the trip. He accused the young prince of having designs to sell Ethiopian interests in return for the *faranji*s (a nickname for all white men) supporting his ambitions.[13] Tafari was forced to slow down. In January 1920 the League of Nations was established in Geneva. When Tafari suggested that Ethiopia join the league, he met strong opposition from the members of the old guard, as well as from many of the European state members of the new international organization.[14]

One of the main arguments against admitting Ethiopia was slavery. Slavery did exist in Ethiopia and was legitimized by the traditional medieval code of the *Fetha-nagast* ("The Wisdom of Kings"). Members of various ethnic groups were enslaved, with thousands owned by emperors. Tafari made a few progressive declarations, explaining that in Ethiopia slavery was not as cruel an institution as elsewhere. He presented reports to the league proving he had acted for liberation of slaves. In his memoirs he wrote that he even turned black slaves from the Nile region into a military orchestra.[15] In August 1922 Tafari managed to send a mission to Geneva that included Heruy Walda-Selassie, one of Ethiopia's intellectual pioneers. After the mission signed the Convention of Saint-Germain-en-Laye of 1919, the French convinced other members to admit Ethiopia to the league.[16] (In the future, Tafari indeed worked against the slave trade and finally outlawed slavery in 1942.)

Ethiopia's official admission to the League of Nations[17] on September 28, 1923, did not change much at home. Ras Tafari was still restrained by the old conservative guard. The British minister even thought that the move only strengthened the reactionaries:

> I would rather compare the case to that of a man with misgivings as to his representability, who finds himself unexpectedly reassured by his election to an exclusive club. Few Abyssinians are afflicted with doubts as to the pre-eminence of their nation, and those who may have been now feel that their mistrust was unfounded. They regard the admission of their country to the League of Nations as an acknowledgement of its merits, and a tribute to the sufficiency of Abyssinian culture. On the whole I think that since the election the foreign Legations have found the Abyssinian Government more difficult to deal with than before. . . . I see no reason to anticipate that a period of upheaval is at hand, or even an age of transition.[18]

The minister, Claud Russel, was wrong for a second time. He grossly underestimated the importance to Ethiopia of its new relations with Europe, as well as the significance of the free African empire's admission to the League of Nations and to its future.

Tafari was not in a hurry to challenge the old guard at home.[19] Rather, he worked to improve his and Ethiopia's image in the West. As noted by historian Angelo Del Boca, the foreign delegations in Addis Ababa ceased to merely advise about reforms but started applying pressure.[20] Tafari responded favorably but cautiously. He was already introducing some changes. In 1920 he brought foreign advisers to the various ministries. In 1921 he abolished punishing criminals by amputation. In 1922 he began importing modern vehicles—cars and motorcycles. The same year he founded Ethiopia's first printing press, which issued holy books as well as pamphlets praising the crown prince. Students were sent abroad to Paris and to other European capitals, and also to Cairo. In November 1922 Tafari traveled to Djibouti and from there sailed with his entourage to the British colony of Aden. There, his hosts exhibited their modern weapons and exposed him to the marvels of modern aviation. In spite of the warnings of his frightened aides, Tafari climbed into an aircraft and sat near the pilot. They flew in a circle above the town. The amazing new adventure drove home more strongly to the prince what was Western might, and whom to befriend in order to inch closer to the throne of Ethiopia.[21]

A Long Trip to Europe

As the "Adwa generation" was growing older, crown prince Ras Tafari grew in confidence. On April 16, 1924, he took the train to Djibouti (the line had been completed in 1917) and from there sailed to the Middle East and Europe.[22] He later wrote that before leaving, "We gave instructions that, while Our War Minister Fitawrari Habta-Giyorgis carried the principal responsibility for the affairs of the government, each minister was to be responsible for the work of his department, and that all of them should report to H. M. Queen Zawditu on everything they had done."[23] For himself, Tafari set three goals: "(1) To see with my own eyes European civilization . . . about which I had read in books; (2) When returning . . . to initiate some aspects of civilization I had observed; and (3) to find a sea-port." The options for a port were those of French Djibouti, Italian Assab in Eritrea, or Zeila in British Somaliland.

The very trip abroad was a courageous move. None of Ethiopia's rulers (excluding the Queen of Sheba) had ever dared to leave the country. According to Ethiopian political culture, a leader should be visible and present. A leader's absence, however short, usually created a vacuum that ambitious contenders were ever ready to fill. Ras Tafari took quite a risk in taking a five-month venture. In any case, Tafari asked his devotee Ras Kassa Hailu to keep an eye on Habta-Giyorgis. He organized an entourage of twelve senior leaders. It included some of his supporters and some potential rivals, who were less dangerous on the road with him. Potential rivals included Ras Hailu Tekla-Haimanot of Gojjam (the region defined by the Blue Nile's curve); Ras Seyum Mangasha, a grandson of emperor Yohannes and ruler of western Tigray; and Dajjazmach Gabra-Selassie, the adviser of Zawditu. Among his trusted supporters were Heruy Walda-Selassie, the empire's leading intellectual and future minister of foreign affairs, and Makonnen Endalkatchaw, Tafari's classmate in Menelik School, a future prime minister.[24] Dressed with traditional black-and-silver cloaks (*kaba*) worn by Ethiopian nobility and wearing big Western-style brimmed hats, they were a sight Europe had never encountered: representatives of a sovereign African kingdom— proud and independent. Europe was curious. For European publics, Africa meant submissive blacks. The Ethiopian princes, radiating self-esteem, drew attention and respect.

France—the Mother of Modernization

On May 14, 1924, the Ethiopians arrived in France. The Paris government did its best to impress them. At the port of Marseille, gunboats fired. A motorcade, led by the president of the republic, toured them through the main boulevards of Paris to the Arc de Triomphe, where speeches were made and the visitors were showered with gestures. Tafari was overwhelmed. In describing this glorious visit he neglected to mention that the French did not grant them access to a free port in Djibouti. Rather, he concentrated on the meeting he had with the Ethiopian students in Paris. Haile Selassie quoted at length the speech made by Andargatchaw Massai, future husband to Tafari's daughter Tananya-Warq and first governor of Eritrea (1952–1959):

> Your Highness! . . . through Your goodness and Your endeavor, the whole world has been impressed by Your sending us abroad for study, thinking that Ethiopia be civilized in wisdom and in knowledge as of old and that she will open her eyes . . . We, Ethiopia's sons, remain unceasingly grateful to You because you have made us study, helping all those of us in difficulty, so that we should follow European civilization and should know Ethiopian history. But now, the distinguished invitation which the European governments have extended to You, and not to any of the kings of Ethiopia in the past, has come because they know that under Your excellent guidance You will cause Ethiopia to be civilized; and Your arrival has made the name of Ethiopia heard all over the world. Ethiopia has the duty to thank You. . . . The whole Ethiopian people, the dead in heaven, the living on earth, are in duty bound to give praise.[25]

Was it an exact quote, or did Haile Selassie later improve the text? In any case, this excerpt surely reflects Tafari's agenda and his concept of himself.

Italy—Mussolini Still Young

After visits to Brussels, Luxembourg, Stockholm, The Hague, and Hamburg, Tafari and his entourage arrived in Rome on June 11. It was not a simple occasion. The representatives of the African empire that had humiliated Italy aroused mixed feelings. Officially, the Italians went out of their way to demonstrate cordiality. King Vittorio Emanuelle came in person to the railway station; to his side stood the prime minister, Benito Mussolini. The crowd cheered. The official reception was held at the Quirinale Palace. The king made a complimentary speech; however, Mussolini was less kind. He arrived late, after the first course was served, walked slowly, bowed to the king, and only nodded at Tafari. Eight days later Mussolini received the prince in his office. After Tafari raised his request for a free port in Assab, Mussolini summoned his advisers, practically closing the meeting. The next day the Ethiopians were handed a draft of a treaty. For a free port in Assab, Ethiopia was to commit to full Italian economic penetration.[26] As Haile Selassie later put it, "For a variety of reasons the draft treaty never came into force."[27]

Mussolini represented a new, Fascist Italy. He himself was also only on the road to absolute power, but he was clearly burdened with the notion of the Adwa humiliation. In time, he would work to avenge it.

Britain—Discord on the Nile

The British were ambivalent about Tafari. Some, mainly Foreign Office officials, saw him as a ray of hope for Ethiopia, a man the British should cultivate. Their voices would gain more weight later. Meanwhile, voices in Britain that were angered by Ethiopia, including her presumptuous prince, were dominant.

Beyond the regular English paternalism, the anger was more concrete. The British ruled in Egypt (as of 1882) and in the Sudan (as of 1898). They saw the whole Nile Valley as a big cotton field—a major economic asset of their great empire. In planning its irrigation, Ethiopia was to have a central role. The British planned to have the Nile basin's biggest water reservoir in Lake Tana, the Ethiopian source of the Blue Nile. There, at over 5,570 feet above sea level, water could be stored to secure an annual supply. In Lake Tana there was little evaporation, no siltation, and the potential to produce hydroelectricity for all. British water experts conceived the Tana Dam in 1902, and their diplomats proposed it to Ethiopia in 1922. For permission to build and manage the Tana Dam, London was ready to give Ethiopia a generous annual subsidy, free electricity, and a free port in Somaliland, at Zeila. But the Ethiopians were suspicious. They, including Tafari, had their reasons to believe that once the British set foot in western Ethiopia, they would never leave, and that they would find a way to annex it to their empire. He feared the British would deal clandestinely or directly with the governor of Gojjam, Ras Hailu Tekla-Haimanot, and with the governor of Bagemdir, Ras Gugsa Wale, and help them to achieve autonomy. When it came to the Nile and the Tana Dam, Tafari did not make life easy for the British, and the latter began losing patience.[28] Edmund Allenby, the high commissioner in Egypt, maintained that the Ethiopians "had to be tamed." The minister in Addis Ababa, Claud Russel, opposed even hosting Tafari in England. When Tafari and his entourage passed through Egypt on their way to Europe, Allenby purposely offended him—twice. (Tafari also went to Jerusalem—we shall come to it later—where the high commissioner, Herbert Samuel, was instructed to offend him once again).[29]

Prime Minister Ramsey MacDonald agreed to receive Tafari only after the Foreign Ministry argued that another insult would be too much. Their conversation was fruitless. Tafari raised the issue of a free port, and the British raised the issue of the Tana Dam. The English press was far more receptive, celebrating the exotic guests. Ras Haylu of Gojjam, the Blue Nile region, was naturally a focus of attention. Even King George was persuaded to host the mission for tea in Buckingham Palace garden (only after being assured they would not stay too long) and have some polite words with Ras Haylu. The king asked Haylu, through an interpreter, if he spoke English? French? Arabic? When he received three negatives, he asked, "Well, what do you speak?" Haylu took the initiative: "Ask him if he speaks Amharic? Gallinya? Guraginya?" When the amazed monarch said no, Haylu responded, "I am glad to see that we are both equally ignorant?" It was said that King George burst out with such laughter that Queen Mary hurried to see if he was alright.[30]

In Cambridge Tafari received an honorary doctorate on July 18. He delivered a speech about the importance of education and committed to sending more Ethiopian students to Europe. Before departing he met again with King George and received a gift: the golden crown of Emperor Tewodros II, whom the British had defeated in 1868.[31] This was perhaps Tafari's only achievement in Britain. The negotiations on the Tana Dam went on leading nowhere, only frustrating the British more. The reports from the British legation in Addis Ababa strengthened the image of Ethiopia as a land of motionless, if not primitive, arrogant conservatism. The annual report for the year 1924, during which Ras Tafari ventured out and reached his hands to Europe, was thus summarized by the minister Claud Russel:

> In my last report I said that Abyssinia is a country where little happens. This statement was amply justified during the past year. . . . It may be said that nothing of political importance has occurred here since the revolution of 1917 [1916?]. In the past year there is no internal event to record of even minor note. Nor, apart from events, was any moral manifestation apparent in the country; no symptom of social change, no whisper of new ideas, no stirring among the people. No new figure appeared upon the scene. The heads of the nation are the same of whom I wrote last year. They pursue the tenor of their way, content in the conviction that all is for the best in the best of all empires. Even death was less busy here than elsewhere. No one died last year in Abyssinia, no one, that is, of any consequence.[32]

"Taming" the Ethiopians

The Ethiopians' visit aroused curiosity but did not weaken European paternalism. In December 1925, as if following the advice of Allenby to "tame" the proud, independent Africans, the British and the Italians exchanged notes. They agreed between themselves to partition Ethiopia into spheres of influence and to help each other diplomatically in promoting their respective interests there. The British sphere included western Ethiopia and Lake Tana. The Italians, in return for their help with the Tana Dam issue, would gain British support to construct a railway from Eritrea to Italian Somalia via Ethiopian territory. All that, supposedly without harming Ethiopian sovereignty.[33] When Ras Tafari heard their designs, he threatened to raise the issue in the League of Nations, and the two powers stepped back.

Meanwhile, Benito Mussolini grew stronger in Italy. In March 1926 the Fascist dictator declared it "a Napoleonic year," in which Italy would begin asserting itself as the successor of ancient Rome in the East. His men in Eritrea interpreted the declaration as a sign to start active subversion in the Red Sea theater, including in Arabia. However, the British were quick to calm *Il Duce* down. When the Fascists understood that the British lion would not allow the Italian tiger to really claim dominance in his own territory, Mussolini opted to wait for better times. In 1928 he even signed a treaty of friendship with Ethiopia.[34]

Tafari, in defiance of the British, invited American experts to prepare a survey of the Blue Nile. The British, perhaps also in an angry response, initiated in May 1929 an agreement between Egypt and Sudan that distributed the Nile waters between the two countries and ignored Ethiopia. The agreement stipulated that Egypt was allowed to build dams without permission from upstream countries and also had the right to veto any water enterprise that might interfere with the flow of the river. This one-sided agreement remained in effect until it was replaced by a similar one in 1959.

Egypt and Jerusalem

Although the Egyptian government was then under British control, Ethiopia had better relations with Egypt than with London. Tafari and his entourage spent time in Egypt on their way to Europe, and they attracted much attention. The year 1924 was full of hope for Egyptian nationalists. The Wafd Party, leading the more liberal-parliamentarian camp, won the country's first free elections and formed the government. Its leader, Saad Zaghlul, now the prime minister, went out of his way to honor Tafari.[35] The ras showed interest in Egypt's ancient sites and its Coptic community. He was well received by Egypt's Christians, the clergy, and the educated young generation. Ceremonies were held in major churches, and meetings were held with Patriarch Cyril. There were also differences, mainly about the Jerusalem monastery of Deir al-Sultan, which sits on the rooftop of the Church of the Holy Sepulchre. Back in 1838 the Coptic monks, who shared the same roof, got control of the keys to the roof yard and began treating the Ethiopians as their dependents.[36]

Tafari journeyed from Egypt to Palestine and stayed there between April 25 and May 1, 1924. He toured Nazareth, the Sea of Galilee, and the Ethiopian monastery on the Jordan River. He spent most of his time in Jerusalem, caring for the welfare of Ethiopian monks. In retrospect, Tafari worked as if he were preparing for a future asylum in Jerusalem (the construction of the Ethiopian consulate was completed in 1928). Back in Egypt, Tafari demanded the keys to Deir al-Sultan from the Coptic church officials. In August 1924, while returning from Europe, Tafari passed through Cairo. He stayed there another full week (until the end of the month) but was denied the keys.

Tafari's main interest in visiting Egypt was studying its modernization process. Tafari toured the new parts of Cairo, Alexandria, and the towns of the Suez Canal. He inspected hospitals and industrial plants and paid special attention to modern schools of higher education in law, engineering, and agriculture. Once he was back in Addis Ababa, his closest adviser, Heruy Walda-Selassie, wrote a book entitled *Happiness and Honor* (published in 1924), which described the whole trip. Its first two chapters were dedicated to Egypt and gave much praise to the modern education system there.[37]

After returning to Ethiopia Ras Tafari established a new school; "Tafari Makonnen" opened its gates in 1925.[38] The school recruited students from all classes and turned them into educated admirers of the modernizing prince. In December 1924 a weekly newspaper named *Light and Peace* (*Berhanena Salam*) made its first appearance, published in both Amharic and French. Members of the newly educated group wrote numerous and frequent articles about the young prince for whom Ethiopia's future waits.

Negus Tafari

In 1926 two major obstacles were removed from Tafari's way. Habta-Giorgis, the minister of defense, died on December 12 at the age of seventy-five. A few days later Abuna Matewos died at eighty-four. Tafari was thirty-four years old and still officially answerable to Empress Zawditu. But the empress was rather busy with her bad health and long prayers. Tafari never gave rest to his mind. "He never goes to bed until the early morning" remembered one of his guards. "He sits alone in his study just thinking and thinking and thinking."[39] The ambitious Tafari was inching his way to absolute power. He appointed a new minister of war, his loyal follower Mulugeta Yigazu, and gave him command of the fifteen-thousand-man imperial guard (the *mahal safari*). The guard was quickly rearmed, dressed in khaki, and equipped with one old tank, a gift from Italy. Another significant innovation was the purchase of two Potez biplanes, with their pilots, French mercenaries.

While Tafari built himself a loyal military force and a layer of loyal, educated bureaucrats (some of whom he sent to represent Ethiopia abroad), he never neglected the religious-national aspect. After the death of Abuna Matewos he conducted tough negotiations with the Coptic patriarchate. His envoys traveled to Cairo to argue that they, the Ethiopians, were the majority, even though their Christianity was somewhat different from the Egyptian Copts and that they (unlike the Copts) are politically independent. Facing such a clear threat to break away, the Egyptian Orthodox Church was forced to change a tradition in place since the fourth century: Ethiopian monks would now be made bishops and serve under a new abuna sent from Cairo. Five Ethiopian bishops were anointed. Abuna Kerilos V arrived from Egypt in 1929, but it quickly became clear that the real head of the Ethiopian church was the king of Ethiopia.

On October 7, 1928, Tafari forced empress Zawditu to crown him as negus.[40] Prior to this, there were two attempts to take control of the capital by men close to the empress. In February there arrived at Addis Ababa Dajjazmach Balcha Safo with his army. He was quickly bribed by Tafari's men. In September other courtiers tried their luck but surrendered to Tafari's superior arms. Now, with a royal crown on his head, it seemed that Negus Tafari had an open path ahead of him.

But not just yet. Ras Gugsa Wale, the empress's estranged husband, had stayed away all those years as a governor of Bagemdir. He never forgot how he was forced to separate from Zawditu, and his hostility grew when Tafari was crowned negus. Beginning in late 1928 Gugsa Wale worked to build a coalition of forces in northern Ethiopia. At a certain stage it seemed that he was joined by the two princes of Tigray, Ras Seyum Mangasha and Ras Gugsa Araya, the two grandsons of emperor Yohannes, as well as by Ras Hailu Tekla-Haimanot of Gojjam. Empress Zawditu, however, willingly or not, avoided supporting her husband. In February 1930 Gugsa was declared a rebel and Tafari ordered general mobilization. Abuna Kerilos declared that he who joins Gugsa Wale betrays Christianity. On March 28 the two biplanes dropped leaflets in this spirit on the rebels' army. Three days later the state and rebel forces collided at Anchiem in the Semen Mountains. This time the planes threw bombs; Gugsa Wale was killed and his army dispersed. Two days later, on April 2, 1930, Empress Zawditu died in Addis Ababa. She was fifty-three years old and suffered from diabetes and typhus. As such, it is possible she died a natural death; however, rumors that she was poisoned by order of Tafari were never disproved.

Emperor, King of Kings, Lion of Judah

One day after the death of Zawditu, Negus Tafari was declared emperor and adopted his baptismal name, Haile Selassie. But he was not in a hurry to celebrate officially. There was no one left to challenge his supremacy. The old leaders were nearly all dead, and most of the young leaders were his making. The hereditary leaders in the provinces still had big armies, but his force in the center was far stronger. In the ancient Ethiopian tension between periphery and center, this time the latter was superior. The empire built by Menelik was finally under a successor capable of maintaining it. Haile Selassie I took his time, believing the coronation should be an event befitting his glory.

All throughout the coming eight months Addis Ababa was cleaned. The Saint George Cathedral was redecorated. Electric lights were installed in the cathedral and on adjacent streets. Invitations for the November 2, 1930, coronation were sent to the kings of England, Italy, Belgium, Sweden, and Egypt; to the queen of Holland; and to the presidents of France, the United States, Germany, Turkey, and Greece. All these and others sent representatives. During the last week of October, dozens of journalists and photographers came to town.[41] On the day before the event, the Duke of Gloucester inaugurated an impressive monument in the square in front of the cathedral. An equestrian statue of Menelik II eternalized the last great emperor. The coronation of Haile Selassie I took place on the site of Zawditu's coronation, but no effort was spared to overshadow it.

At 7 o'clock in the morning the honored guests marched to the cathedral and were seated around the throne, along with the country's great nobles in full traditional dress. Here is the description given by the American minister:

As Sunday, November 2, dawned clear, all in Addis Ababa began to prepare for the impressive event of the morning. The Conquering Lion of the Tribe of Judah and his Empress have just completed a night of prayer and devotion at the most high altar within. Through the early morning the chanting of praises continued, accompanied by the dancing of the priests with their great pulsating drums, the whole suggestive of the Ancient Jewish rites which were in use at the time of King David danced before the Ark of the Covenant.

Proceeded by waving incense burners, His Imperial Majesty, attired in white silk communion robes, entered the ceremonial hall with an escort of aides and clergy, and took his place upon the Throne. The thrilling but solemn silence gently breaks to the throaty voice of his holiness the Abuna Kyrillos:

Ye princes and ministers, ye nobles and chiefs of the army, ye soldiers and people of Ethiopia, and ye doctors and chiefs of the clergy, ye professors and priests, look ye upon our Emperor Haile Selassie the First, descended from the dynasty of Menelik the First, who was born of Solomon and the Queen of Sheba, a dynasty perpetuated without interruption . . . to our times. . . .

The Emperor, whose name is Anglicized as Power of the Holy Trinity, before the questioning of the Abuna gives his sacred pledge to uphold the Orthodox religion of the Church, to support and administer the laws of the country for the betterment of the people, to maintain the integrity of Ethiopia, and to found schools for developing the Spiritual and Material welfare of her subjects. . . .

Following ancient customs, as when Samuel anointed David, and Zadok and Nathan anointed Solomon, so the Abuna anointed His Majesty's head with oil. Seven differently scented ointments of ancient prescription are received on the Imperial head, brow, and shoulders. He then concluded with the words: *That God make this Crown a Crown of Glory. That, by the Grace and the blessing which we have given, you may have an Unshaken Faith and a Pure Heart, in order that you may inherit the Crown Eternal. So be it.*

The centuries seemed to have slipped suddenly backwards into Biblical ritual. The assembly applauded their greeting, and the visiting naval band played the National Anthem, while outside cannons roared a salute of 101 guns, and cheer after cheer came from thousands of subjects massed in the vicinity of the Cathedral.[42]

In the same ceremony, Mennen was declared empress, *etege*. The abuna put a crown on her head, and she was spared only the anointing. Haile Selassie was then thirty-eight, and Mennen a year older. A royal picture was taken of the whole family, with Princess Tananya-Warq, eighteen; Prince Asfa-Wossen, fourteen; Princess Tsahai, thirteen; Princess Zanaba-Warq, eleven; and Prince Makonnen, eight. The empress was then pregnant with Prince Sahla-Selassie, who would be born in the coming February. As was noted earlier, Mennen

The imperial family after the coronation.

Reprinted from Mahtma Selassie Walda-Masqal, Zikr Neger (Addis Ababa: Berhanena Selam, 1947).

was the closest soul to the new emperor, a safe harbor against a sea of challenges and heavy storms that lurked on the horizon.

Notes

1. FO 371/2854, Thesiger to Fallodon, 22.11.1916.
2. FO 371/2854, Thesiger to Balfour, 27.2.1917.
3. FO 371/9993 Annual Report 1923, Russel to MacDonald, 16.2.1924.
4. Asfa-Wossen, *King of Kings*, p. 29, based on a conversation with Dr. Dajjaz-mach Zawde Gabre-Selassie, the emperor's step-grandson.
5. Marcus, *The Formative Years*, p. 28.
6. Hanna Rubinkowska, "New Structure of Power: The Message Revealed by the Coronation of Zawditu (1917)," *Annales d'Éthiopie* 28 (2013), pp. 19–44.
7. FO 371/9993 Annual Report 1923, Russel to MacDonald, 16.2.1924; see also Bahru Zewde, *A History of Modern Ethiopia, 1855–1991* (Athens: Ohio University Press, 2001), p. 128.
8. *HSAB*, p. 82.
9. For a detailed discussion see Bahru Zewde, *Pioneers of Change in Ethiopia: The Reformist Intellectuals of the Early Twentieth Century* (Oxford: J. Curry, 2002).
10. FO 371/9993 Annual Report 1923, Russel to MacDonald, 16.2.1924.
11. Asfa-Wossen Asserate, *King of Kings*, p. XVII.
12. Richard Pankhurst, *Economic History of Ethiopia: 1800–1935* (Addis Ababa: Haile Selassie I University Press, 1968), p. 562.
13. FO 371/3126, Thesiger to Balfour, 26.3.1918, 371/3496 Campbell to Curzon, 12.5.1919.
14. See more in Marcus, *The Formative Years*, pp. 51–55.
15. *HSAB*, pp. 78–81.
16. Jean Allain, "Slavery and the League of Nations: Ethiopia as a Civilized Nation," *Journal of the History of International Law*, Vol. 8 (2006), pp. 213–244; *HSAB*, pp. 76–77.
17. Antoinette Iadarola, "Ethiopia's Admission into the League of Nations: An Assessment of Motives," *International Journal of African Historical Studies*, Vol. 8, No. 4 (1975), pp. 601–622.
18. FO 371/9993 Annual Report 1923, Russel to MacDonald, 16.2.1924.
19. See more details in Marcus, *The Formative Years*, pp. 39–47.
20. Del Boca, *The Negus*, pp. 75–79.
21. Ibid., p. 84; Marcus, *The Formative Years*, p. 50; Imru Haile Selassie, *Kayahut mastawsau,* pp. 105–106.
22. On the 1924 tour see *HSAB* chapters 15–21, pp. 81–123. See more details in Marcus, *The Formative Years*, pp. 59–77.
23 *HSAB*, p. 83.
24. On Heruy Walda-Selassie and Makonnen Endalkatchaw see more in Bahru Zewde, *Pioneers of Change in Ethiopia.*
25. HSAB, pp. 92–93.
26. See Del Boca, *The Negus*, pp. 86–87; Marcus, *The Formative Years*, p. 64; and *HSAB*, pp. 100–102.
27. *HSAB*, p. 103.
28. See more in Erlich, *The Cross and the River: Ethiopia, Egypt, and the Nile,* pp. 79–84.
29. Allenby insisted on prolonged checks of the Ethiopians' passports and on full payments of train tickets to Jerusalem, even though the special train was a gift of the

Egyptian government. Herbert Samuel in Jerusalem was instructed not to receive the Ethiopians at the rail station, and to send them to stay not in the official guest house but in their church on Ethiopia Street. Later, Allenby was instructed by London to apologize and return the money for the train fare to the Ethiopians, which Tafari refused. FO 371/9989, Allenby to FO, 1, 3 May 1924; Allenby to McDonald, 18.5.1924; Samuel to Russel, 30.4. 1924; Allenby to McDonald, 18.5.1924.

   30. Richard Greenfield, *Ethiopia: A New Political History* (London: Pall Mall Press, 1965), p. 158.

   31. *HSAB*, pp. 104–112.

   32. FO 371/10874, "Abyssinia, Annual Report 1924," Russel to Chamberlain, 7.1.1925.

   33. Exchange of notes between Great Britain and Italy, December 20, 1925, *British and Foreign State Papers,* Vol. 121, p. 805.

   34. See Haggai Erlich, "Mussolini and the Middle East in the 1920s: The Restrained Imperialist," in U. Dann (ed.), *The Great Powers in the Middle East, 1919–1939* (New York: Holmes and Meier, 1988), pp. 213–221.

   35. The following is based on Haggai Erlich, "Ethiopia and Egypt: Ras Tafari in Cairo, 1924," *Aethiopica*, Vol. 1 (1998): pp. 64–84; and Haggai Erlich, "Identity and Church: Ethiopian-Egyptian Dialogue, 1924–1959," *International Journal of Middle Eastern Studies* (2000), pp. 23–46.

   36. For the whole issue see the indexes of Haggai Erlich, *Ethiopia and the Middle East* and *The Cross and the River: Ethiopia, Egypt, and the Nile* (Boulder: Lynne Rienner Publishers, 2002).

   37. Heruy Walda-Selassie, *Dastana Kibr* (Addis Ababa, 1924). On Jerusalem, pp. 11–20; on Egypt, 21–30.

   38. Bahru Zewde, *Pioneers of Change in Ethiopia*, pp. 25–27.

   39. Christine Sandford, *The Lion of Judah Hath Prevailed: Being the Biography of His Imperial Majesty Haile Selassie I* (London: J. M. Dent, 1955), p. 46.

   40. See a description of the coronation in ibid., p. 53.

   41. See "Ethiopia coronation 1930 Haile Selassie," YouTube; and https://www.diretube.com/ethiopian-history-the-coronation-of-emperor-haile-selassie-video_1d59a64cc.html.

   42. Report by Addison E. Southard, United States Minister to Ethiopia, *National Geographic*, June 1931.

5

Facing Mussolini

~

Five prosperous years followed Haile Selassie's November 1930 coronation. He was now the lead actor, the master of his own destiny and of his country—seemingly all-powerful, free to reshape Ethiopia and rebuild its status in the world. He became a king of kings, identifying Ethiopia with himself as the embodiment of royalty: no longer "I" or "my" in his speeches and writing, but the *pluralis majestatis,* "We/Ours."[1]

Haile Selassie ruled the free African empire with a mixture of modernization and traditionalism. He was no doubt the greatest reformer of Ethiopia at that time. There were some who envisioned quicker change—"the Young Ethiopians"—but they themselves were of Haile Selassie's own making, sent forward by him as a counterweight to the Conservatives. This is not to say that the Conservatives were uprooted, nor did Haile Selassie have a desire to uproot them. He was a true son of old Ethiopia, an Ethiopian Christian in soul and body. He wanted progress, but only the kind that would grow from Ethiopia's ancient culture. He wanted modernization that stemmed from continuity, and thus he introduced modernity into Ethiopia selectively and cautiously, never disconnecting from two millennia of history. Against the standards of his time and generation, and in these terms, he was a modernizer.

In the international field, which he knew better than any Ethiopian ruler before him, he maneuvered by mixing new ideas with old suspicions. Haile Selassie conceived of Europeans as a model for progress but also as dangerous aggressors. He understood that the 1896 Adwa victory signified a close to the nineteenth century more than it signified an introduction to the twentieth century. He understood that Western ways would have to be adopted in order to persuade Europeans that Ethiopia was ready to walk in their ways. And that membership in the League of Nations was an insurance policy for Ethiopia's independence, no less crucial than its military abilities. At the same time, he understood that Ethiopia must not be overly open to Europe and Europeans—that they were born imperialists looking for opportunities to penetrate and colonialize. How to deal with them without alienating them? How to play their diplomacy game and keep Ethiopia safe? Haile Selassie knew quite well how to do it. In fact, he played their game masterfully. Yet he could not realize—nobody did—that a rude and brutal Italian Fascist would destroy the whole international game. As of the beginning of 1935, Benito Mussolini did precisely that. The Italians' aggression toward Ethiopia that year ignited a chain of global events that culminated in another world war.[2]

The Young Ethiopians

The more important dimension of Haile Selassie's modernization was the introduction of Western education. From today's perspective, this was his major contribution to Ethiopia. For him, higher education was both the key to modernizing and a means to build a new layer of loyal followers. As was previously noted, he established the Tafari Makonnen School. The older school, Menelik II, continued to exist, and some three thousand students had studied within its walls by 1935, but only one-fifth of them finished their studies. The teachers in Menelik II remained mostly Egyptian Copts, and their methods proved too tough. Conversely, Tafari Makonnen was led by an Ethiopian, Dr. Martin Warqneh, who had received British education in India, and most of its staff were Europeans (three were Lebanese Christians). The students of the new school received a better education, and from 1928 to 1931 their number grew from two hundred to three hundred. French remained the first foreign language at both Menelik II and Tafari Makonnen.[3] All 105 of Tafari Makonnen's first graduates were absorbed by the government. By 1935, 853 students had finished their studies: 60 became directors in government, 19 diplomats, 70 in the legal system, 182 in the armed forces, 171 in the Church, and 351 in other functions.[4] Top graduates were sent to study abroad. The preferred destinations were France, Britain, Italy, and Germany, but some required an interim preparatory stage in Egypt, Sudan, Lebanon, or Palestine. Each of the lucky selectees would not leave the country until they had met the emperor and kissed his hand. Those who departed this way never forgot the moment. It served as an oath of eternal loyalty to the royal benefactor, a vow to remain in service of Haile Selassie, "the elect of God."

In his autobiography, which was written in exile seven years after his coronation, Haile Selassie described the reforms he had introduced. He mentioned thirty-two areas he reformed since his appointment as heir to the throne, mainly after becoming emperor.[5] These included reorganization of the ministries, modernizing the legal system, and laying the infrastructure for electricity and telegraph networks and transportation. His autobiography explains:

> Prior to 1922, apart from one motor car, there were hardly any numbers of cars or lorries in Ethiopia. And since, from the Emperor downwards, it was by horse or mule that the nobles as well as the people proceeded . . . it took a long time to reach a planned destination. But since 1922 We had seen to it that many cars, motor-cycles, bicycles, and lorries were imported; consequently operations of all kinds were gradually accelerated.

On establishing a printing press, he wrote:

> All books had to be written by hand; consequently, all the people had great difficulty in finding and in reading books. . . . From 1921–2 onwards We purchased from our private money two book printing presses. . . . The entire people, therefore derived much benefit from reading what they could buy at a low price.

He recalled his experience in founding schools and hospitals, and on the establishment of a central bank, wherein he reorganized Menelik's Bank of Abyssinia into the Bank of Ethiopia in 1931 and tasked it with conducting a national monetary policy, issuing banknotes and coins. He remarked on his reform of the armed forces, their equipment, training, and maintenance:

> The Emperor or the nobles used to retain a large army contingent while moving from one province to another; and the people were forced to produce provisions without payment, such as food, forage,

and wood. But since 1930 We prohibited by proclamation that the peasants be forced to hand over any of their property, except voluntarily and against payment.

Haile Selassie had instituted a national anthem, introduced the beginnings of modern medical services into Ethiopia, and declared its first modern constitution in 1931.

The Emperor used to carry out, in accordance with his own wishes and directions, any sort of peaceful and military operations, as well as administration of the country and anything like this. But now, on 16 July 1931, We promulgated a constitution, set up a parliament, appointed Senators, and caused Deputies to be selected. We appointed presidents for these and directed that all business of government should be carried out on the advice from parliament.

Some of the "Young Ethiopians,"[6] upon whom the modernization enterprise rested, were even older than the emperor. The term was generally applied to those who received education beyond Ethiopia's traditional system. One of the more senior among them was *blatten geta* (doctor, scholar) Heruy Walda-Selassie.[7] Born in 1878, he learned European languages from missionaries and became the prominent pioneer of modern Ethiopian literature. He also became chief adviser on world affairs even before Haile Selassie's ascension to the throne. Heruy published extensively in the new weekly, *Berhanena Salam*, which by 1929 had five hundred readers. After the coronation, Haile Selassie appointed him as foreign minister.

Heruy was also a visionary of reforms. He tried to promote the notion of Japan as a non-Western modernizing power. In 1931 Heruy went there, leading a group of Young Ethiopians. He returned overwhelmed by what he saw, and in 1932 he published a book entitled *The Origin of Light: The Land of Japan*. For many among the new generation in Ethiopia, like others in Asia and Africa, Japan served as a model. (In Japan, too, there were those who thought their country should join hands with Ethiopia, but they were defeated by the advocates of Fascist Italy).[8] Among the Ethiopian admirers of Japan was also Tekla-Hawariat Tekla-Mariam (born 1884), one of the first Ethiopians to tour Europe. During Zawditu's reign he had written a satire criticizing the corruption of the old guard, and Haile Selassie later appointed him Ethiopia's representative to the League of Nations.[9] These intellectuals and others were fully devoted to Haile Selassie. Their admiration reflected old Ethiopian culture of religious respect to men of authority, as well as appreciation shown to a person they consider smarter—someone who sees through them, who looks to the horizon, westward, where progress is.

A Modern Constitution

In his memoirs Haile Selassie wrote he was most unhappy about the medieval legal code in his country. The law book *Fetha-nagast,* "The Wisdom of Kings," was composed in thirteenth-century Egypt by a Coptic scholar. It was translated into Ge`ez in the fifteenth century, and with some adaptations it became the law of the country. The *Fetha-nagast* detailed the Church's organization, the unlimited authority of the emperors, their being divine rulers, and also the penal code, including some crude and cruel procedures, which were based partly on superstitions (the book served well those in Europe who opposed Ethiopia's 1923 admittance to the League of Nations).[10] Tafari had tried time and again to persuade Empress Zawditu to introduce changes, but to no avail.[11] After being crowned he summoned Tekla-Hawariat and entrusted him to prepare a modern constitution. Tekla-Hawariat studied the Japanese Meiji constitution (1890–1947), which stipulated that the emperor is the supreme ruler, but in practice the country was run by a government. Haile Selassie and his advisers, mainly Heruy and Ras Kassa Hailu, changed the draft Tekla-Hawariat presented in order to emphasize the unlimited—indeed, the sacred—authority of the emperor. On July 16, 1931, amid a big ceremony, the new constitution was declared.[12]

The 1931 constitution asserted that Ethiopia identified with the rule of Haile Selassie and his progeny, that he was the direct descendent of King Solomon of Jerusalem and the Queen of Sheba of Ethiopia, and that his personality and his power were holy and unlimited. The constitution also heralded the establishment of a parliament (the House of Advisers), a senate appointed by the emperor, and a chamber of deputies elected by the nobility. Other articles redefined the ministries, the legal courts, the status of foreigners, and more. The constitution did not pretend to establish a representative government. Yet, it was a step forward. It canceled the archaic *Fetha-nagast* and presented in modern language a new order that had some modern dimensions mixed with traditional Ethiopian Christian ones. And, it served as a declaration of intentions: it liquidated the powers of the various regional hereditary rulers and reconfigured Ethiopia as a centralized state under the holy modernizer Haile Selassie.

Centralizing the regime with the backing of a new constitution was Haile Selassie's main objective, and he applied new administrative measures for this purpose. Central among them was transferring taxation from local rulers to the emperor's representatives. Nearly all provincial nobles capitulated. Willing or not, they moved to the capital to serve in the new senate. Their majority, like Ras Kassa Hailu, had long reconciled with the fact that the young emperor was their master. Among the few who found it hard to stomach was Ras Hailu Tekla-Haimanot of Gojjam, whose father was a negus under Menelik. He refused to pay his taxes, attempted to establish contacts with foreign diplomats, and radiated confidence that he was secure in his province, encircled by the mighty Blue Nile. However, the ras of Gojjam stood no chance against the cunning emperor. He was invited to the coronation ceremony, where he was arrested and barely escaped punishment for treason. Back in Gojjam, Ras Haylu was incriminated again, and on April 14, 1932, he was summoned to the capital. He was found guilty of treason and corruption and jailed. Haile Selassie appointed over Gojjam his lifetime friend Ras Imru, a trusted devotee.

The Christian King

It is wrong to describe Haile Selassie strictly by concrete, universal terms—as a shrewd political manipulator, a modernizer, a man of enormous ego and magnetic charisma—though surely he was all that. His power stemmed also from a national-religious dimension. Ethiopian Christianity united the cross and the crown, bestowing an extra element of holiness to earthly authority. In Ethiopian history there were rulers who knew how to combine politics and religiosity, and others who failed to do so.[13] Haile Selassie succeeded perhaps more than his predecessors in fulfilling the ethos of the Ethiopian Christian king "Prester John," as medieval Europeans knew him.[14] By Ethiopian tradition, the emperor was an "elect of God" (*seyuma egziabher*). In keeping with this tradition, Ethiopia's 1931 constitution (Article 5) stated, "the person of the Emperor is sacred, his dignity is inviolable and his power indisputable." Haile Selassie, no doubt, authentically identified with being a descendant of King Solomon and the Queen of Sheba. Many of his Christian subjects worshipped him as such. He derived power and legitimacy from the Bible, both Old and New Testaments. His seal was engraved with the words "The Lion of Judah Has Prevailed." It was an old Ethiopian motto,[15] but no previous emperor was so readily identified with this national-religious symbol.

Haile Selassie worked to successfully control the Church. It was his initiative that allowed Ethiopian monks to be appointed as bishops for the first time. In 1929 he sent four monks from his devotees to Cairo, where they were anointed. He then sent them to various provinces in Ethiopia, where they worked to magnify his image. Abuna Kerilos also arrived from Egypt in 1929 and remained loyal to Haile Selassie till his death in December 1950. The Coptic patriarch himself came in 1930 and took part in the emperor's coronation. At that time, Haile Selassie arranged for sixty young boys to complete their religious studies in Egypt. The boys returned, complaining they were badly treated, so the emperor inaugurated an Ethiopian clerical training academy in Saint George Cathedral.[16]

Another of Haile Selassie's religious initiatives was ordering the translation of the Bible from Ge`ez to Amharic. Only a few Ethiopians, mainly clergymen, really understood Ge`ez. The language had been dead for centuries, like Latin in Europe. By 1934 an illustrated manuscript, with columns written in Ge`ez alongside their translation in Amharic, had been prepared. Mass printing of the new text had to wait until after the Italian occupation, but the book's purpose was clear: to deepen popular religiosity and admiration for Haile Selassie—the king, the defender of the faith, the real head of the Church.

Haile Selassie treated his Muslim subjects in a way befitting a patronizing Christian king. He enabled a registered Muslim-Indian trading firm named Muhammadali Company to administer a branch of the company in Harar and a smaller one in Addis Ababa. The firm paid revenues to his treasurer and provided goods to him and his associates. In 1933 he authorized the opening of an Islamic school in Harar, but he would not yet allow the establishment of a mosque in the capital. By Italian estimates, in 1932 there were 2,625,000 Christians in Ethiopia and 2,250,000 Muslims. Of the latter, only forty-nine were permitted to make the *hajj* to Mecca, and only eleven were granted permission the year after. In the days of Menelik there had been a prosperous, autonomous emirate in the southern region of Jimma under the dynastic rule of Abba Jiffar II. When Abba Jiffar died on September 19, 1934, Haile Selassie abolished the region's autonomy and placed a Christian governor over Jimma. Leaders of political Islam in the Horn of Africa and in the Middle East never forgave Haile Selassie for this act.

Things changed rapidly in 1935 when a crisis broke out with Mussolini. *Il Duce* worked to incite the Muslims of Ethiopia, and Haile Selassie began appeasing them. He finally authorized building a mosque in Addis Ababa and gave speeches on Christian-Islamic brotherhood. Time and again, he preached all-Ethiopian, indeed all-African, solidarity under his leadership. On May 22, 1935, he spoke in Harar. The Italian consul quoted him:

> I am the emperor of all blacks, and all blacks are my subjects. I want to say that not only the black people of Ethiopia should swear allegiance to me. But all black people subjugated under the whites in British Somaliland, in Kenya, Djibouti, Eritrea, Italian Somalia. They are all foreign citizens only legally, not in reality.[17]

In practice, Haile Selassie could rely upon his Christian subjects during the coming war. He was their king and priest. Beyond garnering the allegiance of Christians across Africa, it is apparent that in facing the threat of the aggressive Fascist, Mussolini, he also wanted to become the defender and king of the Horn of Africa, of all its black sons, irrespective of religion. Days would come in which Haile Selassie would conceive himself as the father of all Africa.

The British, the Nile, and Mussolini

Destroying the feudal systems of old ruling families in the provinces had an impact on foreign affairs as well. The British wanted an all-Nile dam at Lake Tana, a plan that Ras Tafari had frustrated throughout the 1920s. He was afraid that the British would make an alliance with the old families of Gojjam and Bagemdir and manipulate western Ethiopia from Khartoum. Now, however, he felt more confident to start talking business with the British. They had promised him an annual subsidy, free electricity, and a port in Somaliland if he enabled the Nile project. But the offer had expired. The Grand Crisis, a global economic calamity that began in autumn 1929, left London hesitant. Haile Selassie, as always, worked slowly. In 1933 he tried to host an international conference on the Tana Dam, but the British did not respond. He tried again in May 1935, but the shadow of Mussolini had already been cast over the area.[18] Construction of a dam on the Blue Nile in Ethiopia would not begin prior to 2011.

From today's perspective we may hypothesize what might have happened had the Ethiopians and the British reached an understanding. What could have been the rate of Ethiopia's economic growth, and what would Mussolini have if the British were so involved in that country? One can also understand why the emperor was suspicious of the British lion. Could he really hug the "lion" without being injured? The British, in any case, remained angry. The dam issue was never their prime consideration when they had to weigh Mussolini against Haile Selassie. Their more central concern was appeasing *Il Duce* in the hope (that in hindsight proved vain) that he would not join forces with Adolf Hitler. In June and July of 1935, at the height of the Italian-Ethiopian crisis, the Inter-Departmental Committee on British Interests in Ethiopia concluded that Italian conquest of Ethiopia would not be that bad:

> In the north, Italy would eventually acquire a protectorate over Tigre. . . . British interests lie . . . in acquisition of control over Lake Tana. . . . It is believed that provision could be made somewhat on this line for a partition of interests between Great Britain and Italy in anticipation for the collapse of the Abyssinian administration, which many authorities consider to be probable.[19]

This report reached the hands of Mussolini (was it leaked purposely?) and convinced him that he was not really risking a conflict in Europe by invading Ethiopia.

Back to Center Stage—Tigray

Another internal Ethiopian issue gained international importance and proved detrimental to the emperor.[20]

As mentioned, the province of Tigray was the only one not directly administered by Haile Selassie's men. The Tigrayans, proud and tough, never really accepted Shoa's domination. After the death of Emperor Yohannes IV of Tigray (1872–1889), the Italians occupied Eritrea (1890), thus dividing the Tigrinya-speaking people.[21] Menelik and his successors did their best to marginalize Tigray, but even Haile Selassie did not dare control it directly. Tigray remained under its traditional leaders—two grandsons of Yohannes: Ras Gugsa Araya ruled eastern Tigray, and Ras Seyum Mangasha ruled the western province. They hated each other, and Haile Selassie knew how to manipulate them. On May 5, 1932, the emperor married his eldest

son, Asfa-Wossen, to Seyum's daughter Walata-Esrael. The emperor
was not slow to balance the equation. On June 16, 1932, he married
his daughter Zanaba-Warq to Haileselassie Gugsa, the son of the rival
ras. The bride was fourteen, the groom thirty-two. He, Haileselassie
Gugsa, was destined to play a leading role in the forthcoming drama.

Italy and "Political Tigrinya"

Ever since Italy penetrated the Horn of Africa in 1885, its Ethiopian
strategy vacillated between two contradicting options. One was to
develop friendly relations through diplomatic and economic chan-
nels. In Rome this strategy was given the code name *politica scioana*
[Shoana], since the imperial center was in Shoa. The other option
was to encourage the creation of buffer zones between the Ethiopian
center and the Italian colonies of Eritrea and Somalia, by helping
centrifugal elements in Ethiopia. This subversive strategy got the
name *politica tigrigna* [Tigrinya], since the region of Tigray was its
prime target. Naturally, the Italian foreign ministry advocated
scioana while the colonial ministry stood for *tigrigna*. Between 1927
and 1932 the tensions between the two approaches grew. The Italian
legation in Addis Ababa supported the reforms of Tafari/Haile Selassie and helped in developing communications, banking, and more.
The foreign ministry pushed for a Treaty of Friendship, which was
signed on August 2, 1928.

In early 1932 Italy began departing from *politica scioana*. The
apparent reason was growing discomfort with Haile Selassie's success in stabilizing Ethiopia. The Fascists believed the emperor was
gradually closing the cracks through which they meant to penetrate
the country. If Italy were one day to avenge Adwa and build its great
empire in the Horn of Africa, the ground should be prepared in
Tigray. The ministries of foreign affairs and the colonial ministries
were asked to submit relevant reports. In March 1932 Emilio De
Bono, the minister of colonies, visited the area. He reported to Mussolini that Tigray was ripe for subversion and that it would not be
difficult to provoke Haile Selassie into a war he would lose. In August, the foreign ministry in Rome concurred, but it advised not to
underestimate Haile Selassie or to overly provoke Britain and
France. Mussolini, it appears, chose the middle ground. He ordered
the intensification of an anti-Ethiopian diplomatic campaign in Europe and promoted subversion in Ethiopia. A special intelligence unit

was established in Italy's Addis Ababa legation. It was tasked with coordinating activities in the five Italian provincial consulates—in Tigray, Wallo, Gojjam, Bagemdir, and Harar. A technician in charge of monitoring Ethiopian wire communications was sent to each consulate, as was a doctor tasked with ensuring the local chiefs' dependency on his services. Tigray was the main interest. Italian colonialists were never free of the "Adwa complex"—the memory of the 1896 calamity, and the duty to revenge it. It was equally clear that a war with Ethiopia would start from Eritrea and an invasion into Tigray. From that point on, the internal order in the northern province that Haile Selassie had arranged through marriages to his children became a factor in the crisis that ensued.

The Death of a Princess

The arrangement in Tigray rested not only on the marriages with the two rival ras but also upon the illusion the marriages created—that the emperor would one day appoint one of them as a negus of Tigray. But soon the equation collapsed. After Ras Gugsa returned to his capital, Makale, he contracted pneumonia, which progressively worsened. On March 25, 1933, his son's new wife, the young daughter of the emperor, Princess Zanaba-Warq, died of the same illness. The Italian doctor who attended the ras and the princess wrote an unflattering report on her husband, Haileselassie Gugsa, the son of the ras, that claimed he neglected his dying wife in favor of seeking pleasure with other women.[22] When the emperor heard of the death of his beloved daughter, he ordered her body to be flown to Addis Ababa. Haileselassie Gugsa flew with her remains. Meanwhile, his father, the ailing Ras Gugsa, was rushed on a mule to Asmara and died on the road on April 26, 1933.

Emperor Haile Selassie was not in a hurry to restore the balance in Tigray. Ras Seyum hoped that his authority would be instated over the whole province, while Dajjazmach Haileselassie Gugsa wanted to inherit his father's domain in eastern Tigray. In retrospect, one may wonder how the emperor failed to perceive Haileselassie Gugsa's treachery, and why he favored Gugsa over Ras Seyum. When the former arrived in Addis Ababa with the body of the princess, the mourning emperor and his wife, Mennen, received him like a son.[23] The Tigrayan showed humility, but he lost no time in plotting with the Italians. In June 1933, while still in the capital, Haileselassie Gugsa wrote clandestinely to the governor of Eritrea and asked to buy a house in Asmara. The emperor, unaware, decided to restore the Tigrayan balance. In March 1934 Seyum was summoned to the capital and was appointed military commander of Tigray. Dajjazmach Haileselassie Gugsa was ordered to return to the province to assume command of the eastern wing under Seyum. He returned to Makale by way of Italian Asmara, where he made a crucial step.

The Traitor and Mussolini's Strategy

On May 27, 1934, Haileselassie Gugsa arrived in Asmara. The next day he met with the governor, R. Astuto, and confided that he was on the side of Italy. The emperor, he said, left no hope for Tigray. He caused friction and promoted anarchy. To prevent further escalation, he was ready to cooperate with Italy. He proposed an Italian invasion from Eritrea and promised to open the road down to the heart of the country. Three days later he presented Astuto with a detailed plan: he had thirty thousand soldiers and would lead the Italians in. Tigray would fall in no time, and the rest of the country would revolt against the emperor. Haile Selassie was hated, he said, and would surely flee to Europe, where he would waste the money he robbed from the people. If Seyum returned to Tigray, Haileselassie Gugsa vowed he would destroy him.

In detailed reports to the minister of colonies, Astuto promised that the Ethiopian traitor was a credible person and that his plan to solve "the Abyssinian question" was a good one. Astuto suggested first preparing the ground with Britain and France and then activating this option. It would be easy to persuade Haileselassie Gugsa to declare himself negus of Tigray and request Italian protection. Britain and the League of Nations ("if still existing") would have no choice but to accept Italian control in Tigray. The emperor, he felt, would also surrender. If he reacted militarily, he would be exposed to an Italian offensive that would reach Addis Ababa.[24]

Haileselassie Gugsa indeed opened the front line in his region to the Fascists in the event of war. The timing of Gugsa's betrayal was arguably historic. That same May, Mussolini had been taking a closer look at the Ethiopian issue. In retrospect, it is quite probable that he took seriously Haileselassie Gugsa's suggestion. It was perhaps not a mere coincidence that on May 31, Mussolini summoned his closest devotees and closed their meeting with his strategy for next year:

1. Completion of defensive arrangements in the shortest possible time.
2. Upon completion of defensive arrangements, study the problem of indirectly provoking an action on the part of Ethiopia.
3. Absolute silence about the policy of military preparation with the governments of France and Great Britain.[25]

In July 1934 Mussolini began to personally supervise the details of a full-fledged Italian policy of subversion in Ethiopia.[26]

Mussolini Drives Escalation

Haile Selassie had a phenomenal memory. Even after the age of eighty he was still collecting pieces of gossip and putting them together. He was also confident that nobody was a better judge than him. Indeed, he was a great judge, but when his judgment failed, it failed greatly. Doubtless, he failed to observe the treacherous character of Haileselassie Gugsa, who went on plotting with the Italians in Asmara. From September to November 1934 he even hosted an Italian agent in Makale, disguised as an engineer invited to build a monument to his father, who was in fact mapping the area.

On December 5, 1934, Mussolini provoked an incident. In a remote location on the border of Italian Somalia and Ethiopia, at a place called Wal-Wal, a skirmish between a Somali garrison (in the service of Italy) and Ethiopian troops resulted in over 150 deaths. Each side protested the actions of the other. While Ethiopia appealed to the League of Nations, Italy outright demanded compensation. Rome issued a humiliating ultimatum to Haile Selassie. All Ethiopian efforts at reasonable appeasement were rejected. The calamity between Haile Selassie and *Il Duce* sent the League of Nations into crisis in January 1935. Ethiopia was a sovereign member, and the league's ability to prevent war and impose mediation and reason was at stake. The concept of "collective security," the most fundamental notion of the international body, was on the table. Britain and France worked to save the League of Nations, but as Mussolini grew bolder, they became more afraid he would join Hitler. Ethiopia and Italy's drama was studied and researched thoroughly. It is worth mentioning that the British remained bitter at Haile Selassie for frustrating their plans for the Tana Dam. In the summer of 1935, London and Paris found a way to assure Mussolini that he was not risking war in Europe by conquering Ethiopia, and that Italy would face only economic sanctions and that both countries would face an embargo on arms sales.

Realizing that a frontal collision with the Italians would be disastrous, the emperor prepared for a guerrilla campaign on the advice of some experts.[27] But guerrilla warfare implied sacrificing Tigray. The only viable plan was to let the Italians in and then conduct hit-and-run operations. Tigray was quite an ideal terrain for guerrillas. But the whole idea of guerrilla warfare was alien to the Ethiopian military tradition, and Ras Seyum, the grandson of Yohannes IV, the pride of Tigray, could hardly accept it. In January 1935 he wrote to Haile Selassie saying he would rather attack and invade Eritrea. At the end of February, Italian intelligence intercepted the emperor's answer:

> The skies are cloudy, a storm is imminent, and the wise are preparing for the floods. So it is with wars, it is incumbent upon us to do so cautiously. The Italians are talking about a peaceful arrangement but on the other hand they prepare for war. As secretly and as quietly as possible you have to put the various chiefs, soldiers and peasants on the alert. It is not necessarily going to be like in Adwa in 1896 [one decisive battle]. We have to position our troops in the mountains and the forests, in valleys and caves, without concentrating them in masses. We have to make them very mobile . . . namely, to act like rebels and block their lines of communication. . . . You have to dig trenches and build small forts in various places. The Italians will most probably try to lure our people from these trenches into the open. Do not allow your men to abandon these trenches and face the tanks. They have instead to move from one trench to another.[28]

To make sure that Ras Seyum would do as he was ordered, Haile Selassie sent Colonel T. Konovaloff, an ex-officer in the Russian czar's army, to Adwa in early July 1935. He stayed with Seyum until a month after hostilities began. Konovaloff's memoirs shed light on the events that ensued. Seyum did try to follow the emperor's instructions, but with difficulty. He and his men did not follow Konovaloff's advice for preparing for guerrilla warfare. According to Konovaloff, Seyum could not read a map and knew nothing about modern warfare. He wrote:

> A military school was to have been started in Adwa and a series of courses given. On this pretext or another this school had never opened. Ras Seyum looked upon the coming of a military school as another of the foolish innovations in vogue Addis Ababa, and was therefore not worth bothering about. . . . The Ras and his chiefs put little faith in modern methods of war or modern war materials, they preferred their swords and considered that these would be quite adequate for what they wanted.[29]

The Ethiopian Defeat

The Italians prepared not only a modern army—in some respects the most advanced of that time—but also bribe money: one million Maria Theresa (MT) silver coins. They failed to bribe Seyum but succeeded with a few of his men. They prepared 150,000 MT for Haileselassie Gugsa and his followers. The emperor started to suspect Haileselassie Gugsa only in late August, but the spy he sent from the capital had been bribed as well. In the meanwhile, another spy had sent a list of suspected persons to Haile Selassie, who in August and September was rather busy finding traitors in Tigray. He cabled to Seyum and to Haileselassie Gugsa, demanding reports. The latter knew how to respond and flatter the emperor. In his memoirs Haile Selassie even quoted one of his cables: "If by any chance the Italians should invade us by military force, I shall resist them to the utmost in my province, until I die." He also reported he was in contact with Eritrean soldiers in the Italian army, and that they would cross the lines and join him when the invasion began. "Some people," Emperor Haile Selassie remembered, "gave Us this news [about the treacherous activities of Haileselassie Gugsa], "but We discounted the reports directed against him and did not suspect that a man who claimed to be a descendent of Emperor Yohannes would betray Ethiopia."[30]

The Italian invasion began on October 3, 1935, on two fronts, from Eritrea and Somalia. Militarily it would have been much easier to reach Addis Ababa from Somalia, but the major effort was from Eritrea into Tigray. One consideration was that if the British intervened, at least Tigray would fall into Italian hands. But the "Tigray first" strategy gave Ethiopia its only chance. If the Ethiopians could conduct efficient guerrilla warfare in this difficult area and could hold the Italians until the rainy season of 1936 (beginning in June), it was possible that Britain and France would finally somehow interfere. For the Ethiopians it meant letting the Italians in, letting the invaders capture Tigray's main towns, and avoiding frontal confrontation. Ras Seyum had his difficulties, but when the invasion began, he pulled back under pressure from the emperor. The Italians were happy to March to Adwa, and they entered the town—the symbol of their 1896 defeat—on October 6, 1935.

Haile Selassie himself was not entirely happy with this strategy. His generals, notably his chief of staff, Ras Mulugeta Yigazu, wanted to make a stand. In late September the emperor decided to form a line north of Makale with Haileselassie Gugsa positioned in its center. The latter was quick to betray the plan to the Italians. Marshal Emilio De Bono, commander in chief, instructed him to wait for the Italian attack and then cross the lines with his men. However, on October 9 the Ethiopian traitor panicked, crossing the lines that night. For the Italians, the road to Makale was now open, but it was a mixed blessing. The premature movement of Haileselassie Gugsa prevented the frontal confrontation they desired. On October 15 the Italians entered Aksum, and on November 8 they took Makale. Nearly the whole of Tigray was now theirs, and the time had come to execute Haile Selassie's guerrilla strategy. Ras Seyum was ordered from Addis Ababa to move to the Tigrayan subregion of Temben, an area with mountainous terrain. Together with forces sent under the command of Ras Kassa Hailu, he managed to withstand the invasion. A frustrated Mussolini replaced De Bono with the tougher Pietro Badoglio, yet the Ethiopians managed to avoid a decisive confrontation. Thus, 1935 ended in an Italian failure, at least according to some British and American experts.[31]

Ras Seyum was not pleased. He was too weak to confront the Italians and too conservative to adopt modern guerrilla warfare. According to a British military observer he was "still imbued with the medieval idea that the only methods of attack were shock movements, either a frontal attack in mass or wide encircling movement to take the enemy in the flank or the rear."[32] "Ras Seyum," wrote Konovaloff,

> had to conduct a guerrilla war, a word which the Ethiopians translate "shiftannet," meaning brigandage. Poor Seyum . . . possessing all to live in comfort . . . and now, over fifty he became by force of circumstances a "shifta." I recall that in a telegram from the emperor advising him not to engage in open battles, Seyum had replied: "I am too old and too tired to become a shifta."[33]

Guerrilla warfare against the Italians—then, and later under occupation—was led mainly by minor chiefs, seldom by sons of elite families.

After the early success of late 1935, the generals of Haile Selassie, headed by Adwa 1896 veteran Ras Mulugeta, began pushing for a frontal battle. On November 28, 1935, Haile Selassie dictated his will and left the capital. Dressed in a khaki uniform, he manned an anti-aircraft gun in the town of Dessie. Foreign journalists and photographers were very impressed by his spirit and conduct.[34] But the Italians were less impressed, and they were also cruel racists.

"The Italians not only spilled Christian blood wantonly," the emperor wrote on December 7,

> but also violated international law by dropping explosives and incendiary bombs on civilians without advance warning, killing many women and children. . . . Moreover, because they are devoid of humanity, they dropped forty bombs on the hospital, which was full of wounded, and on the military doctor's ambulance, even though they were clearly marked with Red Cross symbols that are visible from a distance.[35]

The Fascists used poisonous gas in a way they would not dare doing in Europe. Their military superiority proved overwhelming. Between February 11 and 15, 1936, the Ethiopian armies assembled in Amba Aradam were defeated. It was the decisive battle of the war, in which brave Ras Mulugeta was among the killed. On February 27 the armies of Ras Seyum and Kassa Hailu were routed in Temben. On March 31 the rest of the Ethiopian forces, led by the emperor himself, were destroyed at Maichaw.[36] On May 5 the Italians entered Addis Ababa. Mussolini completed his conquest prior to the rainy season.

On the eve of the Maichaw defeat, March 1936.

Escape

In over two thousand years of history, Haile Selassie was the first ruler of Ethiopia to go into exile. As the front collapsed he returned to Addis Ababa on the night of April 30. There was no one left to defend the capital. Italian aircraft were already bombing the town. Yet Haile Selassie maintained his composure. At six o'clock that morning he summoned the new American minister to present his credentials. Possibly, the emperor was already thinking of Washington as a potential source of salvation. He then convened the twenty-five surviving Ethiopian leaders. Three of them urged Haile Selassie to continue fighting to the end. They mentioned the legacy of Emperor Tewodros II, who (in 1868) chose to commit suicide rather than surrender to the British. Tekla-Hawariat (who had prepared the draft of the 1931 constitution) even dared to call Haile Selassie a coward.[37] However, the majority, headed by Ras Kassa Hailu, argued that he must leave, for as long as he lived, Ethiopia existed. A few hours later, foreign journalists were gathered to hear the emperor's defiant words:

> Do not the peoples of the world yet realize that by fighting on until the bitter end I have not only been performing my sacred duty towards my own people, but have been standing guard in the last citadel of collective security? Are they so blind that they cannot see I have been facing my responsibilities to the whole of humanity?
>
> I wanted with all my heart to hold on until my tardy allies appeared. But if they never come then I say to you prophetically and without a trace of bitterness "the West is doomed."

The American minister who reported these words added: "A truly great ruler and a polished Oriental gentleman has passed from the scene of world politics, and it will be extremely difficult to find his equal among the backward peoples who are striving toward progress and enlightenment."[38]

On May 2, 1936, the emperor boarded a train to Djibouti with his wife Menen and their five children, accompanied by Ras Kassa Hailu and Heruy Walda-Selassie. On May 4 they boarded the British light cruiser *Enterprise.* The captain reported he saw a frightened man who asked if he was safe. "When I told him he was safe like in the Bank of England, he finally smiled."[39] The *Enterprise* sailed to Haifa, where on May 8, Haile Selassie took the train to Jerusalem.

Notes

1. Carmichael, "The Lion of Judah's Pen," pp. 55–83.
2. On the 1930–1935 period in Haile Selassie's life see, among others: Marcus, *Haile Selassie I,* chapters 6–8; Del Boca, *The Negus,* pp. 115–153; Asfa-Wossen, *King of Kings,* chapter 4; and Paul Henze, *Layers of Time: A History of Ethiopia* (London: Hurst, 2000), chapter 7.
3. Zewde, *Pioneers of Change in Ethiopia,* chapter 2; Pankhurst, "The Foundation of Education."
4. See Teshome, "The History of Menelik II School, 1907–1962.".
5. *HSAB,* pp. 65–75. See there for the quotations in this paragraph.
6. See Richard Pankhurst, "Who Were the 'Young Ethiopians,'" www.nesglobal .org/eejrif4/index.php?journal=admin&page=article&op.
7. Bahru Zewde, "Heruy Walda Sellase", *EAE,* III, pp. 20–21.
8. See more in J. Calvitt Clarke, *Alliance of the Colored Peoples: Ethiopia and Japan Before World War II* (Woodbridge, UK: James Currey, 2011).
9. See M. Zabolotskikh, "Takla Hawaryat Takla Mariam", *EAE,* Vol. 4, 2010, pp. 829–830; Zewde, *Pioneers* (see index).
10. Paulos Tzadua, "Fetha nagast," *EAE,* Vol. 2, 2005, pp. 534–535.
11. *HSAB,* p. 178, especially pp. 178–201.
12. Heinrich Scholler, "Constitutions," *EAE,* Vol. I, 2003, pp. 788–791; for an English translation of the 1931 constitution, see Margery Perham, *The Government of Ethiopia* (London: Faber and Faber, 1969), pp. 423–432.
13. Emperor Tewodros, 1855–1868, immaturely tried to control the Church, antagonized the abuna, and ended in disaster. Emperor Yohannes managed to unify the Christian dogma but did not control the bishops of Shoa and Gojjam. Menelik enjoyed the full support of the abuna, but his heir, Lij Iyasu, we saw, failed in trying to rebuild Ethiopia without its Christian elite.
14. Prester John (Latin: Presbyter Johannes) was a legendary Christian patriarch and king popular in European chronicles and tradition from the twelfth through the seventeenth centuries. He was supposed to be an ally against the Muslims during the era of the Crusades. After the mid-fourteenth century, Ethiopia became the center of the search for "the kingdom of Prester John," who was mostly identified with its negus.
15. The Hebrew tribe of Judah was traditionally symbolized by a lion. In Genesis 49:9 the patriarch Jacob blessed his son Judah as a "Young Lion." In Christian tradition, the Lion of Judah is also a term representing Jesus. Revelations 5:5, New International Version: "Do not weep! See, the Lion of the tribe of Judah, the Root of David, has triumphed. He is able to open the scroll and its seven seals." A Ge'ez version of the triumphant Lion of Judah was included among the titles of the emperors throughout the Solomonic medieval dynasty. The motto was revived in modern times by emperors Tewodros II, Yohannes IV, and Menelik II. See Richard Pankhurst, "Lions as Royal Symbol," in *EAE,* Vol. 3, 2007, pp. 573–575.
16. For the above and below in this section, see "Haile Selassie: The Christian King," in Haggai Erlich, *Ethiopia and Saudi Arabia: Christianity, Islam, and Politics Entwined* (Boulder: Lynne Rienner Publishers, 2007), pp. 14–17; and the chapter "Haile Selassie and Islam: Seeking Saudi Help," ibid., pp. 42–46.
17. Paolo Borruso, *L'Ultimo Impero Cristiano: Politica e Religione nell'Etiopia Contemporanea ,1916–1974* (Milano: Guerini e Associati, 2002), p. 178, quoting Italian consul in Harar to Mussolini.
18. See James McCann, "Ethiopia, Britain and the Negotiations for the Lake Tana Dam, 1922–1935," *International Journal of African Historical Studies,* Vol. 14 (1981), pp. 667–699.

19. FO 371/19184, "Report of the Inter-Departmental Committee on British Interests in Ethiopia," Maffey to Foreign Office, 18.6.1935, and especially FO 371/19194, "Committee on Territorial Exchanges in Abyssinia," July 1935.

20. The following is based on Haggai Erlich, *Ethiopia and the Challenge of Independence* (Boulder: Lynne Rienner Publishers, 1986), pp. 135–165. See there for references. The research for these chapters was based on files of the Italian Ministry of Eastern Africa, Series ASMAI 54, British files in FO 371, articles in *Berhanena salam*, and the following books: Corrado Zoli, *Chronache Ethiopiche* (Roma: Sindacato Italiano, 1930.); Corrado Zoli, *Etiopia d'Oggi* (Roma: Societa Anonoma Italiana Arti Grafiche, 1935); Emilio De Bono, *Anno XIII, The Conquest of an Empire,* English Translation, London 1937; Angelo Del Boca, *Gli Italiani in Africa Orientale,* Vol.1 (Roma-Bari: A. Mondadori, 1976) and Vol. 2 (Roma-Bari: A. Mondadori, 1979); *HSAB,* pp. 213–250; Luca dei Sabelli, *Storia di Abissinia* (Rome, 1936–1948) (4 vols.); G. L. Steer, *Caesar in Abyssinia* (London: Hodder and Stoughton, 1936); R. L. Hess, *Italian Colonialism in Somalia* (Chicago: University of Chicago Press, 1966); George Baer, *The Coming of the Italo-Ethiopian War* (Cambridge, MA: Harvard University Press, 1967); T. Konovaloff, *Con le armate del negus: Diarie e memoria* (Bologna: Zanichelli, 1938); and J. F. C. Fuller, *The First of the League's Wars* (London: Eyre and Spottiswoode, 1936).

21. For a detailed analysis, see Erlich, *Ethiopia and Eritrea, Ras Alula, 1875–1897.*

22. ASMAI 54/38, Dr. Pierro Lecco's Report, May 1933.

23. See a short discussion on Haile Selassie's attitudes toward death in Carmichael, "The Lion of Judah's Pen," pp. 55–83.

24. ASMAI 54/38–158, Astuto to De Bono, "Degiac Hailasellassie Gugsa" (top secret), 9.6.1934.

25. Hess, *Italian Colonialism,* pp. 172–173.

26. See Baer, *The Coming of the Italian-Ethiopian War,* chapter A.

27. At the end of the war the Italians had 500 tanks, 1,500 artillery pieces, 350 airplanes, 15,000 machine guns, and 476,000 soldiers. The modern Ethiopian units numbered some twenty thousand soldiers. The other units were half-trained and ill equipped.

28. ASMAI 54/9–27. A translation of a telegram from the King of Kings to Ras Seyum intercepted toward the end of February 1935.

29. Konovaloff, *Con le armate del negus,* p. 36.

30. *HSAB,* p. 247.

31. Foreign Relations of the United States, [hereafter FRUS] Diplomatic Papers, 1936, The Near East and Africa, Volume III. The Chargé in Ethiopia (Engert) to the Secretary of State, Addis Ababa, January 7, 1936. "Time is still playing into the hands of the Abyssinians. . . . It looks as if so far things were going more or less according to Ethiopian plans." See these files in https://history.state.gov/search?q=Haile+selssie.

32. FO 371/ 20934, "Annual Report 1936," section B, "Feudal organization and Generalship."

33. FO 371/20167, An account by Konovaloff, 31 March 1936.

34. Steer, *Caesar in Abyssinia.*

35. Carmichael, "The Lion of Judah's Pen," pp. 55–83.

36. On the battles of the 1935–1936 war see Del-Boca, *The Negus,* pp. 153–177; and the most detailed, Anthony Mockler, *Haile Selassie's War: The Italian-Ethiopian Campaign 1935–1941* (New York: Random House, 1984), Part II, pp. 37–173. Also see *HSAB,* pp. 251–290.

37. John Spencer, *Ethiopia at Bay: A Personal Account of the Haile Selassie Years* (Algonac, MI: Reference Publications, 1984), p. 69; See Haile Selassie's version in *HSAB,* pp. 290–292.

38. FRUS, 1936, The Near East and Africa, Volume III, Minister Resident in Ethiopia (Engert) to the Secretary of State, May 2, May 12, 1936.

39. FO 371/20197, Murray to FO, 30 June 1936.

6

From Refugee to Liberator

~

On May 8, 1936, Haile Selassie and his entourage arrived at the railway station of Jerusalem. He stayed in the city two weeks, no more, but he arranged for his family to stay for many years.[1]

The image of the humiliated emperor captivated the Jewish community in Palestine. Dozens of newspaper articles, including in children's weeklies, described the king as a symbol of exile and catastrophe on the one hand, and a symbol of what Europe was capable of on the other. "At four in the afternoon," the *Haaretz* newspaper reported on May 10, 1936,

> we heard the train entering Jerusalem. The area surrounding the station was filled with police, journalists, and a large crowd impatiently awaiting the arrival of the emperor. . . . Then the Empress appeared in the doorway. She exited first, black, and much older than she looked on her previous trip to Jerusalem two years before. The Emperor appeared after her. Of medium height, black face, tired, he descended the stairs with unsure steps, his head bowed, his eyes full of sadness. . . . When the Negus came out of the station there was a thunder of applause from the surrounding crowd. A little solace.

Haile Selassie cherished the moment: "Even the Jews and the Arabs who had been quarreling amongst themselves forgot their dispute and, standing together, watched Us with pleasure and respect."[2] *Davar* reported:

The next day, at five in the morning, they set off for a visit to Deir al-Sultan. The monks knelt before the Emperor and burst into tears for the bitter fate of the fallen empire. The Empress sobbed aloud and the monks beat their chests with their fists and their shrieks were heard from a distance. The entourage continued on to the building of the Ethiopian consulate on Prophets Street, which was adorned with Ethiopian flags for the Emperor, and from there, they visited the church on Abyssinia Street, where they participated in a mass prayer. The crowd could not ignore the Italian flags that were draped prominently around the Italian hospital near the Ethiopian consulate.

Jerusalem, Haile Selassie said later, was "an Ethiopian sanctuary where there was no smell of scorched buildings and no corpses of priests barred the door, and where we were able to rest in peace before the last effort."[3] However, in his memoirs he devoted only a short passage to the stay in Jerusalem.[4] It probably reflected what he felt. The Lion of Judah, the descendant of King Solomon, was not in the mood for historical inspiration. The glorious Ethiopian empire had just fallen apart, and on his watch. Jerusalem was there with all its biblical legacies, but the future, it was cruelly clear, was to be determined in Europe. From King David Hotel on May 19, Haile Selassie cabled to the Secretary-General of the League of Nations.[5] Europe had betrayed him, and from Europe he would demand salvation. Four days later, he boarded a British ship to exile in England.

Waterloo Station—No Flags

While still in Jerusalem the British high commissioner, A. Wauchope, had to inform Haile Selassie that he would not be an official guest in England but a refugee with no political status. The emperor was told he could bring along just a modest entourage, up to eight persons and two servants. The governor of Gibraltar was ordered to repeat this message and make sure Haile Selassie understood it well.[6] When the emperor reached Waterloo Station in London he had his two sons with him, Asfa-Wossen and Makonnen; his daughter Tsahai; Heruy Walda-Selassie; and Ras Kassa Hailu. In London, he was no longer an emperor of a sovereign state.

Ethiopia indeed officially existed no longer. On May 9 (a day after Haile Selassie arrived in Jerusalem), Benito Mussolini declared the establishment of "Italian East Africa." The territories of Eritrea and Italian Somalia were now annexed together with what was Ethiopia, and the new "Africa Orientale Italiana" was divided into six "governments": Amhara, Harar, Shoa, Eritrea, Somalia, and Sidama. The term *Ethiopia* remained only in the name of the old local Church, and in the title of Vittorio Emanuelle III, now "King of Italy and Ethiopia."

During the next five years the Fascists did their best to uproot "Africa Orientale" from its ancient Ethiopian history. They worked to strengthen the political and cultural identity of the Muslims and to disconnect the Christians from their Egyptian-Coptic affiliation.[7] London did not actively disapprove the new Italian empire. The British's main aim was to appease Mussolini, lest he joined Hitler. In retrospect, it was an illusionary misjudgment; sacrificing Ethiopia proved a catastrophic mistake. Meanwhile, the deposed emperor was an embarrassment for the British, a symbol of a shameful surrender. No official reception awaited Haile Selassie in London at Waterloo Station.

The British government under Prime Minister S. Baldwin was ready to give Haile Selassie refuge, as public opinion would not allow otherwise. In the year and a half since the beginning of "the Ethiopian Crisis," many in England were outraged at the Fascists' racist brutality. One clear voice was Sylvia Pankhurst's, daughter of the pioneering suffragette Emily Pankhurst. Sylvia connected the struggle for women's dignity with Ethiopia's stand against the rapist Mussolini. In 1936 she established a weekly entitled *New Times and Ethiopia News*, and in the coming years she did her best to make the life of the deposed emperor in England as bearable as possible. In her weekly, as well as in many other papers, hundreds of articles depicted the struggle for Ethiopia as one of humanity against barbarism.[8] Nevertheless, Baldwin insisted on playing down the refuge Britain extended to Haile Selassie. The Jewish philanthropist Sir Elly Kadoorie allowed the emperor to stay in his London house, and foreign minister Anthony Eden was allowed to meet with Haile Selassie, but only "privately." An Ethiopian request to meet with King Edward was rejected. Haile Selassie did not give up. As Baldwin was enjoying tea in the garden of the House of Parliament, he suddenly spotted Haile Selassie, who was trying to meet with him as if by accident. The prime minister managed to sneak away, though not very elegantly.[9]

As soon as the occupation of Ethiopia became an accomplished fact, London asked to cancel the League of Nation's sanctions against Italy. The Swiss government offered asylum to Haile Selassie on condition he would not engage in politics. Anthony Eden tried to talk Haile Selassie out of his plan to speak to the League of Nations. But the league remained the only option for the proud exile.

"It is us today. It will be you tomorrow."

In chapter 50 of Haile Selassie's memoirs, entitled "Our Journey to Geneva in Quest of Justice from the League of Nations," the emperor describes the event that made him an icon. Accompanied by Heruy Walda-Selassie and Ras Kassa Hailu, he arrived in Geneva on June 26, 1936. Journalists and photographers came to cover the event, and the Italians among them were instructed to humiliate Haile Selassie. "When We went there on the appointed day and stood at the lectern," he wrote, "the Italians who had come there for news reporting started to whistle continuously with the intention of obstructing Our speech." The Italians yelled mockingly like animals, as racists in a football stand. "At this moment the Romanian delegate remarked to the President of the Assembly, 'for the sake of justice, silence these beasts.' . . . The guards . . . seized them and ejected them." Standing proud and dignified, Haile Selassie was eternalized in photos and newsreels. He apologized for speaking in Amharic, because "in Amharic language alone I am able to speak my mind from my heart and with all the force of my spirit."[10] His speech was translated simultaneously into French and English:

I, Haile Selassie I, Emperor of Ethiopia, am here today to claim that justice which is due to my people, and the assistance promised to it eight months ago, when fifty nations asserted that aggression had been committed in violation of international treaties. There is no precedent for a Head of State himself speaking in this assembly. But there is also no precedent for a people being victim of such injustice and being at present threatened by abandonment to its aggressor. Also, there has never before been an example of any Government proceeding to the systematic extermination of a nation by barbarous means, in violation of the most solemn promises made by the nations of the earth that there should not be used against innocent human beings the terrible poison of harmful gases. It is to defend a people struggling for its age-old independence that the head of the Ethiopian Empire has come to Geneva to fulfil this supreme duty, after having himself fought at the head of his armies. . . . That is why I decided to come myself to bear witness against the crime perpetrated against my people and give Europe a warning of the doom that awaits it, if it should bow before the accomplished fact. . . . What real assistance was given to Ethiopia by the fifty-two nations who had declared the Rome Government guilty of a breach of the Covenant and had undertaken to prevent the triumph of the aggressor? . . . I ask the fifty-two nations, who have given the Ethiopian people a promise to help them in their resistance to the aggressor, what are they willing to do for Ethiopia? And the great Powers who have promised the guarantee of collective security to small States on whom weighs the threat that they may one day suffer the fate of Ethiopia, I ask what measures do you intend to take? . . . Representatives of the World I have come to Geneva to discharge in your midst the most painful of the duties of the head of a State. What reply shall I have to take back to my people?[11]

The speech made quite an impression, the *Times* of London wrote: "For the little good it can now do him—his legend may not be without growing force hereafter—Haile Selassie has taken and will hold a high place in history."[12] Haile Selassie was indeed no longer the man looked down upon by the British minister twelve year earlier: "ignorant, vain and childish . . . wanting in effectiveness."[13] The Geneva speech was quoted time and again, and statements like "[I] give Europe a warning of the doom that awaits it, if it should bow before the accomplished fact," along with the reminder that the "collective security to small states" was the cornerstone of the League of Nations, would prove historic. Twenty-seven years later, Haile Selassie reminded the world: "I spoke then both to and for the conscience of the world. My words went unheeded, but history testifies to the accuracy of the warning that I gave in 1936." Someone among the reporters of his 1936 speech summarized it thus: "It is us today, It will be you tomorrow." In fact, he did not utter these very words, but they remain engraved as his message. The deposed emperor thus earned the reputation of "the conscience of the world," an image that would outlive him.

On July 15 sanctions against Italy were lifted. But appeasing Mussolini proved disastrous, for the Fascist *duce* did join Hitler. They both intervened to assure victory to another Fascist, Francisco Franco, in the Spanish Civil War. Then Czechoslovakia was sacrificed to the Nazis. When the British and the French rose up to defend Poland, it was too late. On the rostrum in Geneva in 1936, Haile Selassie warned that a new world war would break. Those who wanted to prevent that war should have begun by defending Ethiopia against Fascist forces that same year.

On the Sidelines

As the world escalated toward a global war, Haile Selassie was pushed to the sidelines. After his Geneva speech he returned to London, where he was not really welcome. Foreign Minister Anthony Eden supported him personally, but the British government expected trouble—namely, that Haile Selassie would work to damage

the policy of appeasing Mussolini. Dr. Martin Warqneh, the last
Ethiopian official in London, was asked to tell Haile Selassie he
should keep a low profile.[14] Sir Elly Kadoorie returned to his London house and kindly asked Haile Selassie to leave. On August 5,
1936, the deposed emperor and his entourage arrived at the little
town of Bath, west of Oxford. It was to be his home for the next
four years. The quiet English town received him warmly. It was not
Jerusalem, nor London or Geneva, but it offered serenity. After two
months in the Spa Hotel, on October 9 the Ethiopians moved to the
newly purchased Fairfield House. Haile Selassie did his best to give
the new home a royal touch. He bought furniture even though little
money remained for heating. Anthony Eden arranged for some car-
pets and curtains to be shipped from Addis Ababa; Mussolini allowed the shipment, probably in the hope that the exiled emperor
would come to terms with his new reality. But Haile Selassie
showed no sign he would ever accept the fall of Ethiopia. Meanwhile, he busied himself caring for his family and his group of loyal
confidants. Twenty-five persons lived in Fairfield House, and not
all were happy. Princess Tsahai left after a month, returning to London to study paramedicine. Empress Mennen came to visit, found
the British weather unbearable, and returned to Jerusalem.[15]

   With no kingdom, no throne, and no crown, Haile Selassie left
only pleasant memories of himself among the people of Bath.[16] He
loved children and dogs, and he walked with them daily to the town
center, responding to well-wishers by touching his hat, often with a
smile. All the occupants of Fairfield House woke up at six in the
morning for prayer and breakfast. Then Haile Selassie would sit in
his study, dictate his autobiography, read and write letters, and host
visitors.[17] Files in the British archives are full of details about what
kept him busy—mostly matters far from global importance. He gathered pieces of information and gossip, all he could hear on anything,
especially on any other Ethiopian. He also followed international affairs. Much of his time was devoted to financial suits. The most important one was against a British news agency that had cabled from
Addis Ababa during the battles and still owed money to the
Ethiopian post. The agency claimed that the money owed to the government of Ethiopia should now be paid to the Italian government.
Haile Selassie insisted that he was the Ethiopian government. The
issue was dragged out until April 1938, when Britain recognized
"Italian East Africa" de jure. After losing this suit Haile Selassie ran
into financial difficulties. The British government discussed how to

support him without leaving its fingerprints. Finally, "an anonymous donor" was procured to leave a trimonthly sum of five hundred pounds in Haile Selassie's bank account.[18] The Bath municipality, likely on instruction from London, covered the emperor's water and electricity bills. In the end, when Haile Selassie left England, there were fifteen hundred pounds in his Lloyds Bank account.[19]

Another legal issue that consumed Haile Selassie's time was an Italian claim to Ethiopian property in Jerusalem—approximately twenty buildings. The deposed emperor sent a messenger to the Jerusalemite lawyer, Nathan Marein, asking him to defend the Ethiopian case pro bono in the British mandatory court. Marein pursued the case until June 1940, when Italy entered the war and lost that suit. (After the war, Nathan Marein moved to Ethiopia and became a close legal adviser to Haile Selassie.)

Beyond legal affairs, Haile Selassie kept abreast of global politics. Angered at the British and aware of the rising power of the United States under President Franklin D. Roosevelt, Haile Selassie sent a message to him via the American ambassador in London on September 23, 1939, after World War II was declared in Europe:

> It was with satisfaction that I observed in your message [to Hitler and Mussolini, back in April[20]] that you recalled the monstrous injustice committed against my country. The Ethiopian people in their tragic plight turn towards the peace-loving nations in the hope that these will one day liberate them from their present bondage. My people know that the great American nation is firmly attached to the principle of national independence; and they gratefully know that your Government . . . has refrained from recognizing the Italian decree of annexation of Ethiopia. . . . I feel sure, whenever the opportunity may offer, you will desire to use your great influence to secure the restoration to my people of their freedom and complete independence.[21]

By the time of this message, Haile Selassie had already had America on his mind. Relevant developments would soon follow.

Back to History

On April 16, 1938, Britain recognized Italian East Africa de jure. The London government did not bother to inform Haile Selassie. It was a bad year for him. In December 1937 he was involved in a car accident, in which he broke a bone.[22] Later, Ras Kassa Hailu left Bath and returned to Jerusalem. On September 19, Heruy Walda-Selassie,

Haile Selassie's closest adviser and intellectual partner, passed away in Bath. It was rumored that Haile Selassie was left with little money and would have to sell Fairfield House. War in Europe raged while Haile Selassie busied himself in a remote corner. He anticipated a long wait. In March 1940 he bought a new car—a Morris 10—hardly a car for royalty. He loved luxurious cars but had to compromise with a middle-class standard.[23] Haile Selassie surely did not envision having to sell it shortly thereafter.

On May 10, 1940, Winston Churchill became the prime minister of Great Britain. The man who stood up to Hitler and Mussolini was a devout imperialist but also was respectful of Ethiopia and its proud past. Six days after Churchill assumed office, Haile Selassie wrote to the new prime minister, offering his services.[24] Churchill had no time to answer in writing, but Haile Selassie did not have to wait long. On June 8 Italy joined the war on the side of Germany. On June 24 Haile Selassie, code name "Mr. Smith," was on board a British plane flying to Malta. From there he sailed to Cairo, and flew to Khartoum, where he landed on June 27, 1940.

Italy's joining the war aggravated the British situation but also opened the gate for victories elsewhere. These were some of the most difficult months of the war. France had just fallen, and the British Expeditionary Force had barely managed to escape from Dunkirk (the evacuation was completed on June 4). The coming summer and autumn would witness the Battle of Britain. Anxiety about the very survival of the British Islands did not subside before late September. In August the Italians captured British Somaliland, and in September they stormed British forces from Libya and pushed toward Egypt. In February 1941 the Italians were reinforced by the Germans in North Africa, and together they continued threatening Egypt until the last months of 1942. In the Mediterranean theater, the Axis powers went from force to force. By June 1941 they had taken Greece, Yugoslavia, and Crete. But in Italian East Africa the Italians themselves came under siege. This time, unlike in 1935, Mussolini's army could not pass through the Suez Canal through the courtesy of London. The British, in contrast, could concentrate imperial forces around Italian East Africa from all directions. On January 19, 1941, the British army began an offensive from Sudan to Eritrea, and to Ethiopia from Sudan, Somaliland, and Kenya. After fierce battles, the Italians collapsed. The British entered Asmara on April 1, 1941, and Addis Ababa on April 6. The rest of the Italian army in Ethiopia, which was entrenched in Gondar, finally surrendered in November.

For the British commanders in East Africa, having Haile Selassie in Khartoum was a mere nuisance. They had their own plans for the future of Ethiopia (to which we shall return). But the commander in chief of the front, Major General William Platt, and his superior in the Middle East theater, Field Marshal A. Wavell, were ordered by Churchill to host Haile Selassie in the Sudanese capital. The latter had to wait patiently again, biding his time on petty complaints and gathering information. In early July he even toyed with the idea of petitioning Roosevelt to send him arms in return for a future American protectorate in Ethiopia, with an American-built and -controlled dam on the Blue Nile.[25] The British at last began supporting him in September 1940 with two thousand Egyptian pounds.[26] The British command had its own men inside Ethiopia, tasked with organizing guerrilla warfare and gathering intelligence. In August, Brigadier Daniel Sandford was sent for a mission in Gojjam. Sandford had been an adviser to Haile Selassie and knew the country well. His task force, Unit 101, was headed by Sandford until the arrival of Orde Wingate.

Gideon Force

In late October 1940, Churchill and Eden decided to send Major Orde Wingate to Haile Selassie in Khartoum. Wingate was a guerrilla warfare expert who had served in Palestine as an adviser to the Jewish Haganah paramilitary organization during the Palestinian Revolt (1936–1939). In June 1938 he initiated the establishment an of elite commando unit that adopted offensive tactics. He named it "The Gideons," after the biblical leader who preferred "the few and the bold." The unit was, in a way, the nucleus of the future Israeli army.[27] But Wingate's sympathy with the Zionist cause angered the British command, and in May 1940 he was ordered to leave Palestine and never return. The following October he was promoted to lieutenant colonel and sent to work with Haile Selassie and Sandford. In his first meeting with the emperor, Wingate declared that the international community had betrayed Ethiopia in 1935, but he believed that Ethiopia would be the first nation to be liberated. And, he added, the country would not be free and independent if Haile Selassie would not lead it.[28]

For Wingate, the war to liberate Ethiopia was similar to the struggle of the Jewish people in Palestine. Wingate equated Haile Selassie to David and his battle against the Philistines: "The short stature of the emperor was a symbol. The war we are about to enter will be like the one between David and Goliath, and David will prevail."[29] Profound mutual trust between the majestic "Lion of Judah" and the British officer with unorthodox conduct was forged. Wingate knew the area from his days of service in Sudan.[30] In December 1940 he wrote to Wavell, asking to build a force that "will eat into the Italian apple and turn it so rotten that it will drop into our hands."[31] Churchill acquiesced, and Wingate built a force of fifteen hundred men—half Ethiopian, half Sudanese. He called it "the Gideon Force," like the Gideons he had led in Palestine.

Prior to the entry of the Gideon Force in Ethiopian territory, British aircraft scattered leaflets in Amharic. They included the portrait of Haile Selassie with the slogan "The Power of Trinity, the Lion of Judah has prevailed." On January 20, 1941, the force crossed into Ethiopia in Gojjam. Haile Selassie was flown in with his two sons, Asfa-Wossen and Makonnen, along with the *echage* and Ras Kassa Hailu and his young son, Asrate, who had come from Jerusalem. The group conducted a short ceremony on a steep riverbank. A message from Major General Platt was read, and for the first time in nearly five years the flag of Ethiopia was hoisted. Haile Selassie declared he hoped to win with the help of the British.[32]

Haile Selassie—the Nationalist Movement

The Gideon Force's short ceremony near the Sudanese border came to symbolize the beginning of Ethiopia's liberation. In 1941 the entirety of the national liberation movement of Ethiopia was Haile Selassie, his few followers, and the concept of his renewed emperorship. Other factors that were expected to work toward regaining independence were too weak. The intelligentsia was tiny, most its members murdered by the Fascists. The members of the old aristocracy were either torn by rivalry, exiled, or collaborating with the occupation.[33] Ras Seyum of Tigray, his arch-enemy Haileselassie Gugsa (who had been promoted to ras by the Italians), and Ras Hailu of Gojjam were regular guests in the palace of the Italian viceroy.

Nevertheless, the Italians faced resistance from all layers of Ethiopian society. Among the leaders of the resistance were priests, monks, and local chiefs with whom the Fascists dealt with racist brutality. Many guerrilla fighters were not deterred. They continued the *shifta* tactics, now in a modern version. In their first meeting in

Khartoum, Wingate advised Haile Selassie to call the leaders of the resistance "patriots"—*arbanyoch* in Amharic.[34] The prominent patriot (*arbanya*) was Abebe Aregai (who later became ras) of eastern Shoa. He ambushed occupation forces and led acts of sabotage, inspiring other fighters. The Fascists were determined to catch Abebe Aregai, and he pretended occasionally that he was ready to negotiate.[35] However, in spite of his heroism, and of the other *arbanyoch,* they hardly endangered the occupation. The real chance to undermine the Fascists' army, and to start rebuilding Ethiopian sovereignty, was anchored in the strength of Haile Selassie's personality and image of Haile Selassie—in Ethiopia and throughout the world.

This was also what Churchill and Eden thought. On February 4, 1941, two weeks after the Gideon Force entered Ethiopia, Anthony Eden declared in London that the British government "would welcome the re-appearance of an independent Ethiopian State and recognize the claim of Emperor Haile Selassie to the throne . . . [and that the British government had] no territorial ambitions in Ethiopia." He added: "In the meanwhile the conduct of military operations by Imperial Forces in parts of Ethiopia will require temporary measures of military guidance and control. These will be carried out in consultation with the Emperor, and will be brought to an end as soon as the situation permits."[36]

It was a declaration of historical importance, but not all British shared Eden's policy, especially not many of the military commanders in the field or their superiors in the War Office. No less significant was the fact that not all Ethiopian chiefs saw Haile Selassie (at that stage, at least) as the savior of their country.

The Gideon Force's military contribution was negligible. It was a small unit (numbering only two thousand men) with light arms that, at its most influential, disturbed Italian communications. Far more meaningful than its military contributions was Gideon Force's help in reconstructing the myth of Haile Selassie and rebuilding his hierarchy of loyal followers. Nobody in Ethiopia had forgotten that in 1936 the emperor had fled rather than fall on his sword. Orde Wingate and his Gideon Force effectively restored the image of Haile Selassie as a freedom fighter. To Haile Selassie's great fortune, Orde Wingate was a public relations genius. He missed no opportunity to glorify Haile Selassie in biblical terms as the savior of Ethiopia.[37] Wherever the force and Haile Selassie went, the cry *janhoy,* "here is the emperor!" echoed. The Italians tried to recruit local counter forces, but to no avail. After years of cruelly oppressing the Ethiopian masses, they found now just a few willing collaborators. Behind Haile Selassie stood a millennia of Ethiopian pride alongside an assured victory of the British in the Horn of Africa.

Victory Parade

On April 6, 1941, the British army entered Addis Ababa as the Gideon Force and Haile Selassie entered Debra-Markos, the capital of Gojjam. Ras Hailu Tekla-Haimanot, the local hereditary chief who had collaborated with the Italians, presented himself for surrender. The chief, who was old and round, came late for the meeting in his Alfa Romeo car. He bowed down in front of Haile Selassie and was given a chance to deliver a short speech before being handcuffed. After this event, Haile Selassie demanded that the British fly him to his capital. He was denied, and the British explained their position with concern for the lives of the forty thousand Italians in Addis Ababa.

While the emperor was waiting in Gojjam, the British army established two military administrations: one in Asmara for Eritrea, and the other in Addis Ababa for Ethiopia. Haile Selassie, however, would not wait. For him, Ethiopia was not an enemy territory to be administered by the British army. On April 27 he left Debra-Markos with Wingate, a few loyal followers, and the prisoner Ras Hailu. The rest of the Gideon Force followed. After a short ceremony in Debra-Libanos monastery, where the Fascists had carried out a horrible massacre of *arbanyoch* and priests, they reached Entoto Mountain, overlooking Addis Ababa. Haile Selassie surveyed his capital with his binoculars. The legendary *arbanya* Abebe Aregai arrived there, leading fifteen thousand armed men. He bowed before the emperor and cried: "I am your loyal subject. I never submitted to the enemy. I never hoped to see you alive again and I am grateful to God for this day, when I have seen the sun shine."[38] (Abebe Aregai was later promoted to ras and would be a prime minister.)

Aware of the significance of historical symbolism, Haile Selassie waited on Entoto Mountain for May 5, the date on which five years earlier Mussolini had boasted from his terrace in Rome that Addis Ababa was taken by his soldiers. Haile Selassie's parade began at noon. The men of Abebe Aregai stood on both sides of the road forming an honor guard. At half past three, the parade entered the town. Two tanks from the South African Division led the front, followed by Wingate on a white horse, with two battalions of the Gideon Force trailing behind. In the rear, Haile Selassie sat in an open car. He wore a solemn expression that fluctuated between smiles and tears. As they reached the area of Menelik's Palace, they were received by General Alan Cunningham, commander of the British forces that had penetrated from Somalia. A twenty-one-gun salute was heard. Haile Selassie made a speech ordering his people not to harass the Italian prisoners.[39] The prisoners were paraded as the masses rejoiced. The slaughter the British feared never materialized (quite the contrary; the emperor asked the British not to deport the Italians, most of whom were vital, working middle-class residents).

After the ceremony General Cunningham invited Haile Selassie to his headquarters, but the emperor managed to induce the general to come to him. Wingate won some of the emperor's respect, though not an overwhelming amount. In the second volume of his memoirs, Haile Selassie detailed the war for liberation, mentioning scores of names, senior Ethiopians and senior British. Wingate was mentioned here and there. In describing the victory parade the emperor confined himself to the two sentences: "Next came Colonel Wingate riding a white horse. He was the commander of Our Gojjam front from the British army."[40] Gratitude, even to those who served him loyally and efficiently, was not one of Haile Selassie's merits.

Reprinted from Avraham Aqavia, With Wingate in Ethiopia (Tel Aviv: Am Oved, 1944).

May 1941 on the stairs of Genet Lul Palace—submission of the patriots.

Regaining Tigray

His restored prestige, the surrender of chiefs like Ras Hailu of Gojjam, the renewed allegiance of *arbanyoch* like Abebe Aregai, and the presence of the British army and Eden's declaration collectively reconstituted the imperial rule of Haile Selassie.[41]

British political advisers, army officers, and diplomats gathered in Addis Ababa. They included Brigadier Sandford and Major (later colonel) R. Cheesman, who knew Ethiopia well and were committed to fulfilling Eden's declaration to the letter. For them, Haile Selassie was the only man who could put the country together and move it forward. They were also convinced that this was in the best interest of Britain. However, their influence in British circles was limited. World War II was in full swing. Until the end of 1942 there was still the danger that Germany's Field Marshal Erwin Rommel (the "Desert Fox") would conquer Egypt and isolate the British army in the Horn. War strategy was therefore decided by the military rather than diplomats. Many high officers and War Office planners thought that the Eden declaration, or parts of it, should better be ignored.[42] More pointedly, they believed that Tigray should be annexed to Eritrea under the British administration in Asmara.

Brigadier S. Longrigg, the chief administrator (military governor) of Eritrea, was this plan's foremost proponent. He maintained that a "Greater Tigray" state, the reunification of the Christian Tigrinya-speaking heartland Eritrea with the Ethiopian region of Tigray, was a logical continuation of history.[43] Such a state, in his vision, would have linkage to Ethiopia yet prosper under British protection. The key to the fulfilment of the "Greater Tigray" idea was in the hands of Ras Seyum Mangasha, the grandson of Emperor Yohannes IV (1872–1899) and the pride of Tigray. Seyum had his reasons to avoid rejoining Haile Selassie. In 1936 he had been imprisoned by the Fascists and taken to Italy. His daughter and the emperor's son, Asfa-Wossen, separated in exile (and later divorced in 1941). Seyum was not ready to forgive Haile Selassie for what he considered scarifying Tigray in 1935 and 1936. In July 1939 the Italians returned Seyum to Tigray, and he began collaborating with them. Haile Selassie saw Seyum as a traitor. Seyum, however, was well aware of the changing situation. A few weeks before the British invaded Ethiopia, he established secret contact with them. On April 5, 1941, in liberated Asmara, Seyum met with the British political officers. He tried to be ambiguous. He said he was the grandson of Emperor Yohannes but also that he swore allegiance to Haile Selassie. And that he was for the unity of Ethiopia, but Haile Selassie had betrayed him. The British in Asmara were not ambiguous. They appointed Seyum on the spot as governor of Tigray under their administration of Eritrea. On April 8, Seyum wrote to Haile Selassie, swearing allegiance but signing "the grandson of Emperor Yohannes." Following British advice, he did not mention his new appointment in Asmara.

Soon afterward the British in Asmara made another step toward the creation of a separate Tigray state. On April 17 they summoned Seyum's archrival, the infamous traitor Haileselassie Gugsa (a greatgrandson of Yohannes), and appointed him governor of eastern Tigray. The latter did not hesitate to state his favor for Tigray's independence and for a British protectorate. He also wrote on the same day to Emperor Haile Selassie to inform him that he, Haileselassie Gugsa, was the new governor of eastern Tigray.

The British in Addis Ababa were furious. Sandford considered the policy of Asmara a bold deviation from Eden's declaration. He wrote to a colleague:

> The emperor will shortly be left to rule his country. His task will be a formidable one. . . . I would very strongly urge that we put our fingers in the political pie as little as possible. The emperor's record shows him to be extremely astute in handling his own people, and he is not vindictive. Left to himself he will soon have all the important chiefs eating out of his hand—a result very much to be desired.[44]

For its part, the War Office was angry at Sandford and his group. They blamed them for working to return Haile Selassie's control over the whole country, even though this was not an explicit promise of Eden's. The chief political officer of East Africa, Major General P. Mitchell, wrote that Ras Seyum was "by right of birth and descent the Ras of Tigre; whether he becomes in addition an official of some Ethiopian Government under the emperor is another matter which is neither our business nor our interest to try to decide."[45]

Meanwhile, Haileselassie Gugsa managed to disappoint the British in Asmara, and they appointed Ras Seyum over the whole of Tigray. When declaring this appointment, the Asmara officers did not mention the emperor. Instead, they sent a message to Haile Selassie that stated that Seyum would not come to him. On June 20 Haile Selassie wrote directly to the war cabinet in London. He added a bitter letter to Churchill himself, demanding fulfillment of the

Eden promise. It is doubtful that Churchill had the time to consider his arguments. On June 22, 1941, Hitler invaded the Soviet Union. It was a shocking development, one of the deciding moments in global history. Yet the British prime minister found the moment to decide on Africa—Tigray to Ethiopia! Ras Seyum understood the meaning in no time. On July 8 he left Adwa to swear allegiance to Haile Selassie in Addis Ababa.

The return of Tigray to the government of Haile Selassie ensured the territorial integrity of Ethiopia. On January 31, 1942, the emperor and Britain's chief political officer in East Africa, P. Mitchell, signed an agreement in this spirit. Yet the British officers in Asmara did not give up. They still had a card: Haileselassie Gugsa. They avoided extraditing him but finally did so in September 1946. Haileselassie Gugsa was condemned to death in Addis Ababa, but the emperor spared his life. It is doubtful if any other ruler would have done so. But Haileselassie Gugsa was allowed to live in relative comfort.[46] He died in his bed in 1985, another story attesting to the complex personality of Haile Selassie.

Notes

1. This paragraph is based on Haggai Erlich, "In an Hour of Despair, Shelter in Jerusalem," in *Alliance and Alienation: Ethiopia and Israel During Haile Selassie's Time* (Trenton, NJ: Red Sea Press, 2014), pp. 35–40.
2. *HSAB*, p. 295.
3. Del Boca, *The Negus*, p. 185.
4. *HSAB*, pp. 293–296.
5. *HSAB*, pp. 295–296.
6. CO 733/318/5 CO. Dispatches, 23.5.1936.
7. On Church disconnection see Erlich, *The Cross and the River*, pp. 112–117. On the Italians and Muslims during the occupation see Erlich, *Saudi Arabia and Ethiopia*, pp. 67–72.
8. See Richard and Rita Pankhurst, *Ethiopian Reminiscences* (Addis Ababa: Tsehai Publishers, 2013), pp. 13–20.
9. Spencer, *Ethiopia at Bay*, p. 72.
10. *HSAB*, pp. 300–301.
11. Haile Selassie, "Appeal to the League of Nations," June 1936, https://www.mtholyoke.edu/acad/intrel/selassie.htm.
12. *Times*, 2.7.1936.
13. FO 371/9993, Annual Report 1923, Russel to MacDonald, 16.2.1924.
14. FO 371/20197, "Notes and minutes," June–July 1936.
15. See more in Asfa-Wossen Asserate, *King of Kings*, pp. 137–143.
16. See also the BBC film "Footsteps of the Emperor Haile Selassie 1st's Exile to Bath," https://www.youtube.com/watch?v=X8YlK96rEZg.
17. Lutz Haber, "The Emperor Haile Selassie I in Bath 1936–1940," in Trevor Fawcett (ed.), *Bath History*, Vol. 3 (London: Bath: Ruton, 1990). For the latest re-

search see Keith Bowers, *Imperial Exile: Emperor Haile Selassie in Britain 1936–40* (London: Brown Dog Books, 2016).

18. FO 371/22010, Memo by V. Cavendish-Bentinck 29.8.1938; FCO 31/2012, R. Wright to FCO 11.5.1976. It was Lord Maurice Hankey who got the money from Sir John Ellerman. FO 1093/82, including Haile Selassie's letter of thanks, dated 7.6.1938.

19. FO 371/46080, Lloyds Bank Manager to FO, 10.7.1945.

20. On April 14, 1939, Roosevelt sent a letter to Adolf Hitler and Benito Mussolini that read, in part: "The tide of events seems to have reverted to the threat of arms. If such threats continue, it seems inevitable that much of the world must become involved in common ruin. . . . Three nations in Europe and one in Africa have seen their independent existence terminated." See http://www.jewishvirtuallibrary.org/president-roosevelt-message-to-adolf-hitler-and-benito-mussolini-april-1939.

21. FRUS, 1939, Vol. 740.00/1391, The Emperor of Ethiopia (Haile Selassie) to President Roosevelt [Translation], 23 April 1939.

22. Asfa-Wossen Asserate, *King of Kings*, p. 140.

23. Haber, "The Emperor Haile Selassie I in Bath."

24. FO 371/24637, Haile Selassie to Winston Churchill, 16 May 1940.

25. FRUS, 1940, Volume III, 865D.24/1, The Counselor of Embassy in the United Kingdom (Johnson) to the Adviser on Political Relations (Dunn), London, 3 July 1940.

26. FCO 31/2012, T. Cashmore to Mrs. Johnson, 19.5.1976.

27. Among the Gideons were many future commanders of the Haganah and the Israel Defense Forces, such as Yigal Alon and Moshe Dayan. Wingate himself dreamed of establishing a Jewish army in Mandatory Palestine and aspired to be its commander in chief. His contribution to the history of Israel earned him the appellation "the Friend," and his name is commemorated widely throughout Israel.

28. Leonard Mosley, *Haile Selassie: The Conquering Lion* (London: Weidenfeld and Nicolson, 1964), p. 258,

29. On Wingate in Mandatory Palestine and in Ethiopia and for a detailed and reliable description of his life and military contributions, see Avraham Akavia, *Orde Wingate: His Life and Activity* (Tel Aviv: Ma'arachot 1993) (in Hebrew). Akavia had accompanied Wingate in Palestine as his adjutant. Wingate asked for him, and he arrived in Sudan in November 1940 to serve as right hand, friend, and secretary to the British officer all throughout the campaign in Ethiopia.

30. T. Ofcansky, "Wingate, Orde Charles," *EAE*, Vol. 4 (2010), pp. 1187–1188.

31. Mockler, *Haile Selassie's War*, p. 292.

32. Mosley, *Haile Selassie: The Conquering Lion*, p. 246.

33. Alberto Sbacchi, "Italy and the Treatment of the Ethiopian Aristocracy, 1937–1940," *International Journal of African Historical Studies,* Vol. 10 (1977), pp. 209–241.

34. Akavia, *Orde Wingate*, p. 89.

35. David Hamilton Shinn and Thomas P. Ofcansky, "Abebe Aregai, Ras," *Historical Dictionary of Ethiopia* (Lanham, MD: Scarecrow Press, 2004), p. 3.

36. See Perham, *The Government of Ethiopia*, p. 463.

37. Wingate himself won a legendary reputation among Ethiopians. A Jewish doctor, one of the twenty-two Wingate brought from Palestine, testified that he heard Ethiopians talking about an "Israeli prophet" named Wingate who was doing wonders in the country. See Erlich, *Alliance and Alienation: Ethiopia and Israel,* pp. 50–58.

38. Mockler, *Haile Selassie's War*, p. 379.

39. See the second part of Haile Selassie's biography, which details the years 1937–1942, devoted mostly to the battle for liberation; Harold Marcus (ed.), *My Life and Ethiopia's Progress: Haile Selassie I, King of Ethiopia*, Vol. 2 (East Lansing: Michigan State University Press, 1994), pp. 161–165.

40. Ibid., p. 160. Wingate left Ethiopia in June, physically and mentally exhausted. He was later put in charge of anti-Japanese guerrilla activity in Burma, where he was killed. His name was eternalized in Ethiopia. The General Wingate Secondary School (Wingate was promoted to major general before moving to Burma), which was opened after the war, was considered the best in the country. Many leading Ethiopians, including Meles Zenawi (prime minister from 1995 to 2012), were educated there.

41. The following paragraphs are based on "Tigrean Nationalism, British Involvement, and Haile Selassie's Emerging Absolutism: Northern Ethiopia, 1941–1944," in Erlich, *Ethiopia and the Challenge of Independence,* pp. 166–201.

42. See also: FRUS, 1942, Vol. 4, 124.84/157, Memorandum by the Chief of the Division of Near Eastern Affairs (Murray), March 6, 1942.

43. For background see Erlich, *Ethiopia and Eritrea..* Citation refers to 1997 edition.

44. WO 230/16, Sandford to DCPO Ethiopia, Brigadier Lush, 23.4.1941.

45. WO 230/16, CPO to GHQ Middle East, 14.5.1941.

46. See Erlich, *Ethiopia and the Challenge of Independence*, pp. 184–187.

7

Absolutism

~

In May 1941 Haile Selassie was famous in Ethiopia and throughout the world. A quarter of a century had passed since he became the leader of Ethiopia. Time and again he proved resilient, iron willed, and quick minded. He was two steps ahead of all other Ethiopians, a skilled political manipulator, a king who radiated power at all times, even in defeat. An African who could also outmaneuver Europeans, and do so with majestic style.

Haile Selassie, to reemphasize, knew how to read global situations and use them to his advantage at home. Arguably, this was his greatest secret. No Ethiopian who came before or after has ever equaled him. The more complex the game, the better he was at playing it. From the crisis of World War I, he snatched victory over Lij Iyasu (1916). Entering the League of Nations (1923) helped him overcome the elite Shoan establishment. His tour of Europe in 1924 inspired and paved the way for his reforms in Ethiopia. Reconnecting to the Middle East through his visits to Egypt and Jerusalem in 1924 made him the undisputed leader of Ethiopia's Orthodox Church, a title from which he drew substantial political power. At that time, Africa, still occupied by European imperial powers, was not yet in his purview. During the continent's emancipation it would be on top of his agenda, further driving his absolutism at home.

When crowned emperor in 1930, Haile Selassie was already an international celebrity, having appeared on the cover of *Time* magazine.

His second appearance on the magazine's cover was in 1935, when he was elected its Man of the Year. Here and there he failed to understand global affairs. This was especially true when it came to reading Mussolini (in this he was just one of many). Yet, he returned to the throne in 1941 a victorious liberator, a symbol of good staring down evil. The survival of Ethiopia, its territorial integrity, and its opportunity to advance in the world were all dependent on him, and mainly on his masterful ability to play the external-internal game.

British Help

The main challenge facing Haile Selassie from 1941 to 1944 was to maneuver the British to help him build political absolutism throughout Ethiopia.[1]

Not all the British were happy with the Eden declaration of 1941. As we saw, the Asmara military administrators wanted to annex Tigray to their domain. They gave up only in late 1943. The British army officers in Addis Ababa remained powerful; for the duration of World War II, the British army controlled the entire Horn of Africa. The senior British officer in the capital was Deputy Chief Political Officer Brigadier M. Lush, who was not an admirer of Haile Selassie. He did not believe the emperor capable of stabilizing the country, and the two men had occasional differences. Nevertheless, the British in Ethiopia worked to help rebuild the imperial regime. They financed the establishment of new ministries and advised them, and they also equipped and trained a new Ethiopian army.

The Hanging of Belay

In practice, there remained two regional challenges—Gojjam and Tigray. The emperor's men took power (after some difficulties) across the rest of the country, but Gojjam and Tigray had until the late nineteenth century been kingdoms in their own right, and their nobility remained in power. The people of Gojjam, proud and confident beyond the gorge of the Blue Nile, were furious at the arrest of Ras Hailu Tekla-Haymanot. They now followed the *arbanya* (patriot) Belay Zeleka, who defied Haile Selassie's administrators. Belay had been the leader of local patriots who resisted the Italians in Gojjam, and he refused to accept a minor position in a marginal corner. The revitalized central army managed to capture him. Belay was imprisoned, but he escaped and rebelled once again. After the second apprehension, he was hanged in January 1945 in Addis Ababa.[2] His hanging did not improve the image of Haile Selassie among the veteran *arbanyoch*, many of whom were systematically marginalized by the emperor, nor did the execution help popularize Haile Selassie in Gojjam. (In July 1951 there was aborted an assassination attempt on the emperor by some natives of the region.[3])

Tigray–the "*Woyane*"

During the whole of 1942 and early 1943 Haile Selassie tried to impose his control in Tigray, but to no avail. The locals, even without the leadership of their traditional chiefs, opposed any attempt at Shoan domination. The British officers in nearby Asmara went on supporting what they called "Tigrayan nationalism."

Resistance to the central government was centered in eastern Tigray, the domain of Haileselassie Gugsa, who himself was still in British Asmara. The emperor sent bureaucrats from Addis Ababa backed by the army to Tigray. A new taxation system was declared, which increased burdens on the peasants of Tigray, who were also ordered to "host" the soldiers. The resentment turned into revolt that gained momentum, fueled by the angry peasants and the deposed local chiefs. Prominent among them was Haile Mariam Ridda, a former head of a village under the Italians. At the end of 1941 Haile Mariam went to Addis Ababa begging for some appointment, but he had been ignored. Back in eastern Tigray, he gathered Haileselassie Gugsa's followers. In August 1943, open rebellion, which became known as *woyane*, broke out.[4] The rebels took control of the main road connecting Asmara to Addis Ababa. Army units sent from the capital failed to uproot them. By mid-September, the rebels took Makale.

The *woyane* was not the bold expression of "Tigrayan nationalism" that the British in Asmara thought. Asmara-based officers still toyed with the idea that the emperor would accept a "Tigray state" in return for a strip of the Red Sea in Eritrea.[5] But the revolt stemmed less from local ideology than from resistance to oppressive centralization.[6]

As it happened, Haile Selassie managed to mobilize the British based in Addis Ababa to his cause, and the rebels were defeated.

In late August Haile Selassie sent more army units to Tigray under its new commander, Ras Abebe Aregai, the famous *arbanya*.

Additionally, the emperor convinced the British in the capital to help him persuade the people of Tigray to remain loyal to Ethiopia. He signed leaflets in which he mentioned the millennia of Ethiopian unity and promised to pardon the rebels. He also promised that Tigray would be led by its sons under his crown. Tens of thousands of copies were printed, and a British Royal Air Force squadron dropped them on rebel strongholds for three weeks between September and October. The leaflets made little impact. The rebels soon managed to spread their revolt to western Tigray. The Ethiopian army was facing a defeat. In early October Abebe Aregai began calling Addis Ababa for rescue. The British adviser who accompanied the ras, Brigadier A. Cottam, was left with little choice but to recommend bombing the rebels.[7] Being so identified with the emperor, the British could not allow his defeat. On October 6, the British warplanes returned, but this time they did not drop pieces of paper. "Leaflets proved ineffective," the British commander reported, "while bombing was most effective."[8] The rebels dispersed, and on October 14 the central army entered Makale.

The failure of *woyane* removed the last serious challenge to Haile Selassie's absolutism. Ras Seyum, who was suspected of sympathizing with the rebels, was summoned to Addis Ababa and was replaced as governor of Tigray by Abebe Aregai. But just as in the heyday of Menelik, no Shoan could be forced upon the Tigrayans for long. One by one, the army's units left Tigray, and in 1947 Seyum was reappointed over the province. In January 1949 the emperor arranged for his granddaughter, Aida, to be married to Mangasha, Seyum's son.[9] Ras Seyum remained governor of Tigray until his murder in 1960. His son, Ras Mangasha, succeeded him until the 1974 revolution. Of all the provinces of Haile Selassie's Ethiopia, only Tigray was governed by its traditional elite. As for the British, Haile Selassie chose to remember their sting rather than their honey.

Restraining Political Islam

While Haile Selassie struggled to ensure that Tigray would remain in the fold of the empire, he faced another challenge—that of political Islam.

During Italian rule (1936 to 1941), the Italians enhanced Islam in Ethiopia as a political identity. They dreamed of ruling in the whole Middle East and believed such a policy would help them. Italian East

Africa was divided into six "governments," three of which were defined as Islamic: Harar, Somalia, and Sidama. The Muslim elite there was cultivated; Arabic became an official language and was taught in new schools. Hundreds of mosques were built, and the *hajj* to Mecca was subsidized. Back on his throne, Haile Selassie undertook to return the Muslims to their old status—that of tolerated subjects in a Christian kingdom. The central challenge awaited him in Harar.[10]

The Muslim public in Harar was divided. The old local elite maintained a flexible, moderate brand of Islam that had enabled them to prosper under Ethiopian rule since the days of Emperor Menelik and Ras Makonnen. This elite was now led by Shaykh Abdallah al-Harari, who combined orthodox Islam with local popular Islam. The other camp was composed mostly of the town's middle class, who had adopted a more stringent version of Islam mixed with elements of anti-Ethiopian militancy; this group had prospered under the Italians. Hundreds of them, with Italian help, made the yearly pilgrimage to Mecca. Some even stayed in Saudi Arabia for a while and adopted Wahhabi Islamic doctrines. They were led by Shaykh Yusuf Ismail, who, back from Mecca, established a "National Association of Harar."

After his return to Addis Ababa in May 1941, Haile Selassie was informed of the activities of "the Wahhabis" in his native town. They were marching in the streets, waving flags, and carrying slogans in praise of Ahmad Gran, the jihadi leader who had conquered Ethiopia in the sixteenth century. The emperor hurried to respond. Army units were sent to Harar, headed by his son, Makonnen, the duke of Harar. The Wahhabi leaders were arrested, and some were deported. As Harar was thus pacified, the emperor appointed Shaykh Abdallah as the *mufti* of the town and the Harar region.

This was not the end of the story. In 1947 in nearby Somalia there began a struggle over its future. The ex-Italian colony was now held by the British, and they faced a young local nationalist movement. The Wahhabis in Harar regained momentum. Led by Shaykh Yusuf, they expressed identification with Somali nationalism, clandestinely organized a mission to leave for Mogadishu, and began working for the annexation of Harar to a future independent Somalia. The emperor was informed of the matter (possibly by Shaykh Abdallah), and the members of the mission were forced to flee, most of them to Saudi Arabia and Egypt. Arrests were made in Harar, and eighty-one Wahhabis were exiled to other parts of Ethiopia. Only in December 1949 did Haile Selassie pardon the exiles, including those abroad, and enabled them to return. Since then, they were resigned to Christian domination and collaborated with Haile Selassie's policy. Shaykh Yusuf himself became a regular guest in the imperial palace in the capital. He was appointed head of the Hajj Committee (after the Italians were defeated, the number of Muslim pilgrims dwindled anyway), and he headed a team that translated the Koran into Amharic.

Confident that he had neutralized Islam, Haile Selassie made gracious gestures toward his Muslim subjects. He authorized the reopening and redecoration of the Anwar Mosque in the capital's big market, and he publicly rewarded loyal Muslims. For example, in 1954 Harar native Sadiq al-Habashi published a book in Arabic entitled *Ethiopia in Its Golden Age: The Period of Haile Selassie.* The emperor was pleased and appointed him a year later to parliament. Shaykh Abdallah was to gain an international reputation, but not in Haile Selassie's Ethiopia. In 1950 he had differences with the emperor and left for Lebanon. In Beirut Shaykh Abdallah established an association named al-Ahbash, Arabic for "the Ethiopians," which preached intra-religious coexistence and became a worldwide movement. The shaykh himself published dozens of books and became a famed Islamic scholar, perhaps Islamic radicalism's toughest rival. He died in 2008 at the age of ninety-eight.

After the episode in Harar, nobody rose up to challenge Christian hegemony in the Ethiopian empire until the death of Haile Selassie.

From the British to the Americans

The British liberated Ethiopia and put Haile Selassie back on his throne. They trained and equipped his new army, destroyed the *woyane* rebels, and helped build Ethiopia's state machinery anew. Haile Selassie remained an admirer of Britain; he visited England often, savoring its culture. But he never forgot the British patronage, especially not the way they had sacrificed him to Mussolini. He also never forgot that they wanted to control Lake Tana, Gojjam, and Tigray. The British colonialists still surrounded his kingdom—in Eritrea, Sudan, Kenya, and Somalia. The emperor had a measure of gratitude, but he mostly desired to get rid of them. In 1944, as it became clear that the war in this corner of the world was over, Ethiopia and Britain renegotiated their relations. In December they signed a new agreement in which Ethiopian sovereignty was recognized. But Haile Selassie was already charting a new course. He, as already mentioned, had America on his mind. From 1944 until his death, Washington, not London, would be the capital of the big world for him.

In the history narrated so far in this book, the United States of America had quite a marginal role. American relations with Ethiopia can be traced back to Menelik's day and became official in a 1929 agreement. Ras Tafari was among the first to perceive the United States as a potentially less dangerous power in comparison to the European ones. In 1927 he sent Warqneh Eshete, better known as Dr. Martin, to the United States to sign a contract with a private firm to survey the Blue Nile, though nothing came from it. Dr. Martin was also ordered by Haile Selassie to visit Harlem in New York, to meet with African Americans, and to tell them about free Ethiopia. In 1935 the emperor hired the services of an American law professor, John Spencer, who became his trusted adviser until his death. Spencer helped Haile Selassie prepare the December 1944 agreement with the British that facilitated Ethiopia's break from them.

The United States had begun to consider Ethiopia a strategic asset, and Haile Selassie was keen to remind its leaders of that. After his return to Addis Ababa he sent messages full of admiration and commitment to President Roosevelt.[11] Roosevelt responded in kind. On August 4, 1942, the president assured Haile Selassie that the American people followed with sympathy Ethiopia's stand against Mussolini and its reclamation of independence, and promised friendship.[12] In 1943 the United States purchased the old Italian radio station on a hill near Asmara from the British and turned it into its central communication and intelligence base for the entire Middle Eastern and African theater. Renamed Kagenew, it operated until 1977. Haile Selassie sent his men to Washington, and they were told that the United States had an interest in Ethiopia regaining Eritrea.[13]

On February 13, 1945, Haile Selassie and Roosevelt met aboard an American cruiser in the Bitter Lake, in the Suez Canal. The weary US president came from the Yalta Conference, where he had exhausting, and we now know, detrimental negotiations with Joseph Stalin and Churchill. Roosevelt traveled this extra distance to meet with the Arab kings Ibn Saud and Farouk, and with Haile Selassie. It was arranged for the emperor to be flown from Addis Ababa to Egypt in a special American plane that took off at night so that the British would not notice.

Haile Selassie had prepared six points to share with Roosevelt. The first was Ethiopia's claim to Eritrea, and the last was its participation as a founding member in the new United Nations (UN). He boarded the cruiser and after a short ceremony had ninety minutes with the president. Roosevelt, weak and frail—he was to die two months later—made a painful effort to be charming and cordial. Haile Selassie was all smiles. He handed the president a present: a golden globe upon which was marked the meeting spot of the two great men.

Roosevelt was delighted and responded with a more practical present: four American military jeeps (his advisers knew that the emperor was fond of cars). The meeting marked the beginning of a new period in Ethiopia's relations with the Western world. Another episode illuminates the change. When the British in Addis Ababa learned of Haile Selassie's departure to Egypt, they hurried to inform Churchill, who lost no time in inviting Haile Selassie to a meeting in Cairo. It was the first eye-to-eye meeting between the two leaders, and it was quite cold; the picture taken showed no warmth.[14] Churchill was apparently frustrated to find Roosevelt playing in what was still a British backyard as if he owned it. And that Haile Selassie, whom he had saved and whose country he liberated, treated him—Churchill—as a secondary player. When the emperor raised the issue of the Ogaden (some of the British toyed with the idea of keeping it in their Somalia), Churchill avoided discussion. He preferred to compete with the Americans in gestures. He told Haile Selassie that a present of a brand new Rolls Royce car would be shortly on its way to Addis Ababa. The Americans answered by promptly flying a luxurious long Cadillac, sporting the sign "His Imperial Majesty," to the Ethiopian capital. It became Haile Selassie's favorite car, in which he loved to tour Addis Ababa, throwing coins to the masses who would gather along the roads to cheer and bow.[15]

Big Ego, Hard Work

Ethiopia went on modernizing, but one dimension was missing: there was now no sign of political modernization. Since the end of the war, Haile Selassie remained the only source of power. Nobody could challenge his absolute authority. No meaningful contingency of intellectuals survived the occupation, and a new one was still in the making. No other organized bodies emerged from the struggle against the Fascists. The leading *arbanyoch* were either co-opted or destroyed. Regional opposition in the periphery, like what started in Tigray and Gojjam, faded away. Haile Selassie, a Christian king legitimized by a religious-national ethos, was now the only force in Ethiopia. There were no checks or balances of any kind until his end in 1974. The men around the emperor were flattering and obedient. His image, strengthened by performances like throwing coins to the masses, became more and more anachronistic. Though these performances would later be used by some to demonize Haile Selassie, he thought of himself as a gracious, benevolent father, and he loved moments of patronizing generosity. (In one such moment, during a visit to Majorca in 1967, he suddenly gave $250 to each member of his entourage as pocket money. The local Majorcans called him Agha Khan II.[16])

The emperor worked relentlessly to magnify his image. His portrait was to appear everywhere—on coins, bills, and stamps. His picture and only his. Nearly everything new in Ethiopia was named after him. The press—*Ethiopian Herald* in English, *Addis Zaman* in Amharic, and a less important French journal—was busy glorifying Haile Selassie, and so was the radio station. No one dared to become overly noticeable. Great men learned to kiss his legs and to wait hours before getting his attention. Haile Selassie knew them all, and he memorized everything. He did not need written documents but kept millions of details in his mind, where they waited for a useful moment.

Beyond indulging his ego, Haile Selassie worked hard and demanded a lot from himself. He would rise at dawn for prayer and a Spartan breakfast of eggs and butter, which he skipped on fasting days. It kept him lean and healthy for many years.[17] He exercised regularly, and one of his grandsons testified that he once saw him in the early morning by accident, playing tennis in a hidden court.[18] He would arrive at his palace at around nine in the morning, where he received ministers and made plans. In the afternoon he would visit schools, army camps, and clinics. He never showed signs of tiring. In the evening he would stay with his family, occasionally watching a film.[19] Haile Selassie was a family man. His wife Mennen remained his best (and perhaps only) friend. He trusted her. She continued to suffer from a stomach ailment and traveled to Jerusalem whenever she could, for prayers and mostly to see her Israeli physician, Moshe Rakhmilevich.

"Elect of God"

Haile Selassie, like all his predecessors, was declared the "elect of God." He quite possibly believed it. His political power stemmed also from Ethiopian Christianity. After liberation from the Fascists, he renewed his efforts to fully control the Church.

The Ethiopian Orthodox Church had been a bishopric of the Egyptian Coptic Church since the fourth century.[20] The abuna, the head of the Ethiopian Church, was always an Egyptian, appointed by the Egyptian patriarch and dispatched to Ethiopia. This ancient tradition created political problems and Ethiopian dependency on Egypt's rulers. In 1941, back on his throne, Haile Selassie started working to assure that the next abuna would be an Ethiopian. He exerted pressure on the Egyptian Church, including threats to sever relations and hints that the Ethiopians outnumbered the Copts, so that they would one day elect an Ethiopian patriarch. A few weeks after the death of Abuna Kerilos V, in January 1951, the first Ethiopian was named the new abuna, still to be anointed in Cairo and by the Egyptian patriarch. It was Abuna Baselios, a devoted follower of Haile Selassie.[21] Thus, the emperor was made the real ruler of the Church. He dictated a new arrangement that instructed the abuna to appoint twelve bishops, so that in time they could elect a new abuna without dependency on Cairo. In 1959 the two churches separated altogether.

Holy by Constitution

In November 1955 Haile Selassie enacted a new constitution. It contained articles announcing a parliament elected by the people—but without political parties, parliament was hardly more than an advisory body. No representative politics emerged from the new constitution. It plainly defined the unlimited power of the holy ruler:

> Article 2: The Imperial dignity shall remain perpetually attached to the line of Haile Selassie I, descendant of King Sahle Selassie, whose line descends without interruption from the dynasty of Menelik I, son of the Queen of Ethiopia, the Queen of Sheba, and King Solomon of Jerusalem. . . .
>
> Article 4: By virtue of His Imperial Blood, as well as by the anointing which He has received, the person of the Emperor is sacred, His dignity is inviolable and His power indisputable. He is, consequently, entitled to all the honours due to Him in accordance with tradition and the present Constitution. Any one so bold as to seek to injure the Emperor will be punished. . . .
>
> Article 26: The Sovereignty of the Empire is vested in the Emperor and the supreme authority over all the affairs of the Empire is exercised by him as the Head of the State, in the manner provided for in the present constitution. . . .
>
> Article 66: The Emperor has the right to select, appoint and dismiss the Prime Minister and all other Ministers . . . each of whom

shall, before entering upon his functions, take before the emperor the following oath of fidelity to His Majesty and the Constitution.[22]

The Reformer

Haile Selassie became a divine, absolute monarch. No Ethiopian emperor was ever so powerful. He managed to combine ancient political concepts with the power of a new state machinery. In the building of modern government institutions, Haile Selassie was definitely a reformer and an innovator, at least until the early 1960s.

He had begun working toward this before the Italian occupation, but at that time his power was restrained by the provincial rulers. After the Fascists did away with them, he could work freely. He led meaningful changes in three interconnected areas: higher education, military, and bureaucracy.

In 1942 he turned to the British Council for assistance in building a new education system. A ministry of education was opened with British advisers, and American advisers joined up in 1944. The emperor himself served as the minister of education. Every new student received an orange from Haile Selassie for Christmas, an unforgettable token for many.

The exponential growth in school enrollment was impressive. In the school year 1955–1956 there were about 109,000 elementary

Reprinted from Ethiopia Today, prepared by Amafu Makonnen, Addis Ababa, 1960.

Opening the Parliament, 1955.

school students; enrollment climbed to about 430,000 by 1969. During those same years, the number of secondary school students grew from 2,097 to 38,093.[23] Overall, annual growth in education was good in comparison to most other countries, but was hardly enough for Ethiopia's needs. In the late 1940s there were only around one hundred graduates of secondary school in the country. In 1951 the University College was opened in Addis Ababa, and Haile Selassie I University was opened in 1961. Following the emperor's decision, English replaced French as the first foreign language taught in schools. English was taught from the first grade, and some subjects were taught in English as early as the third grade. All students, no matter their background, learned Amharic, the kingdom's official language.[24] Dozens of students were handpicked each year by the emperor and sent for advanced studies abroad. Each chosen student was summoned to the palace to bid farewell, and swore to return. Upon their return, students reported again to the palace to swear allegiance to the emperor, and to be assigned an official role by him personally.

With regard to military reform, the Fascists' destruction of the provincial armies that had existed in Ethiopia from its early history paved the way for change. A modern central army was built, first with British advice, then with help of the Americans, and later, also from Israel. In the 1950s it became the most professional force on the continent. In 1960 Ethiopia's military numbered some 58,000 men: 6,000 of them in the bodyguard (the First Division), 24,000 in three other divisions, and 28,000 national police. A US report in 1962 stated "[An] efficient, modern Ethiopian fighting force has been developed capable of defeating any potential invader."[25] Haile Selassie himself chose the officers and remembered them all. Ethiopia's top soldiers were trained in military academies in Ethiopia and abroad. Everything in the army, any piece of gossip or any officers' meeting, was reported to the emperor, and he masterfully manipulated the information, pitting one officer against the other.[26]

The face of Ethiopian bureaucracy was also transformed. With the exception of Tigray, all provinces came under new administration. Graduates of the education system were appointed to positions with the ministry of the interior that was established in 1942. It was the first time in Ethiopian history that a civil service answerable to the central government became operational and effective. The new bureaucracy was staffed by members of all ethnic, regional, and religious groups who acquired their skills in Amharic. They were selected by Haile Selassie and remained loyal to him.

They were often removed by the emperor to new posts, and they often informed on each other. An all-Ethiopian bureaucratic class was thus created, centrally oriented and obedient. Even though some secessionist movements did arise in various regions, as long as Haile Selassie was there, and as long as the bureaucratic machinery functioned, none succeeded.

Annexation of Eritrea

The climax of Haile Selassie's centralization effort was the annexation of Eritrea.[27] In December 1952 the UN decided in Resolution 390A that Eritrea would be an autonomous entity under the sovereignty of the Ethiopian crown. This decision was perhaps the best fruit that the strategy of reorientation to the United States bore. The British administered the ex-Italian colony as a UN trusteeship while its future was debated. The men Haile Selassie tasked with winning Eritrea in the diplomatic arena were Aklilu Habta-Wald (who will become a key figure in our story) and John Spencer. The former was the son of a priest, well educated, and a future prime minister. With American backing, it was decided that an Ethiopian-Eritrean federal government—namely Addis Ababa—would be in charge of security, foreign relations, and finances. An Eritrean government, freely elected by the people of the Eritrea, would administer internal affairs. Elections for the Eritrean Assembly were held in March 1952, and that July an Eritrean constitution was declared. In September 1952 the British flag was lowered from the governor's house in Asmara and the flag of the autonomy was waived.

The arrangement lasted ten years, until 1962. Aptly defined by one journalist as a "Swiss federation adapted to an African absolute monarchy," the arrangement included within it the formula for its own demise. Ethiopia was already under the full autocratic power of Haile Selassie, and he would not compromise. All Ethiopians were long neutralized from any independent political ability, but Eritreans were accustomed to other standards. The Italians, and then the British (they exercised the "divide-and-rule" strategy), enabled competing political parties and other elements of open politics. But Haile Selassie was not there to play this game. On October 3, 1952, he personally crossed the River Mareb into Eritrea (symbolically on the very day, twenty-seven years earlier, on which the Fascists invaded Ethiopia by crossing that river). Prior to that, the Ethiopian army took over, and Division 2 was put in charge of security. Henceforward the personal representative of the emperor, his son-in-law, Ras Andargatchaw Masai (husband of Princess Tananya-Warq), ruled in Eritrea. With the backing of the army and the local priesthood, he forced the Eritrean Assembly to exercise its right to dissolve. Political parties were soon banned, with the exception of the Unionist Party, which advocated full annexation to Ethiopia. In December 1958 the Assembly abolished the Eritrean flag, in September 1959 the Eritrean constitution was abolished, and finally on November 14, 1962, Eritrea was annexed to Ethiopia as its fourteenth province.

The sons of Eritrea never forgot the liquidation of their autonomy. It was a process conducted with intimidation and violence. Some Eritrean youth, mostly Muslims, fled to Sudan and Egypt. In Cairo, in 1958, they established the Eritrean Liberation Front, which began its armed struggle in Eritrea in November 1961. In the 1960s—to which we shall return—the emergence of Eritrean nationalism and the Eritrean Liberation Front became one of Haile Selassie's main challenges. But for the meantime, the emperor was at the prime of his power.

Notes

1. The following passages are derived from Erlich, *Ethiopia and the Challenge of Independence*, pp. 166–212.
2. Aberra Jembere, "Balay Zallaka," *EAE*, Vol. 1 (2003) p. 456.
3. FO 371/96719 Annual Report 1951, in Busk to Eden, 2.4.1952.
4. Nobody is absolutely sure of the origin of this name, but it became widespread, especially after 1991, when the Tigrayans regained the leadership of Ethiopia. The Tigray People's Liberation Front (TPLF) movement, which led the revolt against the Mangistu Haile Mariam military dictatorship, also called itself Woyane.
5. WO 230/168, "Future Disposal of Eritrea," 12.8.1943.
6. See more in Gebru Tareke, *Ethiopia: Power and Protest—Peasant Revolts in the Twentieth Century* (Cambridge: Cambridge University Press, 1991); Momoka Maki, "The Wayyane in Tigray and the Reconstruction of the Ethiopia Government in the 1940s," in Svein Ege et al. (eds.), Vol. 2, *Proceedings of the 16th International Conference of Ethiopian Studies,* (Trondheim: Norwegian University of Science and Technology, 2009); and Momoka Maki, "Wayyana," *EAE*, Vol. 4 (2010), pp. 1164–1166.
7. WO 01/2690, "Tigre Operations," Ethiopia–1943.
8. FO 371/35608, WO to FO, 22.10.1943.
9. FO 371/73716, Lascelles to Bevin 1.2.1949.
10. This section is based on Erlich, *Ethiopia and Saudi Arabia* , pp. 67–96.

11. FRUS, 1942, Vol. 4, 711.84/30, The Emperor of Ethiopia to President Roosevelt. May 18, 1942, July 28, 1942: FRUS, Vol. 5, 124.841/9–1344, The Emperor of Ethiopia (Haile Selassie) to President Roosevelt, Addis Ababa, August 24, 1944.

12. For more details and analysis on the decline of British influence and the rise of American influence in Ethiopia 1942–1960, see Harold Marcus, *Ethiopia, Great Britain and the United States, 1941–1974* (Berkeley: University of California Press, 1983), p. 14.

13. See more in Spencer, *Ethiopia at Bay*, pp. 139–158; FRUS, 1945, Vol. 8, 884.001, The Minister in Ethiopia (Caldwell) to the Secretary of State, February 27, 1945.

14. Stock photo, "Churchill in Cairo, with Ethiopian Emperor, Haile Selassie," 1943, (1945). No photographer credited.

15. Asfa-Wossen, *King of Kings*, pp. xviii–xix, 169–172; Spencer, *Ethiopia at Bay*, pp. 149, 160–161. See also FRUS, 1945, Volume 8, "Conversations Between President Roosevelt and King Farouk of Egypt, Emperor Haile Selassie of Ethiopia and King Abdul Aziz Al Saud of Saudi Arabia, at the Great Bitter Lake, Egypt, 13–15 February 1945," images.library.wisc.edu/FRUS/EFacs/1945v08/reference/frus .frus1945v08.i0005.pdf.

16. FO 1043/90, Reeman to FO, 9.3.1967. For more stories in this spirit, see Asfa-Wossen, *King of Kings*, pp. 279–280.

17. For details on his daily menu in the memoirs of the emperor's Austrian cook, see "Life and Work at the Court of Haile Selassie I: Memoirs of Lore Trenkler," https://anglo-ethiopian.org/publications/articles.php?type=L&reference.

18. Conversations with Dajjazmach Dr. Zewde Gebre-Sellassie, a grandson of Ras Seyum of Tigray and a step-grandson of the emperor.

19. Asfa-Wossen, *King of Kings*, p. 202; Del Boca, *The Negus*, p. 240.

20. The following section is derived from Erlich, *The Cross and the River*, pp. 123–143.

21. Bairu Tafla, "Baselyos, Abuna," *EAE*, Vol. 1, pp. 495–496.

22. Ethiopian 1955 constitution, www.chilot.me.

23. John Markakis, *Ethiopia: Anatomy of a Traditional Polity* (Oxford: Clarendon, 1974), p. 148.

24. See Perham, *The Government of Ethiopia*, pp. 249–256.

25. FRUS, 1961–1963, Volume 11, Africa 276. Telegram from the Department of State to the Embassy in Ethiopia, Washington, May 19, 1962.

26. See Erlich, *Ethiopia and the Challenge of Independence*, pp. 225–248.

27. The following is based on Tekeste Negash, *Eritrea and Ethiopia: The Federal Experience* (Piscataway, NJ: Transaction, 1997); Erlich, *Ethiopia and the Challenge of Independence*, pp. 213–224; L. Ellingson, "The Emergence of Political Parties in Eritrea," *Journal of African History* (1977), pp. 261–281; and Ruth Iyob, *The Eritrean Struggle for Independence: Domination, Resistance, Nationalism, 1941–1993* (Cambridge: Cambridge University Press, 1995).

8

The Road to Loneliness

~

Haile Selassie, like anyone else, understood the world according to ideas molded in his youth. He was arguably the smartest, wisest, and most sophisticated Ethiopian of his time. The fact that he had reclaimed Ethiopia's sovereignty must have caused him to feel superior to all other Ethiopians, as evidenced by the religious, national, and constitutional legitimacy he accorded to himself as an emerging absolutist. Indeed, he managed to reconstitute Ethiopia's standing among the nations of the world. The old Adwa legacy of victorious Ethiopia had been shattered by Mussolini, but Haile Selassie regained independence, outmaneuvered the British, and built sturdy new relations with the United States. His revived Ethiopia became a founding member of the United Nations and regained Eritrea. In this chapter we shall trace the dialectical dynamism between the emperor's external relations and his power at home. The 1950s and the early 1960s saw Haile Selassie in his prime. He controlled his game. Years of decline would follow later. While on top, he was the sole ruler—supreme, self-isolated, and increasingly lonely.

In the United States:
"And He Shall Reign Forever and Ever"

The way to regain Eritrea was through Washington and the UN. Aklilu Habta-Wald roamed the corridors there, together with Haile

Selassie's American adviser John Spencer. Aklilu represented Ethiopia when fifty nations gathered in San Francisco on October 24, 1945, to declare the establishment of the new international organization. On November 13, Ethiopia became an official member, proudly representing Africa, a continent still under the yoke of imperialism. Aklilu and Spencer, with the backing of the United States, pulled strings that led to the resolution that returned Eritrea to Ethiopia. Winning American goodwill, however, was not easy. There were many in Washington who resented Haile Selassie's dictatorial regime. In May 1951, President Harry Truman instructed the State Department to avoid inviting Haile Selassie to visit.[1]

One way of placating the Americans was to help in the Korean War. The war on the Korean peninsula, which took place between 1950 and 1953, was pivotal in the struggle between the Western and Eastern blocs. It was a bloody war, but Haile Selassie did not hesitate to send his best troops to fight together with the UN forces, namely, the Americans. Over three thousand Ethiopian soldiers, the best of Division 1, saw action in Korea. Of those, 121 were killed and over five hundred were wounded.[2]

On May 22, 1953, an agreement was signed reaffirming the US lease on the Kagnew military base[3] and securing US military and economic aid for Ethiopia. Haile Selassie, as always, wanted to cement this in person. He instructed Aklilu and Spencer to organize a state visit.[4] Foreign Secretary J. F. Dulles agreed only after he was advised that a visit from the Ethiopian king would help the administration's relations with the African American community. On May 18, 1954, the emperor boarded an American plane in Addis Ababa and sat near the pilot. During the flight to France, one of the engines failed, and all the Ethiopian passengers panicked—except Haile Selassie, who kept smiling. In France they boarded a luxurious liner named *United States* and marveled at its air-conditioning and microwave. The emperor was flown to Washington, where he was disappointed to learn that only the vice president was to receive him at the airport.[5]

The meeting with President Dwight Eisenhower at the White House reflected some differences between the leaders. After all the niceties and the ceremonial signing of documents, Haile Selassie raised new issues. Eisenhower, who had gained extensive diplomatic experience dealing with ego-driven generals in World War II, managed to elegantly avoid discussing practicalities.[6] No harm was done, but something kept the Ethiopians and Americans from connecting easily. This was not the only such instance.

A visit to New York brightened Haile Selassie's spirits. A motorcade took him along Broadway, while hundreds of thousands cheered. Many came to salute the freedom fighter who stood up to Mussolini. A rain of confetti came down on him. The normally stoic leader smiled, once and even twice! He would cherish the warm greeting he received in Harlem, where African Americans awaited him. Speeches full of inspiration were made in the local church, praising him and Ethiopia as a land of pride and freedom. A chorus of two hundred singers performed "Hallelujah" from Handel's *Messiah*. It did so with deep devotion, repeating and repeating the line: "And he shall reign for ever and ever. King of Kings, Forever and ever! Hallelujah, hallelujah!"

New York was also the site of a meeting at the UN that would prove meaningful for Haile Selassie. On June 1 the emperor was hosted by Secretary-General Dag Hammarskjöld. Haile Selassie savored the moment:

> After eighteen years, I again find myself in a center where are concentrated the passionate hopes of the thousands of millions of human beings. . . . The League of Nations failed and failed basically because of its inability to prevent aggression against my country. . . . So it is that here in the United Nations we have dedicated ourselves anew to those high and indeed essential ideals, essential if the world is to continue on the path of peace.[7]

The Americans helped Haile Selassie, and they were instrumental in securing Ethiopia's control of Eritrea. Their interests in the Red Sea area were compatible with Ethiopia's independence and made an alliance feasible.[8] But somehow, a full mutual trust was not built, in spite of American aid in all fields. Haile Selassie wanted more arms, but Washington maintained that Ethiopia needed economic aid rather than more military equipment.[9] Vice President Richard Nixon's visit to Ethiopia in 1957 did not bridge those differences.[10] The Ethiopians, it appears, favored the British's sophisticated paternalism to American directness.

With the British Lion, Again

After state visits to Canada and Mexico, the emperor traveled to Great Britain on October 14, 1954. He spent two weeks there, and his stay was quite different from the one in the United States.

The British went out of their way to shower Haile Selassie with honors and cordial gestures. In Portsmouth's harbor, Ethiopian flags were hoisted on all vessels, and a battleship fired a twenty-one-gun salute. A royal reception awaited him at Victoria Station. In attendance were the young Queen Elizabeth (who seemed to have taken a real liking to Haile Selassie), Anthony Eden, Britain's top army generals, and Winston Churchill, now prime minister again. Sylvia Pankhurst, his ardent supporter from his days of exile, was also present. A stream of receptions followed: in Buckingham Palace, Westminster Abbey, Oxford, and of course, in Bath, where Fairfield House was well preserved. Haile Selassie received a medal from the queen, and the press celebrated him with long, admiring articles. Britain embraced Haile Selassie as if expressing regret. The British people loved the emperor's majestic conduct and shared his love of pompous ceremonies. The Haile Selassie of Victoria Station 1954 bore no resemblance to the embarrassed refugee who arrived at Waterloo Station in 1936.[11]

Haile Selassie was moved. Even though he'd had a French education and his strategic considerations directed him to the United States, he remained an anglophile. He admired the British and tried to adopt British style in his personal conduct. Most of all he admired Churchill, the man who had played such a central role also in Ethiopian history. Even though Haile Selassie seldom showed gratitude, for Sir Winston he did his best. The name of Addis Ababa's main street, which led from the railway station to the piazza, was changed from Railway Street to Churchill Road. The name remains today.

The British Empire was in decline, but it was still very present in Ethiopia's sphere. The British were in Sudan until January 1956, in Egypt until April 1956, and in Kenya, Uganda, South Yemen, and Somalia. The issue of Somalia was discussed by Haile Selassie and Churchill in London. In 1948 the British had returned Ogaden to Ethiopia, and now the emperor demanded that the whole of Somalia be under his imperial rule, just like Eritrea. His request was, of course, overly ambitious and patently unrealistic. The British agreed to return only the Haud region to Ethiopia, and they signed the area over in November 1954. Eventually, an independent Somali republic was established on July 1, 1960, and it demanded the Ogaden from Ethiopia. The issue has remained unsolved.

The Changing World—Bandung

Haile Selassie enjoyed repeating his 1924 tour thirty years later, though this time, he skipped Italy.[12] The emperor returned to Ethiopia in November 1954, six months after his departure.

Africa and Asia were changing. In July 1952 a revolution in Egypt toppled the monarchy, and the Algerian revolt began in November 1954. But in Ethiopia, nothing changed politically. Singers sang for the beloved emperor, calling him like lost sons to return home. Intellectuals prepared a constitution that defined his power in biblical terms. There were those in government who feared that staying away for so long was a risky matter, but no one dared to tell Haile Selassie that. He loved standing on the global stage.

It would be wrong to say that the emperor neglected his country in the 1950s. Ethiopia moved forward in the fields of education and administration, and the middle class expanded.[13] He dealt with these matters at home, but the things that were left undone, as we shall see, would affect Haile Selassie in coming years. Whatever his achievements in the domestic realm, it was clear that he preferred dealing with external affairs. There was hardly a twentieth-century head of state who toured the world like Haile Selassie. Now, back from the West, he probably understood that it was time to rethink his positions on foreign affairs.

The international game was opening for new players—not only for Western Europe, the United States, and the Soviet Union. New maneuvers and new challenges to the old order were on the horizon. Other countries could no longer be ignored as new forces emerged. Josip Broz Tito of Yugoslavia and Zhou Enlai of China demonstrated their independence from the Soviet Union. Jawaharlal Nehru of India posited an ideology of a nonaligned international movement. Kwame Nkrumah of the Gold Coast (future Ghana) was making a name as an all-African anti-imperialist freedom fighter. Gamal Abd al-Nasser of Egypt was on his way to becoming the hero of pan-Arab revolutionary unity, as well as a rising force in Africa. Haile Selassie must have realized that he could not go on remaining the anti-imperialist icon merely by virtue of the legacy of his confrontation with Mussolini in the 1930s. He was aware that a new generation and a new reality were leaving him behind, and that in comparison to these new leaders, his image would quickly be demoted to an old-school reactionary. He needed to rebuild his international standing without losing his medieval grip on Ethiopia. It was quite a challenge, one that had to be dealt with patiently. (As we will see in the following chapter, he accomplished this image reconstruction flawlessly.)

In April 1955 an international conference was held in Bandung, Indonesia. Twenty-nine nations were represented. The resolutions adopted were tantamount to declaring the establishment of "a third bloc." In Bandung, the principle of nonalignment was adopted, and the conference carried a spirit of defiance against existing structures and old orders. Haile Selassie understood he better not attend. How could he aspire to shine in such a gathering while dictating a new constitution in Ethiopia (to be declared in November) that defined his rule in biblical terms? The emperor even avoided sending his senior diplomat, Foreign Minister Aklilu Habta-Wald, to the conference. Instead, he dispatched his prime minister, Makonnen Endalkatchaw, an old nobleman who spoke little French and English. He was tasked with listening. The show in Bandung was stolen by Gamal Abd al-Nasser. With his charismatic presence and his large, reassuring smile, the Egyptian became a man of the future, a leader for the times. At that time, Nasser was already interfering in Ethiopian affairs. He supported Somali nationalists and helped the Eritrean exiles in Cairo. Makonnen Endalkatchaw returned from Bandung and reported what the emperor surely wanted to hear—that Nasser was not a serious statesman but an unsophisticated showman and a shallow person.[14]

Nasser—Smiling and Disconnecting

Relations between Nasser and Haile Selassie were of mutual appreciation and mutual suspicion. The emperor was twenty-six years Nasser's senior, which probably gave him the illusion of some paternalism. Nasser for his part knew how to flatter the Ethiopian ruler. Egypt's Revolution Day, July 23, corresponded to Haile Selassie's birthday, and Nasser was careful to make mention of it. He also recalled to the emperor how he'd admired Haile Selassie as a young officer posted in Sudan, preparing to face the Fascists. But beyond these niceties, there was growing mistrust. After the 1956 Suez War, Nasser became an all-Arab hero and deepened his involvement in what he called Egypt's "African Circle." While helping the Somalis and the Eritreans he cynically offered a treaty to Haile Selassie, which the latter rejected. In 1957 the emperor resorted to various excuses to decline invitations to visit Cairo.[15] He knew he needed to engage Nasser patiently on the new court of all-African diplomacy.

Until 1958 Ethiopians hardly saw themselves Africans. However, as Africa was emancipating, Haile Selassie began tapping this new energy. Ghana won independence in 1957, and Nkrumah convened an all-African conference in Accra. Before the conference, on November 12, 1958, Haile Selassie made a significant statement. In his annual Crown Speech, he declared that Ethiopia was always a part of Africa. "The speech was a declaration on foreign policy of historic importance," according to the view of the Israeli consul in Addis Ababa. He posited:

> Ethiopia is now doing its utmost to count itself among the African peoples which obtain independence. . . . The Nasserite threat increased to the extent that it forced Ethiopia to look for allies not only to her north, but also to her south and her west. Relying on Africa will be the most natural result of the Arab and Islamic pressure.[16]

Connecting to the new circle of inter-African diplomacy was slow and hesitant. However, in time it would be of the utmost importance for Haile Selassie. In Africa he would gain a major victory, and later, toward his end, would sustain fatal blows. Africa would be at the crux of his renewed rise and also of his future fall.

Meanwhile, Nasser represented a double challenge: he was an ardent opponent of monarchy who proposed to unite the entire region in revolution. The Egyptian president worked to transform the Muslims of the Horn of Africa into revolutionary Arabs—in Eritrea, in Somalia, and potentially in Ethiopia proper.

There was another major factor in these relations: the Nile. In 1959 Egypt began concrete preparations for building the Aswan High Dam, and Nasser negotiated with Sudan toward a water agreement (signed in November) that ignored Ethiopia altogether. Haile Selassie responded by again inviting American firms to conduct surveys on the Blue Nile. (Their final report was submitted in 1964 and included the building of four dams along the river.) But while the emperor was doing practically nothing, the Egyptians (and the Soviets) were building. Work on the Aswan High Dam began in January 1960 and was completed in 1971.

The Aswan High Dam in Egypt—or so it was thought at the time—ended Egypt's ancient dependency on Ethiopia as the source of four-fifths of the Nile waters. Nasser invited Haile Selassie to Cairo in June 1959 and even organized him a tour of the dam site. Haile Selassie was ready to play the polite guest, but behind his smile he came to disconnect from Egypt in the spiritual sphere. On June 28, 1959, he attended a ceremony in Cairo's main Orthodox church, during which the Coptic patriarch recognized Abuna Baselios as a patriarch, his equal. The Ethiopian Orthodox Church became fully independent, thus ending sixteen centuries of Christian connection between Ethiopia and Egypt.

The Lion of Judah and Israel

From Cairo, Haile Selassie flew to Moscow. He spent two weeks there, exchanging compliments and signing agreements of little significance. The emperor would not allow the Soviets to penetrate and influence Ethiopia, but he enjoyed feeling he was playing them wisely. He also played wisely with Israel.

Haile Selassie's relations with Israel were intricate. He was, after all, a descendant of King Solomon. Jerusalem was for him a part of his very identity. Whenever he met with Israelis, he would emphasize that he was one of them, but he never visited the capital of the Jewish people after 1936. Haile Selassie was careful not to alienate the Arabs, and he voted against Israel in every international forum. In January 1949 Ethiopia voted against admission of Israel to the UN. Haile Selassie recognized Israel only de facto in 1956.

David Ben-Gurion, the prime minister of Israel, was not deterred. In 1958 he envisioned an alliance with three non-Arab states—Turkey, Iran, and Ethiopia. His biggest success was with Haile Selassie. The emperor, discerning the Israelis' eagerness to be accepted, was ready to open wide a side door. He invited the Israelis to help in nearly everything related to Ethiopia, from paving roads to internal security. He was also convinced that the Israelis could work wonders in Washington, persuading the Americans to support him more generously. An alliance was built, though not openly. As of the late 1950s, Israel never invested in any other country the way it did in Ethiopia. The best minds and muscle of Israel were sent there to advise, train, and build. Thousands of Ethiopians studied and underwent training in Israel. Haile Selassie placed such trust in the Israelis that even the man in charge of the wireless communication on his plane was an Israeli Mossad agent.

The Rebels of 1960

One of the most dramatic events of Haile Selassie's life occurred when he was on a flight to Brazil on December 13, 1960. A coup was attempted, and it developed into the most serious threat to the emperor's supremacy between 1941 and 1974. It was led by some of the young whom he raised but also had paternalistically humiliated.[17]

The coup had an ideological dimension, introduced by the civilian among the mutineers. Girmame Neway, a son of the nobility, had graduated from the Haile Selassie Secondary School in Addis Ababa and was sent for further studies in the United States. At Columbia University, Girmame wrote his master's thesis on British colonialism in Kenya. He studied Marxism and the writings of black activists in America, and on campus he organized student meetings. In 1954 Girmame returned to Ethiopia and was positioned in the ministry of interior. The comfortable job did not mellow him. In place of a formal suit he sported khakis and a red tie, and he was known to speak endlessly. It was not long before word reached the emperor and Girmame was sent away to the region of Wollamo. There, he began distributing land to peasants, and when he was summoned to explain, he told Haile Selassie that he had to take care of the hungry. Consequently, he was removed and appointed over a district in Harar. There, Girmame discovered that monies intended for purchasing equipment for the local clinic had been allocated elsewhere. Girmame hurried to Addis Ababa to report the irregularity, but nobody wanted to hear. Toward the end of 1960 he began contemplating a revolution. The first step was to persuade his brother, Mangistu Neway, the commander of the First Division, Ethiopia's imperial bodyguard.

Mangistu Neway, born in 1919, was not a revolutionary. He was destined to be an officer and had already fought in the war against Mussolini. After Italy invaded Ethiopia he fled to Sudan, where he joined a British military academy. He returned to Ethiopia after the liberation and joined the renewed army, where he excelled, was promoted, and served in Korea. In 1956 he became the commander of the bodyguard with the rank of brigadier general. Unlike his brother, he was a happy person, admired by his soldiers. When Girmame decided to convince Mangistu to turn against the emperor, he gave him a copy of Anwar al-Sadat's 1957 book, *Rebellion on the Nile and the Egyptian Revolution,* in which the future president of Egypt described how he and his fellow "free officers" deposed the corrupt King Farouk in 1952. Indeed, the Nasserite revolution in Egypt was echoing in the hearts of Ethiopia's young generation, as it did elsewhere in Africa and the Middle East. In his trial prior to his hanging Mangistu showed no remorse, nor did he present himself as an ideologue. He said he only wanted to open Haile Selassie's eyes so that he would rid himself of the corrupt people around him.

What really motivated him? Perhaps some of the answer is to be found in the story of the third leader of the coup, Warqneh Gabayhu, the head of the imperial secret service. Born in 1925 to a poor family from the Gondar area, Warqneh was lucky to be educated in Addis

Ababa's Menelik II Secondary School. He joined the bodyguard, and in time Mangistu Neway placed him in charge of the division's intelligence unit, a position for which he underwent training in Israel. In 1959 the emperor appointed him over the national secret service with the rank of colonel. Close to Haile Selassie's ear, Warqneh became one of the powerful men in Ethiopia. Why did he join Girmame and Mangistu to form a revolutionary committee? In a moment of truth, he poured his heart out before his Israeli counterpart, Isser Harel: "The emperor summons me in the early morning and then lets me wait for hours, till the evening. He treats me like a little boy, purposely humiliates me. He has for us only contempt. He does that to all of us!" Another Israeli who was close to the fourth conspirator, Chief of Police Tsege Dibo, later explained: "They were simply ashamed that their ruler behaved like he was a god. They saw how things were in the West and among us [Israelis]. They wanted more freedom and respect, not really a democracy."[18]

The Coup and Its Suppression

On the evening that the emperor flew to Brazil, the mutineers sprang into action. Warqneh's secret service men seized the radio station, the central bank, and other key posts, while the bodyguard soldiers under Mangistu encircled the other army units in the capital. The soldiers were told that they were defending the emperor from other generals who were aiming to invade Addis Ababa and topple the regime. Using the same trick, senior members of the elite were asked to assemble for their protection. Many of them gathered in the imperial palace, Genet Lul, in the main hall, "The Green Salon" (today's Makonnen Hall in Addis Ababa University). Empress Mennen and heir Asfa-Wossen were led to another room. The next morning Asfa-Wossen was forced at gunpoint to read a declaration over the radio. It mentioned the backwardness of Ethiopia compared to other African nations and heralded the end of Haile Selassie's rule. Ethiopia, the crown prince read, would become a constitutional monarchy under Asfa-Wossen, with Ras Imru as the prime minister. To reiterate, Ras Imru grew up alongside Haile Selassie like a brother, and he felt secure enough to speak his mind as a progressive prince, calling to open the system and implement land reform, for which he was nicknamed "the red ras." The rebels then published an eleven-point plan that promised far-reaching changes, and as news of the coup spread, students led demonstrations against Haile Selassie.

However, the mutineers' steps were not perfectly calculated. Some of the leading personalities managed to avoid arrest. Nearly all other commanders of the army were out of the loop. Dajjazmach Asrate Kassa and General Merid Mangasha coordinated the counteraction. They instructed the tank unit and the commander of the paratroops stationed near the capital to move in. Abuna Baselios signed a pamphlet excommunicating the rebels as traitors to God and his messiah.

When the leaflets were dropped over Addis Ababa, many of the soldiers found out they were not defending their emperor but rather betraying Christianity. The next morning, December 15, fierce battles began. They lasted three days and cost two thousand lives. As the tanks approached the palace, the rebels understood they had lost. Girmame asked the US ambassador to mediate but was refused. General Tsege Dibo was killed, and Colonel Warqneh Gabayhu tried to hide, exchanged fire, then shot himself. The two brothers, Mangistu and Girmame, ran to the Green Salon and sprayed the hostages with their machine guns, massacring fifteen people, among them Ras Seyum of Tigray and Ras Abebe Aregai, who was prime minister at the time. The two brothers fled through a cellar and climbed Mount Entoto, and from there ran to their native region of Mojo. Meanwhile, aboard his plane, Haile Selassie was informed.

As soon as the coup started, Asrate Kassa called the ambassadors of Great Britain and the United States, but they apparently avoided action. A British official later explained that both the Americans and the British had sympathy for the rebels, though the picture is not entirely clear.[19] Asrate also alerted the Mossad agents stationed in Addis Ababa, and they informed their superiors in Tel Aviv. Israeli prime minister Ben-Gurion asked, "Who will the people support?" When he understood that Haile Selassie had popular support, Ben-Gurion gave instructions to help the emperor. Mossad's director, Isser Harel, advised Haile Selassie to land in Liberia and wait for him there. From West Africa the emperor flew to Asmara, where his son-in-law General Abiy Abebe coordinated their next steps with Asrate. Once the rebels were defeated, Haile Selassie flew back to Addis Ababa. On December 18 he spoke on the radio, with the tone of a betrayed, vengeful father:

> You all know how much authority We reposed in those few who have risen against Us. We educated them. We gave them authority. We did

it in order that they might improve the education, the health and the standard of living of Our people. We confided to them the implementation of some of the many plans We have formulated for the advancement of Our nation. And now Our trust has been betrayed. . . . The judgement of God is upon them; wherever they go, they will never escape it.[20]

On December 24 the two brothers were spotted by the army. Girmame shot himself, and Mangistu was wounded and captured. He was quoted as saying before his judges: "I have done what you say, but I am not guilty. Ethiopia has been standing still, while our African brothers are moving ahead in the struggle to overcome poverty. What I did was in the best interests of my country."[21]

On March 29, 1961, Mangistu Neway was hanged (together with two other conspirators) in a square near the Saint George Cathedral. The public that gathered there was instructed to show him no sympathy.[22]

The hanging of Colonel Warqneh Gabayhu.

Courtesy of Israeli Defense Forces Archive, Tel Aviv.

Loneliness

The emperor felt betrayed. He no longer liked the palace where his men were massacred. Genet Lul ("the paradise of a prince") had been built in 1930, the year of his coronation, on property inherited from his father, Ras Makonnen. Haile Selassie preferred it to Menelik's palace, known as "the Old Gebi [palace]," and in 1932 moved to Genet Lul. He loved this palace—it was inviting and pleasant and surrounded by beautiful gardens. The occupying Fascist governors also felt at home there. In 1941 Haile Selassie was happy to return to Genet Lul, but as his power grew, it became too small. In 1955, in celebration of twenty-five years on the throne, the emperor inaugurated the Jubilee Palace, a much larger compound complete with marble halls and majestic decorations but lacking the air of intimate comfort that was about Genet Lul. In 1974, in Jubilee Palace's entrance hall, a short and humiliating deposition ceremony was staged for Haile Selassie. From there, as if closing a circle, he would be driven back to "the Old Gebi," where he would be imprisoned and later murdered.

On February 11, 1962, Empress Mennen died. Mennen was a devout Christian, always busy inaugurating churches, orphanages, and schools. She initiated the first school for girls in Addis Ababa and supported the Ethiopian monastery near the Jordan River in the Holy Land. Unlike Taytu, Menelik's wife, who had intervened bluntly in her husband's business, Mennen kept a low profile. Behind the scenes, she was Haile Selassie's chief adviser—loyal, sober, and dependable. The 1960 rebels, fortunately, kept her outside the Green Salon when they massacred their hostages.

Mennen's life was not easy. She saw the death of six of her ten children (four of them born before she married the emperor). She suffered from stomach ailments and was often treated in Jerusalem's Hadassah Hospital. After her death Haile Selassie summoned the Israeli architect Zalman Enav and asked him to design a mausoleum for the couple, in the shape of Solomon's star. The mausoleum never materialized, but in the year 2000, Haile Selassie and Mennen were reburied next to each other in the eastern wing of the Trinity Cathedral.

Haile Selassie was approaching the age of seventy when Mennen died. He would not remarry. Though he had twelve more years of active life ahead, they were also years of deepening loneliness and sadness. A few months after Mennen's death, Prince Sahla-Selassie died of pneumonia. Observers noticed that the emperor had often some difficulty focusing.[23] He was never fond of his elder son, Asfa-Wossen, and now even less so, especially given his role in the 1960 coup. No doubt the prince had been manipulated and threatened by the rebels, but his father never really forgave him for their naming him emperor in his stead, and for reading their declaration (a fact that would acquire importance later on). Many believed that Haile Selassie thought that Asfa-Wossen should have died rather than betray him.[24] The emperor's fatherly love was concentrated mostly on Prince Makonnen, born in 1923, whom he declared "Prince of Harar" at the age of seven and probably hoped would one day inherit Ethiopia's crown. But on May 12, 1957, Makonnen was killed in a car accident. His funeral was held three days later at the Trinity Cathedral. Mennen could hardly stand on her feet, and Haile Selassie stood at one corner, immersed in grief.[25] These tragedies no doubt hardened and isolated Haile Selassie. However, he remained sentimental about his granddaughters and about his eldest daughter, Tananya-Warq, who was a tough, opinionated woman, ever on guard to preserve the old order.[26]

In 1961 Haile Selassie authorized the opening of Haile Selassie I University. He donated Genet Lul as the central building of the new campus (today it is the Institute of Ethiopian Studies of Addis Ababa University). While Haile Selassie felt betrayed by the young officers and students, his punishment of the country's youth was just symbolic—a temporary denial of some benefits. His establishment of the university shortly after the failed coup was perhaps the most meaningful step toward modernization he made. Lonely and isolated, he became more conservative, even reactionary. Yet he envisioned the future of Ethiopia—only after his death—as one led by the young and the educated.

Notes

1. See FRUS, Vol. 5, 775.56/5–1651, Memorandum by the Secretary of State to the President, May 16, 1951; 775.5/6–2351; Paper Prepared in the Bureau of Near Eastern, South Asian, and African Affairs," May 23, 1951.

2. https://en.wikipedia.org/wiki/Kagnew_Battalion. A small Ethiopian unit remained in Korea until the early 1960s. In 1960 Haile Selassie sent an Ethiopian unit to join UN forces in Congo. There, no combat was recorded.

3. Haile Selassie called the Ethiopian brigade sent to Korea "Kanyu Force." *Kanyu* in Amharic means "tough, strong leader," and it had been the name of Ras Makonnen's warhorse. By old Ethiopian tradition, a warrior is also known by his horse's name. Ras Makonnen was "Abba Kanyu," and naming the force after him was a gesture of Haile Selassie toward his father. Many Ethiopian words were transmitted to other languages through Italian spelling. Thus, *Kanyu* became *Kagenew*, the name of the American military base near Asmara.

4. For a detailed discussion of Haile Selassie's visits to the United States, see Theodore Vestal, *The Lion of Judah in the New World* (Santa Barbara, CA: Praeger, 2011).

5. Spencer, *Ethiopia at Bay*, pp. 268–269; Asfa-Wossen, *King of Kings*, pp. 188–191.

6. FRUS, 1952–1954, Africa and South Asia, Vol. 1, Part 1, 775.11/5–2954, Memorandum of Conversation, by the Director, Foreign Operations Administration (Stassen), Washington, May 29, 1954, participants: Emperor Haile Selassie, President Eisenhower.

7. Asfa-Wossen, *King of Kings*, pp. 186–192; Vestal, *The Lion of Judah in the New World,* p. 60; www.lionofjudahsociety.org/free-pdf-book-selected-speeches-of -haile-selassie-i/.

8. See also Harold Marcus, *The Politics of Empire: Ethiopia, Great Britain and the United States 1941–1974* (Lawrenceville, NJ: Red Sea Press, 1995).

9. FRUS, 1958–1960, Africa, Vol. 14, National Security Council Report, December 30, 1960.

10. FRUS, 1955–1957, Africa, Volume 18, 115, Memorandum of a Conversation, Addis Ababa, March 12, 1957, Vice President Richard M. Nixon, Haile Selassie I, Emperor of Ethiopia.

11. Asfa-Wossen, *King of Kings,* pp. 192–197; on detailed British preparations for Haile Selassie's visit see files at FO 371/108286; on the visit, speeches, ceremonies, and more see FO 371/108287.

12. The privilege to represent the restored Ethiopia in Rome was left to the legendary runner Abebe Bikile, who won the marathon in the 1960 Olympics against the background of the Colosseum.

13. The literature on Ethiopia's development is too rich to be summarized here. Among other studies see Christopher Clapham, *Haile Selassie's Government* (London: Longman's, 1969); Patrick Gilkes, *The Dying Lion: Feudalism and Modernization in Ethiopia* (London: J. Friedmann, 1975); Paul B. Henze, *Layers of Time: A History of Ethiopia* (London: Hurst, 2000); Robert L. Hess, *Ethiopia: The Modernization of Autocracy* (Ithaca, NY: Cornell University Press, 1970); John Markakis, *Ethiopia: Anatomy of a Traditional Polity* (Oxford: Clarendon Press, 1974); Margery Perham, *The Government of Ethiopia* (London: Faber and Faber, 1969); Zewde Reta, *Yaqadamawi Haile Selassie Mengest* (Addis Ababa: Shama Books, 2012); and Seyoum Haregot, *The Bureaucratic Empire: Serving Emperor Haile Selassie* (Trenton, NJ: Red Sea Press, 2013).

14. Erlich, *Alliance and Alienation,* p. 71. The passage on relations with Nasser is based on pp. 70–76 as well as Erlich, *Ethiopia and the Middle East,* chapters 10–12; and Erlich, *The Cross and the River,* chapter 7.

15. FO 371/125392, Furlonge to FO, 25.1.1957, and later reports in this file.

16. See Erlich, *Ethiopia and the Middle East,* pp. 133–138; and Hess, *Ethiopia: The Modernization,* pp. 234–239.

17. The discussion of the 1960 coup is derived from Greenfield, *Ethiopia: A New Political History,* pp. 337–452; Christopher Clapham, "The Ethiopian Coup d'Etat of December 1960," *Journal of Modern African Studies,* Vol. 6 (1968), pp. 495–507; Del Boca, *The Negus,* 254–264; and https://en.wikipedia.org/wiki/1960 _Ethiopian_coup_attempt.

18. Erlich, *Alliance and Alienation*, pp. 86–90.

19. FCO 31/1470, C. Hart to FCO, 23.2.1973, "American Involvement in the 1960 Coup." An American source hints that Americans did help the emperor: "Haile Selassie, who may have been harboring fears concerning US intentions under precisely such emergency conditions, has probably been reassured by the assistance rendered by the US for the Emperor's cause during the rebellion—[3 lines of source

text not declassified]." FRUS, 1961–1963, Vol. 21, Africa, Special National Intelligence Estimate, January 24, 1961, Ethiopian Prospects After the Abortive Coup.

20. Del Boca, *The Negus*, pp. 265–266, quoting the *Ethiopian Herald*, December 19, 1960.

21. Donald Levine, "Haile Selassie's Ethiopia: Myth or Reality?," *Africa Today*, May 1961, pp. 11–14.

22. See YouTube, "General Mengistu Neway Caught and Hanged," https://www.youtube.com/watch?v=BKPw9C5tXsg.

23. FO 371/165338, Joy to FO, 7.3.1962.

24. See, for example, FO 371/190145, "Ethiopia—an Introduction," by J. Russel, 6.12.1965.

25. FO 371/125392, Embassy to FO, 16.5.1957.

26. Hanna Rubinkowska, "Asfa Wasan Hayla Sellase," *EAE*, Vol. 1, p. 366–367; "Makonnen Hayla Sellase", *EAE*, Vol. 3, p. 685; "Tanana Warq Hayla Sellase," *EAE*, Vol. 4, pp. 858–859.

9

We Are Not God

~

On March 29, 1961, General Mangistu Neway was publicly hanged. The bodies of Colonel Warqneh Gabayhu and another mutineer were hanged too. Haile Selassie wanted to make an example of them for all Ethiopia to see. It was an uncharacteristic way to draw a red line, clear and brutal. As Ras Tafari, he had abolished the cruel punishments that had been prescribed in the medieval *Fetha-nagast*. But now, he ordered a public display of horror. Doubtless, he was personally offended by the coup d'etat: "Our trust has been betrayed. . . . The judgement of God is upon them."[1] At the same time the emperor tried to underplay the significance of the coup and inspire calm. "These military coups are in fashion" he said somewhat later. He continued, "I'm not a bit surprised that certain people tried to put one on here too; but all it does is to slow down our economic and political development; and then I can't accept the murder of fifteen dignitaries of the empire."[2]

Coups and revolution were indeed in fashion in Africa and the Middle East, spheres that at that time were more relevant to Ethiopia than Europe's waning colonial powers. The British empire was dismembering, and France was not as influential as before. The United States emerged as an important power—the main source of aid, both military and economic. But Washington invested far less in Ethiopia than the emperor expected. Much to his frustration, he felt America took Ethiopia for granted. The American diplomatic style and Washington's gestures were hardly favored by Ethiopians. In March 1961 President John F. Kennedy initiated the establishment of the Peace Corps. Tens of thousands of young Americans were sent to Asia and Africa to volunteer and spread the word of liberalism. Altogether, over three thousand young Americans spent years in Haile Selassie's Ethiopia (they were finally sent home by the revolutionary regime in 1976). But the idealistic youngsters from American campuses were not accepted with open arms. Like the European missionaries of the nineteenth century, they were met with suspicion. The Ethiopians would not depart from their ways. Ultimately, the Peace Corps contributed to Ethiopia more by creating a new generation of Ethiopianists in America[3] than by creating bridges between Ethiopians and Americans.

The Middle East and Africa were relevant strategic arenas in the 1960s. Nasserite revolutionary ideas had influenced the rebelling officers of December 1960. Such ideas became Haile Selassie's biggest challenge. Mangistu Neway's public hanging conveyed a message: no one would get away with undermining the emperor's absolutism. Indeed, Ethiopian internal politics remained (until the emperor's demise in 1974) a competition for his favor. The only change was widening the scope of this competition by creating new layers of educated youngsters. Haile Selassie managed to neutralize any meaningful cooperation among members of the elite by encouraging them to denounce each other. Thus, everyone and everything revolved around his exclusive power.

No One Would Dare

In 1961 the emperor declared the opening of Haile Selassie I University and donated the palace of Genet Lul for its campus. The lecturers of University College (established ten years earlier), mostly Catholic missionaries, were replaced by young promising Ethiopians. Among them were the doctors Sergew Habla-Selassie, Abraham Demoz, Duri Muhammad, Mesfin Walda-Mariam, Asmarom Legese, Bereket Habta-Selassie, and Getachaw Haile, who would lead the university up to the 1974 revolution. None of them was an admirer of the emperor. In secret they spoke against him, and they even dared meeting with army officers like Aman Andom.[4] But beyond that, they did little. The university's best graduates were sent abroad to complete higher degrees. Upon returning, Haile Selassie allowed them to speak quite freely on campus, as he was confident they would stay in line.[5] The students were chatting in the cafeterias, toying with revolutionary slogans, like "better be a lion for a day and die than live the life of a lamb for a thousand days."[6] But as long as the Lion of Judah was in his prime, they did not roar, at least not before 1969.[7] In July 1962 Haile Selassie celebrated his seventieth birthday. Most observers noted that Ethiopia progressed steadily, albeit slowly, under his paternalistic authoritarianism. A leading British Ethiopianist concluded an article entitled "Haile Sellasie at Seventy" stating that the influence of the Queen of Sheba in Ethiopia was still greater than that of Karl Marx.[8]

Haile Selassie was confident that the educated young would only seek jobs. He could also rely on his parliament, to which he was preaching to initiate change, knowing well that the members would not. They fully understood what was expected from them: to prepare agendas for next meetings. The emperor could complain that nobody dared to shoulder the responsibility of creating change and that everything was pushed up to his busy desk. He indulged in this seemingly sophisticated game, expanding the circle of senior dignitaries without allowing them any freedom, except to undermine each other. On February 6, 1961, he promoted those who had proven themselves loyal in the previous December. Dajjazmach Asrate Kassa became head of the senate, General Merid Mangasha was appointed minister of defense, son-in-law Abiy Abebe became minister of the interior, and Colonel Tamrat Yigazu became governor of Jimma. On April 17 he made Aklilu Habte-Wold, Asrate's archrival, prime minister. Various committees tasked with modernizing government were appointed, and their members went on pretending they were active. New army officers were trained and commissioned, and the best were sent for advanced training abroad. Frustrated young officers in the army's thirty-six battalions could cautiously pour their hearts out to each other. At the time, nobody dared do more.

The only one who apparently tried to move Haile Selassie to initiate some change was Asrate Kassa. He was convinced that without opening the system it would collapse. Asrate composed a fifteen-point "Memorandum to His Majesty" recommending a revision of the constitution and making the government answerable to the parliament. The petition was signed by General Merid, Abiy Abebe, Tamrat Yigazu, and Germachaw Tekla-Hawariat (the son of Tekla-Hawariat who had been behind the 1931 constitution). In May 1963 they finally dared to approach Haile Selassie with their petition.

Asrate Kassa later told his son that the emperor ordered him to read the paper aloud. Asrate Kassa did as he was told, stopping after each line to look at his master. Haile Selassie was full of contempt. Asrate admitted he became pale. When he finished, the emperor said nothing. He just stared each in the eye, one by one, then left the room. Haile Selassie's retribution was swift. Shortly after presenting the petition, Abiy Abebe was removed from the interior ministry and appointed to the senate. Asrate Kassa was appointed over Eritrea, away from the capital. Tamrat Yigazu and Germachaw Tekla-Hawariat were sent to other provinces. Only General Merid Mangasha remained in office as minister of defense until his death in 1966.[9]

The following episode testifies to how anxious and petty-minded Haile Selassie was about his exclusive status. In early October 1963 he made another visit to the United States. The National Security Council prepared a memorandum for President Kennedy that read:

> This is primarily a personal exchange between two world statesmen. The Emperor is very vain and will want to discuss world affairs. He will be particularly flattered if you take him aside for private sessions, not only on world affairs generally but soliciting his views as a predominant leader . . . on African affairs. . . . The Emperor is very protocol conscious and was unhappy on his 1954 visit because Eisenhower did not meet him at the plane. . . . He is a little resentful that the President of the Ethiopian Senate Assrate Kassa, whom you saw on July 25, was treated too well here. Play any mention in low key.[10]

The Nasserite Threat

The autonomy arrangement for Eritrea that was formed in 1952 had no hope to coexist with Haile Selassie's absolutism.[11] Eritrea's formal definition as a "federation under the sovereignty of Haile Selassie" was paradoxical. For the emperor, there could be no compromise between his divine authority and the representative political institutions prescribed by the UN. Eritrea—at least its mountainous heart—was indeed Ethiopian, as it was by its Christian Tigrayan population, history, and culture. In Haile Selassie's mind, Eritrea had been usurped by the Italians in 1890, and it was high time to retrieve it and bring it again under his imperial authority. When the emperor compelled the Eritrean Assembly to vote itself out of existence— thus abolishing Eritrea's flag, political parties, and constitution— Haile Selassie was as motivated by the Nasserite threat as he was by imperial yearnings.

The Egyptian ruler, the standard-bearer of pan-Arabism, also had his hands in Eritrea. Many of the young Eritreans who fled from Haile Selassie's men headed to Cairo. Nearly all of them were Muslims, but there were also some Christian Tigrayans who fought for Eritrean independence among them. In the Egyptian capital they met at "Eritrea House," a building Nasser gave them, where they learned from Algerian FLN (Front de Liberation Nationale) guerrilla experts. Radio Cairo enabled them to broadcast their message to Eritrea. In 1958 an "Eritrean liberation movement" was declared in Cairo, and the Eritrean Liberation Front (ELF) was formed in 1961. In November of that same year, armed struggle began in Eritrea.

While Nasser and Haile Selassie were exchanging personal compliments, the Nasserite threat to the Ethiopian regime grew. Nasserism radiated antimonarchical ideas, inspired Eritrean nationalism, and defined itself as antireactionary and contra-Zionist. Cairo considered the Eritrean struggle part of a victorious, all-Arab revolution. Nasser aimed to convert the Muslims in the Horn of Africa into fellow fighters for Arab unity "from the Atlantic Ocean to the [Persian] Gulf."

The declaration of the independent Republic of Somalia on July 1, 1960, added another dimension to the challenges of the Ethiopian empire. Somalia was composed of ex-British and ex-Italian colonies, and it also claimed for its territory the mostly Somali-inhabited Ogaden region, which stretched over a fifth of Ethiopia. Somali territorial claims were made on the basis of ethnic Somali nationalism and Nasserite ideology and were supported by Egyptian agents. This was at least what Haile Selassie suspected. At the heart of the Somali claim to Ogaden was the town of Harar, Haile Selassie's birthplace. The town had been the capital of the sixteenth-century Islamic holy warrior Ahmad Gragn, who destroyed Ethiopia in 1529–1543. Gragn benefited directly from the Ottomans' momentum in the Middle East, and Haile Selassie did not fail to see the similarities. Nasser was for him a new Ahmad Gragn, ready to inspire militancy against his Christian empire.

Beyond seeing himself as the unifier of Arab nations, Nasser also saw himself as the champion of African emancipation; Eritrean separatists and Somali nationalists were waiting for a great Nasserite victory. But Nasser's failures in the Middle East were beginning to mount. In late 1961 the United Arab Republic, the 1958 political union between Egypt and Syria, was dissolved. From September 1962 forward, Nasser was bogged down in a fratricidal Arab war in Yemen. The Yemen War (which would last seven years) would not

only determine who would benefit from the Arab Peninsula's re-
sources but would decide the future of the entire Arab world. From
Haile Selassie's point of view, the war would also be meaningful to
the status of the Ethiopian empire within the Horn and how much influence the ideas of a greater Somalia and Arab Eritrea would have.
He decided to act. On November 14, 1962, the emperor declared the
final annexation of Eritrea to Ethiopia, its fourteenth province.

Turning to Africa

Africa was emancipating, and it was a time of rising expectations.[12]
Haile Selassie was not slow to grasp the significance for himself and
for his empire. For centuries, Ethiopia was the only independent
African country (with the exception of Liberia, though Liberia's independence was not on account of its own military prowess, like
Ethiopia's); it was a symbol of pride for the black continent. The
new winds in Africa brought with them opportunities and risks.
From now on, the continent became the more important international
diplomatic system for Ethiopia.

Risk stemmed from the revolutionary dimension in the anticolonial struggle. Ghana, which gained independence in 1957, sought
the leadership in Africa. Kwame Nkrumah, one of the prominent
members of a new generation of Western-educated Africans, was
anxious to accomplish his vision of freedom and social progress.
Nkrumah spoke of uniting the whole continent, abolishing the borders created by colonialism, and promoting an all-African economic, social, and cultural revolution. His vision was in many ways
parallel to that of Nasser's in the Arab world, and the two of them
were friendly (Nkrumah even married an Egyptian woman who admired Nasser). In December 1958 Nkrumah hosted a conference in
Accra that established the All-African Peoples' Congress. Haile Selassie cautiously sent his son Sahla-Selassie to attend and report
back to him. The Accra conference was attended by representatives
of the already independent states of Ethiopia, Ghana, Guinea,
Liberia, Morocco, Tunisia, and the United Arab Republic (Egypt),
and by twenty-eight liberation movements from across Africa. The
atmosphere was one of revolution and defiance. A second gathering
of the All-African Peoples' Congress was held in Tunisia in January
1960, and a third meeting followed in Cairo in March 1961.
Nkrumah and Nasser managed to organize a group of states adher-

ing to their ideology that included Algeria, Guinea, Morocco, Mali, and Libya. In 1961 they met in Morocco and became known as the "Casablanca Bloc." Haile Selassie perceived the bloc as a threat to Ethiopia's borders and the exposure of his imperial regime as archaic and reactionary. Simultaneously, another group of states— Nigeria, and most of francophone Africa, including Senegal and Cameroon—convened in Monrovia. The new "Monrovia Bloc" towed a different line: the right of the newly independent African states to maintain their own identities, territories, and economies. They believed in promoting African solidarity, but they did not support revolutionary all-African unification.[13]

Haile Selassie was all for the Monrovia line, but his chance to shape an all-African consensus at that time seemed slim. The continent's centers of political momentum were in its west and its north, far away from Addis Ababa. In July 1962 the emperor was already seventy years old, gray-haired, and looking his age. Yet he did not have to reinvent himself in order to gain seniority. Practically all of the young leaders of emancipating Africa had been teenagers when Haile Selassie took his heroic stances against colonialism—stances that doubtless made him something of a hero to them. His image as the brave African standing alone against brutal Mussolini and against European indifference was well engraved in their minds. There is no other way to explain Haile Selassie's esteemed status in Africa in the 1960s other than the legacy he established for himself in the 1930s as defender of the last citadel of African freedom. He remained an inspirational symbol and a father figure. Nelson Mandela, for example, no less a symbol of African pride, wrote that he decided in 1943 to begin his fight when a friend quoted to him from Haile Selassie' speeches.[14] Already an experienced freedom fighter by 1962, Mandela managed to escape from South Africa to Ethiopia, where Haile Selassie rendered him and his colleagues some help. Mandela was overwhelmed at having reached Addis Ababa on an Ethiopian Airlines plane:

> Here I experienced a rather strange sensation. . . . I saw that the pilot was black. I had never seen a black pilot before, and the instant I did I had to quell my panic. How could a black man fly an airplane? . . . Once we were in the air, I lost my nervousness and studied the geography of Ethiopia, thinking how guerrilla forces hid in these very forests to fight the Italian imperialists.

Mandela went on:

Ethiopia was the birthplace of African nationalism. Unlike so many African states, it had fought colonialism at every turn. . . . In 1930, Haile Selassie became emperor and the shaping force of contemporary history. I was seventeen when Mussolini attacked Ethiopia, an invasion that spurred not only my hatred for that despot but of fascism in general. . . . Here, for the first time in my life, I was witnessing black soldiers commanded by black generals, applauded by black leaders who were all guests of a black head of state. It was a heady moment. I only hoped it was a vision of what lay in the future of my own country. . . . Ethiopia has held a special place in my own imagination, and the prospect of visiting Ethiopia attracted me more strongly than a trip to France, England, and America combined. I felt I would be visiting my own genesis, unearthing the roots of what made me an African. Meeting the emperor himself would be like shaking hands with history. . . . I was surprised by how small the emperor appeared, but his dignity and confidence made him seem like the African giant that he was. . . . I was fascinated. He stood perfectly straight, and inclined his head only slightly to indicate that he was listening. Dignity was the hallmark of all his actions.[15]

Africa Comes to Addis Ababa— the Organization of African Unity

Beyond his iconic image as a symbol of anticolonial sentiment throughout Africa, Haile Selassie also had his masterful diplomatic skills to rely upon.

As he was entering the all-African diplomacy game, Haile Selassie must have remembered how he had been isolated, deserted, and betrayed in the League of Nations. His new foreign minister, Katama Yifru, advised the emperor not to neglect the new international African scene and to try to lead it. Katama, like all African foreign ministers, was invited to the meetings of both the Casablanca and Monrovia Blocs.[16] Haile Selassie, he wrote, usually consulted his senior advisers but always made final decisions himself. He sent Katama to attend the Monrovia Bloc Conference in January 1962 in Lagos, Nigeria. Only once Katama cabled from Nigeria that the road was clear and all were waiting for Haile Selassie did the emperor fly to Lagos. In his speech there Haile Selassie championed the establishment of an all-African organization and offered himself as a mediator to bridge the differences between the two blocs. He then invited all African heads of state to convene in Addis Ababa.

On June 15, 1962, the Casablanca Bloc met in Cairo. Nkrumah delivered a speech about revolutionary African unity. Katama was sent by the emperor to observe and to invite Nkrumah's close friend, Ahmed Sékou Touré of Guinea, to Ethiopia. Thirty years Haile Selassie's junior, Sékou Touré would not refuse. On June 28 they met in Addis Ababa and agreed that all leaders of the Casablanca Bloc should come to Ethiopia in May 1963, and that Sékou Touré would persuade them. Katama was sent to tour the continent to hand-deliver Haile Selassie's invitation. He told Nasser he was not allowed to return home empty handed, and Nasser agreed on the spot.

In May 1963 the town of Addis Ababa was cleaned thoroughly. Beggars were put on trucks and dropped off in far places. Green tin walls were erected to save visitors the sight of poor shacks. Menelik Palace ("the old Gebi") and the Jubilee Palace were redecorated, and other buildings were repainted. The Africa Hall in Addis Ababa, which was completed in 1961 and housed the UN offices, had its main hall refurnished to host all heads of state with their entourages. A huge feast was prepared in Menelik Palace.

Haile Selassie personally went to the airport in a motorcade to receive each of the arriving leaders. One by one, like Mandela a year before, they "shook hands with history." All curiously awaited Nasser's arrival. The tall Egyptian and the short Ethiopian nearly fell into each other's arms. A famous picture, all cordial smiles, seems to reflect the leaders' authentic affection. Tens of thousands of Ethiopian Muslims came to the airport and cheered, "Nasser, Nasser."[17] In May 1963 Nasser's stature in the African context had already mellowed. He had his hands full with the war in Yemen, which, it was clear, was not to end shortly. In the year that passed since the previous gathering of the Casablanca Bloc in Cairo, Nasser had to adapt. The all-African revolutionary dream had to wait for better days, but in the meantime, Nasser embraced Haile Selassie. Indeed, throughout the three-day conference (from May 22 to 25) the two leaders exchanged compliments and sat next to each other often.

Haile Selassie was declared chairman of the conference and conducted the deliberations in Africa Hall. He paid personal attention to each of the thirty-two heads of state, and they all must have felt privileged. The harder work was left to the foreign ministers, who convened in another hall. They had three different proposals for an African charter to discuss—one authored by Ethiopia, and the other two offered by the Monrovia and Casablanca Blocs. The Ethiopian proposal contained six voluntary resolutions (such as cooperation in combating colonialism, racism, and more) and the commitment to establish a permanent all-African body.

In the plenary, all thirty-two leaders delivered speeches. Tension was mounting in advance of Nkrumah's speech, which he gave on May 24. The leader of the Casablanca Bloc would not relinquish his position on all-African unity:

> Our objective is African union now. There is no time to waste. We must unite now or perish. I am confident that by our concerted effort and determination, we shall lay here the foundations for a continental Union of African States. . . . No sporadic act nor pious resolution can resolve our present problems. Nothing will be of avail, except the united act of a united Africa. . . . African unity is, above all, a political kingdom which can only be gained by political means. The social and economic development of Africa will come only within the political kingdom, not the other way around. . . . By creating a true political union of all the independent states of Africa, with executive powers for political direction, we can tackle hopefully every emergency and every complexity.[18]

Meanwhile, the foreign ministers agreed on the Ethiopian proposal, namely, on maintaining states' sovereignty and existing borders and the principle of mutual nonintervention. The text was distributed as the leaders convened for the closing session on May 25. Haile Selassie did not mince words:

> But while we agree that the ultimate destiny of this continent lies in political union, we must at the same time recognize that the obstacles to be overcome in its achievement are at once numerous and formidable. Africa's peoples did not emerge into liberty in uniform conditions. Africans maintain different political systems; our economies are diverse; our social orders are rooted in differing cultures and traditions. Furthermore, no clear consensus exists on the "how" and the "what" of this union. Is it to be, in form, federal, confederal, or unitary? Is the sovereignty of individual states to be reduced, and if so, by how much, and in what areas? . . . We should, therefore, not be concerned that complete union is not attained from one day to the next. The union which we seek can only come gradually, as the day-to-day progress which we achieve carries us slowly but inexorably along this course. . . . Thus, a period of transition is inevitable. Old relations and arrangements may, for a time, linger. Regional organizations may fulfill legitimate functions and needs which cannot yet be otherwise satisfied. But the difference is in this: that we recognize these circumstances for what they are, temporary expedients designed to serve only until we have established the conditions which will bring total African unity within our reach.[19]

Even Nasser understood that he could not challenge these conservative principles if an all-African body was to be declared. Only

Nkrumah felt frustrated and betrayed. He rose up from his seat and attempted to leave the room. From the rostrum Haile Selassie asked Sékou Touré, urging him in a fatherly way, to talk to Nkrumah. The latter complied and signed the charter together with all the rest.[20]

The final session was held behind closed doors. The Italian architect Arturo Mezzedimi, who had built Africa Hall, was the only non-African in attendance. He was tasked with ensuring the proper functioning of all the building's equipment. Mezzedimi later reported that when the charter of the Organization of African Unity (OAU) was approved, the heads of state rose to their feet and began applauding Haile Selassie, the mastermind behind the summit. "They went on clapping their hands for ten minutes. I could not believe my eyes. I'd never seen anything like it. The emperor, who was also on his feet, enjoyed his triumph but, as always, he maintained complete control. He held his body rigidly, and not a muscle moved in his face."[21]

Africa's Eldest Statesman

That same evening, an extravagant banquet was held in Menelik Palace. The Ethiopians have a tradition of imperial feasts but one like that had never been seen. The finest dishes and drinks were served to the leaders of Africa.[22] An Ethiopian orchestra played African music and Viennese waltzes. The evening peaked with a performance by the South African–born singer Miriam Makeba. Still young but already a symbol of freedom fighting, Makeba would gain the moniker "Mama Africa." That night she inspired all the great men of the continent. We are told that even Haile Selassie was moved. Doubtless, establishing and heading the Organization of African Unity was one of the major events in his life—both a personal achievement and an assurance that his ancient empire was safe. For the next ten years, Haile Selassie would be the great patriarch of Africa, the continent's eldest statesman.

In December 1966 the British ambassador, John Russel, finished his term in Addis Ababa and sent his "Last Impressions from Ethiopia" to London. In them, he analyzed the complex character of Haile Selassie: humanly wise and cruelly cunning, with all possible shades in between. More than three years after the establishment of the OAU, he concluded that the emperor managed to open Ethiopia to the world, ending its isolation in its "Alpine citadel," and to do so

Celebrating the establishment of the Organization for African Unity, 1963.

even though the Ethiopians were so much different from the rest of the Africans. He added:

> By any account Emperor Haile Selassie is the most eminent figure in Africa today. I use the expression "eminent" advisedly: it excludes brilliant opportunists like Nasser, corrupt demagogues like the Nkrumah stamp, decent, frightened men like Nyerere, or unsure ones like Kaunda. Sophisticated second-rate Francophones like Bourguiba or Senghor, even sincere patriots like Kenyatta. As a world figure of a real class and proven durability, Haile Selassie stands on his own.[23]

The emancipating African continent had its share of new problems, conflicts, and rivalries. No one could be better than Haile Selassie in mediating and stabilizing the continent. During the next ten years, Haile Selassie went on touring the rest of the world as well. He traveled to Europe and America, but Africa became the source of his prestige and power. Between the ages of seventy-two and eighty-one he flew from one summit to another, reveling in his special status. The second OAU conference was convened in Cairo in July

1964. Haile Selassie showered compliments on its host, Nasser, and took pride that the organization had become a living fact.[24] Indeed, the flexible structure of the OAU (quite like the Arab League) ensured its survival.[25] In Cairo it was also decided that Addis Ababa would be the organization's permanent headquarters, and Haile Selassie was unofficially crowned as the senior figure in Africa. Becoming central to African diplomacy and positioning his capital as the arena of African politics was the crowned jewel of his post–World War II career. In the not very distant future, maintaining this status would come at a price.

Ethiopia Lags Behind

While Haile Selassie traveled from one country to another enjoying international fame, Ethiopia lagged behind. The spirit of awakening that characterized the country in the 1940s and 1950s had all but disappeared. Haile Selassie had ceased initiating change, but change was desperately needed. Even Nelson Mandela, who admired Haile Selassie in 1962, was disappointed in what he saw:

> Addis Ababa, the imperial City, did not live up to its title, for it was the opposite of grand, with only a few tarred streets, and more goats and sheep than cars. . . . Contemporary Ethiopia was not a model when it came to democracy, either. There were no political parties, no popular organs of government, no separation of powers, only the emperor, who was supreme.[26]

The young educated generation wanted representative politics, and rural Ethiopia required land reform. But Haile Selassie had little patience for internal affairs. The Italian architect Mezzedimi, who wrote that the emperor had been always ready to listen to him, noted that after the establishment of the OAU the emperor only pretended at listening.[27] More frustrated was Dajjazmach Asrate Kassa, the head of the senate. In July 1963 he poured his heart out to an Israeli diplomat:

> Ethiopia is in crisis and on the eve of a revolution which will destroy the system. The public is of the opinion that there should be a change, either by peaceful means or by violence. Till recently this was what the educated ones thought, now it is also the mood among the masses. . . . There are three foci of tension. One is the army, in which the rank and file hate the high officers. The junior and intermediate officers, lieutenants and majors are clearly revolutionary. The higher officers

are rivalry-torn, they hate each other. The other focus is the intelligentsia. Its members can render support to the young officers, but not lead a change by themselves. The third focus are the masses in the peripheral provinces. They want their regional autonomy back, and they are capable of challenging the imperial system. Indeed, we must go back to some decentralization. This is a precondition to further reforms . . . The emperor knows all this and knows he should delegate some power to the people and its representatives. But after forty years in absolute power, it is difficult for him to make the right choice.[28]

These were prophetic words. The lieutenants of 1963 would lead the bloody revolution of 1974 and obliterate Ethiopia's elites. They would be supported initially by the intelligentsia, but once in power, they would systematically destroy the educated layer. In 1991 liberation fronts representing the peripheral regions would finally destroy the dictatorial military regime of Mangistu Haile Mariam.

But Haile Selassie preferred the flattery of his prime minister, Aklilu Habte-Wold, whom he credited for a number of diplomatic successes, including regaining Eritrea, the establishment of the OAU, and appeasing Nasser. Aklilu, a son of a priest, had no source of power other than the emperor's patronage.[29]

Meanwhile, the Eritrean Liberation Front intensified its pro-Arab propaganda and scored some successes in the field. In 1964 Haile Selassie appointed Asrate over the province, thus removing him and his nagging advice from the capital. The emperor also authorized him to change the army's tactics against the rebels. Asrate strengthened relations with local Eritrean Christians and recruited their sons to new antiguerrilla units trained by Israelis. For a while, it worked. It also deepened the rivalry between Aklilu and Asrate. The latter kept telling the emperor that his prime minister diverted his attention from needed reforms. Aklilu, for his part, repeated accusations that Asrate was preparing a private army in Eritrea in order to capture power. Asrate developed a strong bond with Haile Selassie's heir and eldest son, Asfa-Wossen. But on Aklilu's advice, the emperor would not delegate any authority to his designated successor.

Global Standing and Personal Cult

The more Haile Selassie enjoyed international status, the less patience he had for his fellow Ethiopians. His prestige and glory in Africa inflated his ego. Kings, prime ministers, and rulers from all over the world came to pay him respect in his capital. The queens of England and the Netherlands, the Shah of Iran, the presidents of Yugoslavia and France, and the chairman of the Communist Party of China all came to visit him. Even President Kennedy hosted him in Washington (the Americans spoke among themselves about the need for reform in Ethiopia, but they continued to trust that Haile Selassie would serve their regional interests[30]). The list of Haile Selassie's adventures abroad and the trove of world celebrities he hosted is too long to be presented here.

The urges to tour the globe so intensively, to seek glory, and to meet with famous figures may be attributed to Haile Selassie's growing loneliness. In July 1963 one of his grandsons, Lij Samson, was killed. The prince drove recklessly after a night in Addis Ababa's bars and crashed his automobile. British ambassador Russel reported:

> For all his strength and authority and for all the political strength and success which the Emperor derived from the African Summit so recently held here, there are many occasions when Haile Selassie is a lonely old man. In the last six years he has lost many of those who were closest to him—his Empress, his favorite son the Duke of Harar, his third son prince Sahle Selassie, now Lij Samson; and his three closest old friends, Ras Kassa [Hailu, died 1956], Ras Makonnen [Endalkatchaw, died February 1963], Ras Ababa [Aregai, murdered 1960]. To add to this he has, since their involvement in the coup d'etat two-and-a-half years ago, lost practically all confidence in the Crown Prince and in one other remaining old friend, Ras Imru. It is, I think, this loneliness in his own generation that moves the Emperor to find much comfort in the constant companionship of his grandchildren, indeed in all children. He always has a flock of them (and a little dog) around his heels on State occasions. Two or three times a week he goes down to the Imperial stable to watch them ride. (He was a great horseman all his life and still takes a most active interest in horses.) And most days of the week the whole Royal family lunches or dines with him en famille.[31]

On October 6, 1963, Haile Selassie addressed the UN assembly again and took pride at the establishment of the OAU under his leadership. African unity, he reemphasized, was the ultimate defiance against racism. His words resonated:

> On the question of racial discrimination, the Addis Ababa Conference taught, to those who will learn, this further lesson: that until the philosophy which holds one race superior and another inferior is finally and permanently discredited and abandoned; that until there are no longer first class and second class citizens of any nation; that until the

color of a man's skin is of no more significance than the color of his
eyes; that until the basic human rights are equally guaranteed to all
without regard to race; that until that day, the dream of lasting peace
and world citizenship and the rule of international morality will remain but a fleeting illusion, to be pursued but never attained. And
until the ignoble and unhappy regimes that hold our brothers in An-
gola, in Mozambique and in South Africa in subhuman bondage have
been toppled and destroyed; until bigotry and prejudice and malicious
and inhuman self-interest have been replaced by understanding and
tolerance and good-will; until all Africans stand and speak as free beings, equal in the eyes of all men, as they are in the eyes of Heaven;
until that day, the African continent will not know peace. We Africans
will fight, if necessary, and we know that we shall win, as we are confident in the victory of good over evil.[32]

A month before Haile Selassie addressed the UN, Dr. Martin
Luther King Jr. delivered his famous "I Have a Dream" speech,
which became a hymn to human equality. The African American's
speech overshadowed the emperor's. A year later, both were nomi-
nated for the Nobel Peace Prize, and King won it.

One of the highlights of Haile Selassie's dialogue with the
greater world was his 1966 visit to Jamaica, especially with respect
to the Rastafarians centered on the Caribbean island. Haile Selassie,
it must be said, never took them overly seriously. He of course knew
of Marcus Garvey's prophesy that connected him to the myth of return to Africa. Those who called themselves after him, the Rastafarians, saw his 1930 coronation as a sign of redemption, and the emperor himself as a messiah heralding independence, freedom, and
prosperity in the mother continent (Rastafarians celebrate Haile Selassie's birthday, his coronation day, and the declaration of the 1931
Ethiopian constitution that declared him a descendant of King
Solomon). In Jamaica the cult won tens of thousands of adherents,
and among them were some who wanted to immigrate into Ethiopia
promptly. In 1948 Haile Selassie allotted them land in Shashamane,
southern Ethiopia (the Jamaican community there numbered around
two thousand).[33] Beyond this, the whole story was no more than an
episode for Haile Selassie. When he ordered Jamaica be included in
one of his tours, he was in for a surprise.

On the tarmac of Kingston airport tens of thousands of worshippers were waiting on April 21, 1966. The atmosphere was ecstatic.
Haile Selassie appeared in the door of the Ethiopian Airlines plane,
and thousands began storming toward him, chanting slogans that declared he was God. The stunned emperor hurried back into the plane

and for a moment considered ordering the pilot to take off. Finally, his guards ventured out, ready to shoot.[34] He then made his way to the city in an open car, waving to the masses.[35] The main ceremony was held in the Kingston Stadium. The stadium had seen many glorious world records, but never a sight like this. Jamaica, now four years independent, saluted Haile Selassie. A delegation of the Rastafarians was invited to meet the emperor, and they repeated their gestures of worship. "We are not God," Haile Selassie responded. "We are not a prophet. We are a slave of God."[36] Some of the Rastafarians were disappointed. "They expected someone between God and Cassius Clay [the iconic world heavyweight champion, Muhammad Ali]," a British representative reported.[37] Others became even greater believers. The week before Haile Selassie's arrival experienced heavy rains, but as the emperor's plane landed, the sun came out and shone directly on Haile Selassie's face. For many, it was a sure sign of Godly holiness.[38] The emperor, in any case, went on touring the island, and he departed amid a similar gathering of tens of thousands in the airport.

Although the young Jamaican singer Bob Marley missed the emperor's visit, he became the most famous preacher of Rastafarianism and contributed more than anyone else to the belief in Haile Selassie's divinity. In the 1970s Marley composed music based on some of the emperor's speeches, most notably Haile Selassie's UN speech of October 6, 1963. Entitled "War," the song was first performed in 1976: "Until the philosophy which holds one race superior and another inferior is finally and permanently discredited and abandoned, everywhere is war, Me say war. . . "[39]

After Haile Selassie's deposition and murder, Bob Marley met the emperor's son and heir in exile. The prince gave the admired singer his father's ring, which Bob Marley asked to be buried with.

"A Man Who Has Made Us What We Are Today"

In 1966 Haile Selassie made a few steps toward opening the government. On February 23 he declared he would give more autonomy to the provinces. On March 22 he authorized Prime Minister Aklilu to appoint his ministers himself. The emperor said again that he wanted officials to shoulder more responsibility rather than refer everything to him. But observers remained skeptical.[40] Every morning dozens of ministers and senior officials gathered in the Old

Gebbi, waiting for the moment the emperor's secretary would allow them to approach his majesty and present their case. They all knew they should not risk any independent initiative but rather humbly argue whatever they had in mind. Haile Selassie kept complaining to foreigners he was overworked, but he continued to humiliate his men, and nothing changed. Aklilu remained submissive, an obedient servant. Only a few dared to suggest new ideas, and they did so very politely. Ras Imru, "the red ras," was one of them.[41] On one occasion, in a public audience, Imru asked Haile Selassie if it would be more appropriate if parliament would elect the prime minister. The emperor gave him his dismissive stare and left the room.[42] The CIA concluded in March 1966:

> Haile Selassie still reigns as supreme authority in Ethiopia, but his de-clining vigor, his absorption in external affairs, and the growing com-plexity of government are leading to general immobility of the Impe-rial system. The elite of the bureaucracy and the army are increasingly alienated from the regime, and the armed forces are hard pressed to put down insurgencies in the provinces. Even with the inspiration of successful coups elsewhere in Africa, however, the odds are against the Ethiopians turning out their Emperor. Nor is the Emperor likely to change the system in any meaningful way. The outlook is for growing internal discontent, continued insurgency in the provinces, and de-mands on the US for more military aid.[43]

The British ambassador at that time wrote that Haile Selassie was so confident that he was the elect of God that he never really cared for his personal safety.[44] For who in Ethiopia would dare raise his hands to his divine majesty?

On May 5, 1966, Haile Selassie celebrated the twenty-fifth an-niversary of his 1941 reentry to Addis Ababa as a liberator. It was a good occasion for more appointments—namely, for widening the circle of rivalries among his men. Since Aklilu had seemingly re-ceived more power, Dajjazmach Asrate deserved a promotion. He was summoned from Eritrea and elevated to ras. Ras Asrate, loyal to the end, confided three days later in his diary:

> The emperor is very reluctant to give up his powers. To begin with, he shows no willingness to abdicate, bestowing no power upon his eldest son, whom he considers to be unworthy. But if he persists in clinging to power, things could get out of hand and we would be incapable of controlling events. The coup of 1960 was nothing but a dress re-hearsal. The armed forces are clearly in the process of launching a second coup. And this time they are very likely to be successful be-

cause the Crown's image has been seriously tarnished in the past seven years. . . . Very few people now understand what a military regime could do to our country. . . . They would try to uproot the entire elite in our country, because the military would never feel entirely safe as long as we are in circulation. What madness! . . . We will be the first to be eliminated, but then it will be the turn of the man in the street. Because they are suspicious of everyone and they will throw into prison Ethiopians from every walk of life, while mass execution of our people will be an everyday occurrence. They will pit one group against another and soon the slender thread of solidarity that has slowly formed among the various peoples of Ethiopia will be cut out of the mindset of the Ethiopians . . . but our hands are tied by our loyalty to a single man, who has made us what we are today.[45]

Notes

1. Del Boca, *The Negus*, pp. 265–266, quoting the *Ethiopian Herald*, December 19, 1960.
2. Ibid., p. 265.
3. See Theodore Vestal, "Peace Corps," *EAE*, Vol. 4, pp. 127–128.
4. See Erlich, *Alliance and Alienation*, pp. 154–159.
5. Tadesse Tamrat, a prominent historian and future head of the Institute of Ethiopian Studies, told me he had come back from Israel and told Haile Selassie he would like to establish a kibbutz, a socialist community of farmers. He remembered vividly Haile Selassie's dismissive, forgiving smile.
6. Del Boca, *The Negus*, p. 269.
7. R. Balsvik, "Student movement, Ethiopian," *EAE*, Vol. 4, p. 752.
8. Edward Ullendorff, "Haile Sellasie at Seventy," *Times* (London), July 23, 1962.
9. Del Boca, *The Negus*, p. 270–271; Asfa-Wossen, *King of Kings*, 238–241.
10. FRUS, 1961–1963, Vol. 21, Africa. Memorandum from William H. Brubeck of the National Security Council Staff to President Kennedy, September 30, 1963.
11. The following is based on Haggai Erlich, *Ethiopia and the Challenge of Independence*, pp. 213–224; Haggai Erlich, *The Struggle Over Eritrea 1962–1978* (Stanford, CA: Hoover Institution, 1983), chapters 1–3; and Haggai Erlich, *Ethiopia and the Middle East,* pp. 127–140.
12. In 1951 Libya became independent, and Sudan, Morocco, and Tunisia followed in 1956; Ghana and Guinea became independent shortly thereafter. In 1960 eighteen countries became independent, including Somalia, Cameroon, Togo, Madagascar, Congo, Dahomey (Benin), Nigeria, Ivory Coast, Chad, the Central African Republic, Gabon, Senegal, Mali, Mauritania. A year later: Sierra Leone and Tanganyka (Tanzania). In 1962: Algeria, Uganda, Rwanda, and Burundi.
13. For a discussion and literature on the OAU (also from the Ethiopian point of view), see Ashlid Samnoy, "Organization of African Unity," *EAE*, Vol. 4, pp. 50–52.
14. Mandela, *A Long Walk to Freedom,* p. 84.
15. Ibid., pp. 254–255.
16. See also www.tadias.com/05/25/2013/ketema-yifru-the-architect-behind-the-oau; Aberra Jembere, "Katama Yifru," *EAE*, Vol. 3, pp. 359–360.
17. Bereket Habte Selassie, *Conflict and Intervention in the Horn of Africa* (New York: Monthly Review Press, 1980), p. 155.
18. "Africa Must Unite or Sink—Kwame Nkrumah," AfricanGlobe.net, February 13, 2013.

19. See full text in Haile Selassie, "Towards African Unity," www.blackpast .org/1963-haile-selassie-towards-african-unity.

20. Asfa-Wossen, *King of Kings*, p. 254.

21. Del Boca, *The Negus*, pp. 283–284.

22. See also "Life and Work at the Court of Haile Selassie I: Memoirs of Lore Trenkler," the Austrian cook of the emperor, https://anglo-ethiopian.org/publications /articles.php?type=L&reference.

23. FO 371/190146, Russel to FO, "Last Impressions of Ethiopia," 5.12.1966.

24. "Speech at the 1964 O.A.U. Summit (1964)," in Ministry of Information, *Important Utterances of H.I.M. Emperor Haile Selassie I, 1963–1972* (Addis Ababa: Berhanena Selam, 1972), pp. 368–379.

25. In 2002 it was renamed the African Union. Fifty-three of the continent's fifty-four states were members.

26. Mandela, *A Long Walk to Freedom*, p. 255.

27. Del Boca, *The Negus*, 287.

28. Israeli State Archives, Ethiopia 1963, Bar-On to Africa Department, July 15, 1963.

29. See Aberra Jembere, "Aklilu Habte-Wold," *EAE*, Vol. 1, pp. 170–172; see also a short autobiography written by Aklilu in the Derg's prison before he was executed in November 1974: Aklilu Habte-Wold, *Aklilu Remembers* [Amharic and English texts] (Addis Ababa: Addis Ababa University Press, 2010).

30. See FRUS, 1961–1963, Volume 21, Africa, 309, National Policy Paper. December 19, 1963.

31. FO 371/172852, Russel to FO, 16.7.1963.

32. Full text in Ministry of Information, *Important Utterances of H.I.M. Emperor Haile Selassie I*, pp. 460–471.

33. Giulia Bonacci, "Rastafari/Rastafarianism," *EAE*, Vol. 4, pp. 339–340.

34. FO 371/19015, Collins to FO, 22.6.1966.

35. YouTube, "Haile Selassie State Visit to Jamaica, 21 April 1966."

36. Asfa-Wossen, *King of Kings*, p. 259.

37. FO 371/190175, Murray to FO, 20.5.1966.

38. See www.africasacountry.com. *Erin Macleod*, when-emperor-haile-selassie -went-to-jamaica-on-this-in-1966. https://africasacountry.com/location/ethiopia.

39. https://aslyrics.com, Bob Marley lyrics. See also the YouTube Guide, Bob Marley and Haile Selassie speech.

40. FO 371/190146, Russel to FO, "Ethiopia After Haile Selassie," 26.5.1966.

41. FO 1043/66, "Notes on the Imperial Family," 17.3.1965.

42. Del Boca, *The Negus*, p. 295, quoting the diary of Asrate kept by his son Asfa-Wossen.

43. FRUS, 1964–1968, Vol. 24, Africa, Prospects for Ethiopia, Special Memorandum Prepared in the Central Intelligence Agency, Washington, March 31, 1966.

44. FO 371/190146, Russel to FO: "Ethiopia After Haile Selassie," 26.5.1966.

45. Del Boca, *The Negus*, p. 297–298, quoting Asrate's diary.

10
Nothing New Under the Sun

~

Was Haile Selassie a descendant of King Solomon? Skeptic observers and professional historians have their doubts. Romantic men would perhaps toy with the similarities. It was said that King Solomon wrote three books. When young he composed the Song of Solomon (Song of Songs). As a mature man he wrote the Book of Proverbs. As an old man he wrote Ecclesiastes: "The words of the Preacher, the son of David, king in Jerusalem. Vanity of vanities, sayeth the Preacher, vanity of vanities; all is vanity." King Solomon's words bespoke pessimism toward the end of his life, along with understanding that one should cling to life: "However many years anyone may live, let them enjoy them all."[1] We have reviewed Haile Selassie's youth—his Song of Solomon chapters. We followed his years as a middle-aged king, maneuvering and balancing between change and conservatism. The chapters that follow are Haile Selassie's book of Ecclesiastes, the ruminations of an old man. In 1967 Haile Selassie was seventy-five years old, aged in body and spirit. He had already begun to identify with the aging Solomon: "What profit hath a man of all his labour which he taketh under the sun?" But the emperor was still full of life, ready to devour what life may still offer. At the age of eighty, the Lion of Judah was still on his throne, still roaring, "who will not fear?"[2]

Israel and the Six-Day Salvation

In 1967 there came word from Jerusalem, and it was one of relief.[3] Haile Selassie was ambivalent toward Israel. On the one hand he trusted Israel and was happy to rely on the abilities of her sons. The official newspaper, the *Ethiopian Herald* (and the Amharic *Addis Zaman*), published more articles on Israel than on any other country. Practically every week a piece full of admiration for the young country appeared in its pages, lauding the country's social, agricultural, and scientific achievements. Israelis were invited to advise in nearly all fields, including the more sensitive ones of security and armed forces. (Israel, yearning for international recognition and anxious to build its position in Africa and Asia, invested more in Ethiopia than in any other country in its history.) On the other hand, Haile Selassie would not engrave any official stamp on this special relationship. Only in 1962 did he recognize Israel de jure, and even then he did not open an embassy in Tel Aviv. He would never return to Jerusalem, his own beloved holy city, even though he visited dozens of other capitals, many of which were in the Middle East. Many leading Israelis were invited to talks with him. The talks were always cordial but were held mostly in secret. The emperor told the Israelis that he trusted only them, that he knew the Arabs were after his hide—arming and inciting the Eritreans and Somalis and trying to undermine his leadership in Africa and the OAU. He expected his Israeli partners to understand why he could not provoke the Arabs by exposing his special relations with them. Furthermore, he expected they understood that he must vote against Israel and denounce it in international bodies. He was just pretending, and, between brothers, Israel should turn a cheek to it.

A moment of truth came on May 22, 1967. Nasser closed the Straits of Tiran in the Red Sea, declaring he would blockade Israel. For the emperor it was a double threat. First, Egyptian control of the northern gates of the Red Sea would mean it would become "an Arab lake"—that Eritrea would be consumed by Arab influence, and that Ethiopia would have no access to the sea. Second, an Arab victory in the inevitable war that was about to commence would spell an existential danger for Ethiopia—at least so was the feeling among many in Addis Ababa. Haile Selassie summoned his aides. Ras Asrate Kassa later testified that all were alarmed, but the general consensus was not to provoke Nasser.[4] The Israelis were furious to learn that Ethiopia was among the signatories of a resolution proposal at

the UN recommending moving the issue to The Hague International
Tribunal, a move that would practically render Nasser's illegal maneuver successful.[5]

Israel's ambassador to Ethiopia at that time was General Haim
Ben-David. "The emperor requested more details," he reported at the
end of the first day of the June war. Ben David continued:

> I explained the situation to him on a map that I brought with me. . . . I
> asked the emperor if we could rely on his help should we need it and
> of course in top secrecy. The emperor responded: "How could you
> have any doubt? The Arabs are our enemies; they drink our water [the
> Nile] but want to destroy us. We still remember Ahmad Gragn's inva-
> sion of Ethiopia in order to destroy Christianity here. We know you
> are the only friends in the region, and we can rely only on you." He
> asked me to keep his words to myself.[6]

June 1967 saw Ethiopia's churches full with worshippers praying for an Israeli victory. When news came of the Arab defeat, joyous cries were heard all over. In the years that followed, Israeli involvement in Ethiopia deepened. In practice, there was a substantial
alliance. Israeli advisers not only worked with Ethiopians in top administrative positions but also were in close daily contact with junior
army officers. Israeli majors and captains lived with their Ethiopian
counterparts in the field, sharing their grievances. No less important
was the myth shared also by the emperor, that Israelis were most influential in Washington. That there, in the American capital, they
could work wonders.

American Negligence

The Israeli victory of 1967 neutralized fear of an all-Arab invasion
of Ethiopia. But the threat from the Arab world had merely changed
form. In the two years that followed that war, new regimes emerged
in the Arab world that were no less dangerous to imperial Ethiopia.

Another relevant consequence of the 1967 war was the closure
of the Suez Canal (it would be reopened only in 1975), which badly
effected Ethiopia's already poor economy. More significant, the Red
Sea, no longer an oil artery for the West, lost importance in the eyes
of Washington. The Americans went on using the Kagenew Base and
equipped the Ethiopian army according to the 1953 agreement, but
they refused necessary upgrades. The United States assumed that

Ethiopia faced no real danger, that the Ethiopians could not use more sophisticated weapons, and that if they became overly confident they would themselves attack their neighbors. In March 1968 an Israeli official was told by Haile Selassie: "The Arabs will do their best to destroy us. . . . The Americans do not help. . . . They do not mind if the USSR controls the Red Sea. If the Arabs understand that we co-operate with you [Israel], they would invade Ethiopia. They would also leave the OAU."[7]

US national security advisor Henry Kissinger shaped American policy toward Ethiopia more than anyone else. Prior to Haile Selassie's visit to the White House in the summer of 1969, he wrote a long memorandum to President Nixon:

> Ethiopia is our closest friend in Africa. Our purpose in this visit . . . is to reassure Haile Selassie of our support without being drawn into his own parochial and exaggerated view of threats to Ethiopian security. The Emperor has an appetite for U.S. arms which we can neither satisfy under present military aid limitations nor justify in terms of our own estimate of his position. Moreover, military concerns divert the Emperor from economic development—where we can help and where prompt action is crucial to Ethiopia's stability and thus to our interests in the country. . . .
>
> At 76, on the throne for over half a century, Haile Selassie sees himself as one of the towering figures of modern history. He assumes not only his acknowledged role as Africa's elder statesman, but also a stature and wisdom in world affairs beyond the Continent.
>
> His outlook was clearly shaped by the Italian conquest of Ethiopia in the thirties—his dramatic but futile appeal to the League of Nations, a bitter wartime exile, a restoration only to find court intrigue and Communist efforts at subversion. Added to these experiences was the traditional fear of Christian Ethiopia being overwhelmed by surrounding Moslems. The product in the Emperor is a virtual siege mentality, in which Soviet arms aid to neighboring Somalia, Sudan and Yemen seems larger than life. The West, he fears, will repeat the mistakes of the thirties if it underestimates the threat to Ethiopia. Thus, the Emperor sees a common interest with the U.S. in making Ethiopia a bulwark against a Communist-Moslem thrust into the Horn of Africa.
>
> To these views (and most others) the Emperor brings both a passion from tragic experience and a sensitivity born of a royal self-esteem. Yet, as you know from your earlier meeting with him, these deeper qualities that determine his thinking may be deceptively obscured beneath a quiet, almost somber exterior in his personality.[8]

Nixon was attentive to this sober analysis. On July 8, 1969, he hosted Haile Selassie in the White House. In his welcome speech, he lavished the emperor with compliments. He noted that Haile Selassie was the only head of state who had met four different American presidents, a record that would probably never be broken. Nixon equated Haile Selassie to his ancestor King Solomon, and he quoted the Lord's promise to the king of Jerusalem: "I will give you a wise and discerning heart, so that there will never have been anyone like you, nor will there ever be."[9] With this "wise heart," Nixon waxed poetic, Haile Selassie was an inspiration for the world:

> We honor him also for what he means to history . . . the spirit that inspired us all in 1936, when we saw him standing tall and proud before the League of Nations talking for what all of the pragmatists, all of the realists said was a lost cause. . . . What His Majesty leaves, that heritage, on the pages of the history books of the world means more than the leadership of a nation, or a continent, or, for that matter, of the world. And for that moment of inspirational leadership we are all in his debt.[10]

Haile Selassie responded with compliments in kind, but he had not traveled to Washington for nice words. He brought a list of desired arms, which the Americans politely ignored. Namely, they established a committee to study the request and make recommendations. Meanwhile, the heads of the Ethiopian army, practically all ranks, became frustrated at what they saw as America's blind negligence. Washington would only supply outdated, used arms: old Sherman tanks and P-86 jet fighters, and a few F-5s. In April 1971 Prime Minister Aklilu confided to the Israeli ambassador, Uri Lubrani, that he did not get along with the US State Department.[11] The Israelis, who approached the Americans time and again on behalf of the Ethiopians, were told there was "no way the US would increase the military aid. It would be just a waste. . . . All of Africa gets 18 million dollars' worth of military aid, of that Ethiopia gets 13 million. There is no doubt that they have military needs, but all should be done within this financial framework."[12]

There was one moment of grace for Haile Selassie during his July 1969 visit to the United States. After secret preparations it was agreed that he would fly from Washington to Atlanta to pay respect at the grave of Dr. Martin Luther King. The emperor spent two hours there, received an honorary doctorate from the local university, made an emotional speech, and laid a wreath at the grave of the civil rights leader.[13]

The Americans, though never meeting the Ethiopians' expectations, remained the main supporter of Haile Selassie's regime. American military advisers worked with the Ethiopian army, young

Peace Corps volunteers did their best in the countryside, and be-tween 1968 and 1970, around four thousand Ethiopian officers were sent to the United States for advanced training. Among them was the fearless and unrestrained Lieutenant Mangistu Haile Mariam. In his six months at the Maryland Military Academy, he accumulated what he considered racist insults. He returned to Ethiopia anti-American to the bone.

New Challenges in the Region

By the time Haile Selassie visited Nixon, the Middle East and the Horn of Africa had seen changes that presented Ethiopia with new challenges.

On May 25, 1969, Colonel Ja`far al-Numayri captured power in Sudan and began building a pro-Soviet military regime. In the short term, from 1969 to 1971, Sudan returned to active enmity with Ethiopia. It enabled the Eritrean ELF to act freely, within and out-side Sudanese territory, and traded threats with Ethiopia's imperial government.

With young army officers, 1964. The cadet Mangistu is in the upper row, above Haile Selassie.

Courtesy of Israeli Defense Forces Archive, Tel Aviv.

In September 1969 Colonel Mu`ammar Qaddafi captured power in Libya (and would not be ousted until 2011). Like Numayri, he joined the pro-Soviet Arab bloc. Qaddafi began aiming for continental leadership, and he quickly collided with Haile Selassie. Bold and young, he resorted to indelicate language to expose the emperor as an old reactionary. In 1970 Qaddafi opened an Eritrean office in Tripoli and declared an Islamic war against the Christians of Ethiopia.[14] In the following years he worked persistently to undermine Haile Selassie's standing in the continent.

In October 1969 General Siyad Barre took power in Somalia. Barre did away with the parliamentarian system and began expanding the Somali army with Soviet aid. He added a Marxist ideology to the Somali nationalist claim to Ogaden, inspiring ethnic Somalis and also Oromos in southern Ethiopia to rebel against Haile Selassie and secede from Ethiopia.

In the same year, the Palestine Liberation Organization (PLO) managed to establish a state within a state in Jordan, which had implications for Eritrea and Ethiopia. The PLO adopted the Ba'thist ideological line that Eritrea was a part of the Arab world and that fighting the Ethiopians was part of the Arab revolutionary struggle against imperialism and Zionism. Palestinian guerrilla experts trained Eritreans in their camps in Jordan, Lebanon, Syria, South Yemen, and in the Afar Desert on the Eritrean coast.

Qaddafi was the main financial supporter of the Eritrean-Palestinian collaboration, which was duly supported by Nasser. Earlier in 1968, a new regime emerged in Iraq (with Saddam Hussein as its number two), which began arming the Eritreans through Sudan. The aid from the Libyans and Palestinians came through South Yemen. Thus, the Red Sea became the main channel for arms against Haile Selassie's regime.

Searching for Moderates

In 1970 the situation in Eritrea was deteriorating at the hands of the new pro-Soviet Arab regimes. Haile Selassie continued to look for moderates in the Arab world and hoped that his friend Nasser would restrain his enemies. The Egyptian leader kept promising he would do so, provided the emperor cease his reliance on Israelis. Though Haile Selassie never really trusted Nasser, he was willing to play the game. In May 1970 Nasser messaged the emperor to say that he was out for an Arab summit in Khartoum, and that on his way back he would bring Qaddafi and Numayri to Cairo. He also pledged to try to bring the presidents of Syria and Iraq. The emperor, he wrote, was invited to meet with them, and they would solve the Eritrean issue together.[15]

The meeting in Cairo was held the second week of June 1970, but none of the said presidents came. It was attended by the vice prime minster of Sudan and the Libyan ambassador to Cairo. The latter told Haile Selassie bluntly that any friend of Israel was the enemy of the Arabs and of Libya, and that Libya would continue supporting the Eritreans. The emperor's men reported later that Haile Selassie angrily admonished Nasser like a father admonishing a son, but reports from Cairo indicated that Nasser responded in kind.[16] Nasser, in any case, was no longer in control of inter-Arab affairs and surely had no hold on young leaders like Numayri, Qaddafi, and the PLO's leader, Yasser Arafat. Exhausted and ill, the Egyptian leader was to die some two months later, on September 28, 1970. His successor, Anwar al-Sadat, would lead Egypt differently, also in the Ethiopian context.

Prior to his visit to Cairo in early June 1970, Haile Selassie flew to Moscow. Speeches were made by the guest and his hosts, and old relations and the legacies of the struggle against Mussolini were mentioned. The Union of Soviet Socialist Republics (USSR) considered Ethiopia the main power in the Horn and key to controlling the Red Sea. The emperor must have believed that the visit would enhance his status among the nonaligned nations and would perhaps shake up Washington. In reality, the Americans were unimpressed, and little came from the Moscow tour.

In the same month, a pivotal OAU meeting was convened, wherein Egypt, Algeria, and Libya denounced Israel as an imperialist state occupying African territory in Sinai.[17] The pronouncement put Haile Selassie on the defensive. From that point on, Arab representatives continued blaming the emperor for collaborating with Zionists and thusly promoting imperialism. This pressure would gradually increase and would have a growing impact on the emperor and his fate.

A New Challenge at Home: The Students

In the academic year of 1969–1970, the Haile Selassie I University campus became a focal point of political unrest. The previous year had seen the rise of the young generation in Western Europe, the

United States, and even in Egypt—a wave that inevitably reached Ethiopia. The impassioned students of Haile Selassie University were the most active protesters in Africa that year.

The emperor was probably not surprised. Haile Selassie trusted no one, least of all youngsters, whom he considered ungrateful by nature. He remembered how the students had supported the December 1960 coup, and he had no illusions about their contemporaries. He was always doubtful that education could change the ungrateful human nature,[18] but he was certain he could control—or, if necessary, oppress—their youthful spirit. He was resolved that as long as he sat on the throne, Ethiopia's students would prepare only for the distant future.

The campus at Sidist Kilo Square (formerly the Genet Lul Palace) was expanded to include new dormitories, cafeterias, and a new library. A new five-year bachelor's degree program was introduced in 1964, in which students spent their fourth year in distant provinces teaching peasant children and gaining exposure to the problems of the country. Fifth-year students prepared hundreds of papers reflecting on their experiences and oral testimonies they had collected in Ethiopia's rural peripheries. Through this system students became better exposed to the harsh realities of feudal Ethiopia. They were also influenced by their foreign professors as well as by the many African diplomats and officials residing in Addis Ababa as representatives of their new republics.

Haile Selassie was not afraid of the youth he cultivated. He enabled the establishment of a student union and its newspaper, *News and Opinions*, which began publication in 1966. But it became slowly apparent that the student paper would not follow in the obedient steps of the *Ethiopian Herald* (or of *Addis Zaman*). The paper published articles and poems that hardly concealed their criticism of country and king. In typical Ethiopian fashion, messages were conveyed indirectly. The demonstrations that followed were not against the emperor but mainly against his Parliament. The students adopted the slogan "Land to the Tiller"—a call for land reform aimed at Ethiopia's feudal elite. The emperor saw the gesture as just one more tool to put to use in his sophisticated political game; he spoke out in favor for such land reform but left it to Parliament to initiate and legalize it. Everyone understood the rules of this game: Haile Selassie would remain a man of progress, the young would let out steam, Parliament would endlessly discuss the matter, and the land would stay in the hands of the emperor's loyal feudal elite (and the Church).[19]

In 1967 a more militant student leadership emerged. The student union was renamed the Union of the Students of Addis Ababa University (USUAA), avoiding the name Haile Selassie I University. In place of *News and Opinions* came a periodical entitled *Struggle* (*Tigil*), and its contents became more radical. For example, the November 1969 issue included an editorial titled "Feudalism Must Be Purged" and featured articles that supported the fight of the Vietnamese people against the United States and analyzed the guerrilla tactics of Ho Chi Minh and Che Guevara. Again, Haile Selassie was not directly mentioned, but everything connected with his regime was attacked, especially any aspect of policy connected to the United States, like the Peace Corps volunteers "who undermine our culture." Strikes, demonstrations, and riots were held not only on the university campus but also in secondary schools, in the capital, and elsewhere. On December 29, 1969, the student leader Tilahun Gizaw was assassinated near the university campus. Nobody doubted that the murder was perpetrated by the imperial security services (though these suspicions seemed not to consider the fact that Tilahun's sister was the widow of the late Prince Makonnen, the emperor's favorite son). Angry students stormed the hospital and carried out Tilahun's body. A huge demonstration ignited on campus when soldiers opened fire and killed twenty-three students. Haile Selassie hurried to the TV studio and announced the dismissal of the minister of education. Off camera, he gave his men free rein with their tactics for calming the campus.

From then until the end of Haile Selassie's regime in 1974, no murderous events of the scale of what occurred in 1969 were repeated. The student movement became fragmented, as nobody dared anymore to openly act in the manner of Tilahun Gizaw. The campuses, nevertheless, remained disquieted. Students continued to demonstrate—and to be beaten, jailed, and interrogated. Some were tortured and sent to distant places. In 1972 the USUAA was outlawed.

On November 3, 1971, Haile Selassie gave his annual speech. He reemphasized the priority he attached to education: eighty-four new secondary schools had been opened the previous year, and the education budget had increased by 27 percent. Haile Selassie lamented that the students remained, in his estimation, ungrateful:

It grieves Us that the availability of educational opportunities falls short of Our expectations. The few who are fortunate enough to benefit from these limited opportunities and yet fail to make the best use of their time should regret the opportunities they are squandering. Obviously, such an unfortunate state of affairs cannot but grieve Us. Therefore, it is the sacred duty and responsibility of students and parents to see to it that the mistakes of the past are not repeated and that time which should be devoted to the pursuit of learning is not wasted by students heedlessly, following the instigation of a few misguided trouble-makers who have yet to understand the value and true meaning of education.[20]

His paternalistic approach did not improve as he approached the age of eighty. In June 1972 when a British diplomat asked Haile Selassie about the restive campus, he answered

It is the duty of the parents and the older people to guide their children, so that they should develop not only physically but also mentally. Youth are sometime easily exposed to external influence. It is the duty of the elders to show them which of these influences are useful, and which ones are not, and thereby to convince them where they went wrong.[21]

All Is Quiet at the Top

Haile Selassie did not like to hear even the slightest criticism. Ras Asrate, who had the courage to politely suggest change, had to pay for it. Prime Minister Aklilu kept accusing the ras of building a private army in Eritrea. According to Asrate's son, the historian Asfa-Wossen Asserate, Israeli and American agents did suggest to him, separately, to consider acting against the emperor, but he was too loyal to Haile Selassie.[22] Instead, Asrate accumulated frustrations.[23] At the end of January 1970, he left Asmara and flew to London, where he stayed for a few months. In his absence the Ethiopian army tried to teach the rebels a lesson its own way. In June Ras Asrate returned to Asmara in despair. The Eritreans, inspired and trained by PLO experts, turned to spectacular acts of sabotage, which they filmed and publicized. In October they managed to blow up the Asmara-Massawa railway line on camera, and on November 21 they ambushed and killed the commander of the Ethiopian Second Division. In response, Haile Selassie declared martial law in the province and removed Asrate from Asmara.[24]

Over the next years Asrate, now head of the meaningless Crown Council, was practically sidelined. The aging emperor went on pushing aside anyone with some spark of independent thought. Former minister of defense Abiy Abebe was "parked" in the senate, the "garage." The capable foreign minister Katama Yifru was appointed in August 1971 to the Ministry of Agriculture and Commerce. Only obedient prime minister Aklilu remained Haile Selassie's adviser. Aklilu complimented the emperor for maintaining status quo and for basically doing nothing with regard to land reform, to distribution of power, or to enacting some autonomy in the provinces.

The American "National Intelligence Estimate" of June 1970 summarized:

> Haile Selassie, on the dual basis of the authority of his office and his own shrewd manipulation of nearly everyone and everything in the Ethiopian Government, so far retains fairly effective control over his ramshackle empire. Though nearly 78 years old, with gradually diminishing vigor and flexibility, he still makes all major and most minor decisions, moves ministers, governors, and generals in and out of office, and maintains a network of informants who pervade the government and provide information to the palace. In practice, he is both the chief architect of such modernization as has taken place in Ethiopia and the zealous preserver of an ancient feudal order.[25]

In December 1970 Abuna Baselios died. He was Haile Selassie's age and one of the few individuals the emperor liked. The old abuna felt close enough to occasionally express an opinion. For example, back in 1960, when he helped save Haile Selassie, Baselios promised the loyal soldiers a salary raise. When the emperor did not fulfill this promise, the abuna closed himself in Debra Libanos Monastery. Haile Selassie selected Tewoflos as the new abuna. Tewoflos was a strong-minded and conservative person who firmly advised against land reform (by tradition the Church owned one-third of the land). After the Revolution of 1974, Abuna Tewoflos continued to oppose the new reforms; he was arrested in 1976 and murdered in jail three years later.

The imperial elite remained obedient. Its members enjoyed landownership and control of the peasants. Land was an import element in the emperor's power. He could endow position, title, rank, and land, and he could also rescind them. The system had its traditional name, *shum-shir*, "appoint and remove," and the cycle of appointments was nicknamed the *masob*. The *masob* is the round straw table or tray that diners rotate as they eat. Nearly every morning Haile Selassie would be driven to Menelik Palace to perform the *shum-shir*. At night he would consider appointments and removals, and in the morning he would announce them to the crowd that anxiously awaited him at the *masob*.[26]

The Parliament was supposed to give the system an appearance of modern representative politics. By the 1955 constitution, Ethiopia held parliamentary elections that held some air of competition. But the Parliament itself was little more than a toy for Haile Selassie, and he found it especially useful in torpedoing any move toward land reform. The members of the House needed nothing spelled out to them: they understood that their job was to conduct fruitless debates. Haile Selassie's November 3, 1971, annual speech before Parliament provided an apt example of the emperor's sheer paternalism:

> Forty years ago today, We established for the first time in the history of Our country the legislative branch of the government. While the tradition of counsel has always been a part of our national ethos, We brought into being this institution of counsel—the Parliament—as a vital entity and distinct part of Our Government, so that it will share a part of Our responsibility and deliberate on matters affecting the welfare of Our people and the progress of Our country. Over the years We have witnessed the growth and strengthening of Our Parliament. We have also witnessed the foundation We laid for democratic and responsive administration develop on an ever-secure base. And for this, praise be to the Almighty who has blessed our labours. With the passage of time and as the Parliament becomes more mature, it is but natural that the increasing duties and responsibilities devolving upon you, Parliamentarians, demand far-sightedness and profound insight. It is thus proper that We should review here today some of the main achievements and performances of Our government during the past twelve months and indicate the highlights of its major plans.[27]

"Alas, the Wise Man Dies–Just Like the Fool" (Ecclesiastes 2:16)

Haile Selassie respected very few Ethiopians. As a young man he admired his father and Emperor Menelik. Later, he respected pioneers of modern scholarship like Heruy Walda-Selassie, who died in 1938. From what we know of his final decades, it is difficult to point to many other Ethiopians whose opinion he considered worthwhile. As was noted earlier, his trusted wife, Mennen, died in 1962. He even mistrusted his half-brother, the "red ras," Imru Haile Selassie, after the 1960 rebels declared him prime minister. Believing Imru too naïve to be an adviser, the emperor appointed him ambassador in distant countries.

Yet Haile Selassie maintained affection and respect for his eldest daughter, Tananya-Warq. Like her father, she was a tough person. The emperor spent hours with Tananya-Warq, nearly every evening, and relied on her judgment of character.[28] The British Embassy reported that she was "a formidable woman. . . . Her house is a center for the royal family, whose members are used to acting as she wishes. The Princess is a shrewd business woman, she can be ruthless and . . . has the reputation of a schemer. Her manner can range from regal inscrutability to pleasant good humor."[29] The emperor despised the rest of his court. The more they flattered him, the deeper his scorn. Conversely, those who did not flatter enough were removed.

The aging Haile Selassie found comfort in endless travels abroad. There, in distant countries, he could indulge in honors and meet with people he could converse with on equal footing. Detailing his travels in 1971, or any other year, would be exhausting. In his November 1971 annual speech, he explained how personal diplomacy was effective and counted some of his visits abroad that year: Italy, the Vatican, Spain, Rwanda, Burundi, China, Somalia. Additionally, he hosted numerous heads of other states. His trip to Iran is worth mentioning. In October the shah, Muhammad Reza, hosted festivities for the 2,500th anniversary of the Persian empire. The shah prepared megalomaniacal ceremonies in the ancient capital of Persepolis. It was such a demonstration of corruption and waste that some observers believe that the celebrations in Persepolis began the countdown to Iran's 1979 Islamic Revolution. Haile Selassie was formally the most senior guest. Ten kings attended, along with dozens of princes, presidents, and prime ministers, but Haile Selassie was the only emperor. A king of kings, equal to the host, the shah of shahs. (In 1968 the shah had visited the emperor in Addis Ababa, an event that was eternalized on an Ethiopian stamp.) In official photos of the Persepolis event, both emperors appeared often together. Muhammad Reza Shah, however, did not live to enjoy old age. He was deposed at the age of sixty and died in exile a year later. In contrast, Haile Selassie was entering his eightieth year in 1971.

The aging emperor of Ethiopia was now more and more restless, and was often out of focus.[30] A French journalist who knew him well wrote: "Haile Sellase only has a few hours of lucidity in the morning. His character is terribly embittered. He insults his cabinet ministers and refuses to listen to them. In the afternoon he often takes a long nap before spending the evening only with members of his family. The man who was once a symbol for the world and for Africa is nothing now but an old man, whose faculties are dwindling."[31]

In July 1970, as Haile Selassie's seventy-eighth birthday approached, the British began preparing drafts of eulogies and messages to the Ethiopian people. An American journalist who saw the emperor on his seventy-ninth birthday wrote that he was walking like a marionette, his voice hardly audible, "a lonely and confused man." In 1971 the British foreign ministry officials corresponded about preparations for a royal funeral.[32] In April 1972, as the emperor prepared to visit Britain, the British ambassador reported to his prime minister that Haile Selassie had difficulty interacting with men he had not known before—that he may be "gaga" one day and as sharp as a razor on another.[33] The Polish journalist Ryszard Kapuscinski was among those who worked to demonize Haile Selassie and portray him as a devilish dictator, growing senile as he aged. Kapuscinski's book *The Emperor: Downfall of an Autocrat* was a combination of some research with sensationalized stories mixed with grains of truth. According to Kapuscinski, one of the emperor's servants testified:

> In old age, he became even smaller. He weighed fifty kilograms [about 110 pounds]. He ate less and less, and he never drank alcohol. His knees stiffened up, and when he was alone he dragged his feet, swaying from side to side as if on stilts. But when he knew someone was watching him, he forced a certain elasticity into his muscles, with great effort, so that he moved with dignity and his imperial silhouette remained ramrod-straight. . . . His Majesty never forgot about this infirmity of old age, which he did not want to reveal lest it weaken the prestige and solemnity of king of kings. But we servants of the royal bedchamber, who saw his unguarded moments, know how much the effort cost him.[34]

"How Old Could He Be?"

Haile Selassie made endless speeches. He loved to preach in big moments. Some people, like Henry Kissinger, had little patience for listening to him.[35] Only a few managed to conduct a straightforward conversation with the emperor. In June 1972, as he was approaching eighty, the queen of interviews, the Italian journalist Oriana Fallaci, came to his palace. Courageous and bold, she had managed to open up some of the great men of the century.[36] Fallaci was instructed to give the questions in advance and told not to wear pants. She agreed to the emperor's attire request, but she would not allow even the king of kings to have all the questions in advance. During the interview she deviated from protocol by ignoring the interpreter and manipulating Haile Selassie into answering her directly in French. There was no chemistry between them. When Fallaci went too far, Haile Selassie angrily waved her out. She took her revenge by describing him as an old bird:

> How old could he be? Actually eighty, as we read in his biographies? I'd say ninety, a hundred. . . . The eyes were round, astonished . . . swollen with forgetfulness. Eyebrows, whiskers, beard, and hair all over him like feathers. Beneath that bird's head with the pharaoh's face, the body twisted and turned, as fragile as a child's body made up to look like an old man.[37]

The interview was published a year later in the *Chicago Tribune*.[38] It is worth reading the full text as perhaps the best document reflecting the mind of the old king: "The words of the preacher. . . . Vanity of vanities." A lion in the winter.

ORIANA FALLACI: There is a question, Your Majesty, that has been troubling me since I saw the poor running after your car and fighting over an 18-pence dollar. What do you feel, Your Majesty, when you distribute alms to your people? What are your feelings when you are faced with their poverty?

HAILE SELASSIE: Rich and poor have always existed and always will. Why? Because there are those that work and those that don't, those that wish to earn their living and those that prefer to do nothing. Those that work, that want to work, are not poor. . . . Yes, We too are aware distributing alms serves no useful purpose. Because there is only one means to solve the poverty problem: work.

ORIANA FALLACI: Your Majesty, I'd like to make sure I've understood you right. Do you mean, Your Majesty, that whoever is poor deserves to be?

HAILE SELASSIE: We have said that whoever doesn't work because he doesn't want to is poor. We have said wealth has to be gained through hard work. We have said those who don't work starve. And now We add that the capacity to earn depends on the individual: Each individual is responsible for his misfortunes, his fate. It is wrong to expect help to fall from above, as a gift: Wealth has to be deserved! Work is one of the commandments of Our Lord the Creator!

ORIANA FALLACI: Your Majesty, what do you think of the new, disconnected generation? I mean the students rioting in the universities, especially in Addis Ababa and . . .

HAILE SELASSIE: Young people will be young people. You can't change the uncouth manners of the young. Besides, there is nothing new in that: There is never anything new under the sun. Examine the past: You'll see that the disobedience of the young has occurred all through history. The young don't know what they want. They can't know it because they lack experience, they lack wisdom. It is for the head of the state to show the young which path to tread and to punish them when they revolt against authority. It is up to Us. But not all the young are wicked and only the most irreducible culprits must be punished unbendingly. The others must be reduced to reason and then persuaded to serve their country. That's what We think and that's how it must be.

ORIANA FALLACI: Punished even to the point of a death sentence, Your Majesty?

HAILE SELASSIE: . . . the death penalty is just and necessary. For disobedience, for instance. Why? Because it is in the interests of the people. We have abolished many things. We have abolished slavery, too. But not the death penalty, We can't abolish that. It would be like renouncing punishment for those who dare to defy authority. That's what We think and that's how it must be.

ORIANA FALLACI: Your Majesty, I would like you to tell me something about yourself. Tell me: Were you ever a disobedient youth? But maybe I ought to ask you first whether you have ever had time to be young, Your Majesty?

HAILE SELASSIE: We don't understand that question. What kind of question is it? It is obvious that We have been young: We weren't born old! We have been a child, a boy, a youth, an adult, and finally an old man. Like everyone else. Our Lord the Creator made Us like everyone else. Maybe you wish to know what kind of youth We were. Well: We were a very serious, very diligent youth. We were sometimes punished, but do you know why? Because what We were made to study did not seem enough and We wished to study further. We wanted to stay on at school after lessons were over. We were loath to amuse Ourselves, to go riding, to play. We didn't want to waste time on games.

ORIANA FALLACI: Your Majesty, maybe I wasn't clear enough . . .

HAILE SELASSIE: *Ça suffit, ça suffit!* Enough, enough!

ORIANA FALLACI: Your Majesty, of all the monarchs still occupying their thrones you are the one that has ruled longest. Moreover, in an age that has seen the ruinous downfall of so many kings, you are the only absolute monarch. Do you ever feel lonely in a world so different from the one you grew up in?

HAILE SELASSIE: It is Our opinion that the world hasn't changed at all. We believe that such changes have modified nothing. We don't even notice any difference between monarchies and republics: To Us they appear two substantially similar methods of governing a nation. Well, tell Us: What is the difference between a republic and a monarchy?

ORIANA FALLACI: Actually, Your Majesty . . . I mean to me, it appears that in republics where democracy reigns the leader is elected. But in monarchies he isn't.

HAILE SELASSIE: We don't see where the difference lies.

ORIANA FALLACI: Never mind, Your Majesty. What is your opinion of democracy?

HAILE SELASSIE: Democracy, republic: What do these words signify? What have they changed in the world? Have men become better, more loyal, kinder? Are the people happier? All goes on as before, as always. Illusions, illusions. Besides, one should consider the interests of a nation before subverting it with words. Democracy is necessary in some cases and We believe some African peoples might adopt it. But in other cases it is harmful, a mistake.

ORIANA FALLACI: Your Majesty, do you mean to say that some nations, your nation in fact, are not ripe for democracy and therefore don't deserve it? Do you mean to say that freedom of speech, of the press, couldn't be tolerated here?

HAILE SELASSIE: Freedom, freedom. . . . Emperor Menelik and Our Father, both illuminated men, examined this word in their day and studied these problems closely. They raised them, in fact, and granted many concessions to the people. Later on We granted further concessions. We have already mentioned that We it was who abolished slavery. But, We repeat, some things are good for the people and others are not. It is necessary to know Our people to realize this. It is necessary to proceed slowly, cautiously, to be a watchful father for one's children. Our realities are not yours. And Our misfortunes are endless.

ORIANA FALLACI: Your Majesty, have you ever regretted your kingly fate? Have you ever dreamed of living the life of an ordinary mortal?

HAILE SELASSIE: We don't understand your question. Even at the hardest, most painful moments, We have never regretted or cursed Our fate. Never. And why should We have? We were born of royal blood, authority is ours by right. Since it is Ours by right and since Our Lord the Creator has deemed We might serve Our people as a father serves his son, being a monarch is a great joy to Us. It's what We were born for and what We have always lived for.

ORIANA FALLACI: Your Majesty, I am attempting to understand you as a man, not as a king. So I beg to insist and I ask you whether this job ever constitutes a burden, for instance when you have to use force to accomplish it. It's hard to feel indulgent to human beings.

HAILE SELASSIE: A king must never regret the use of force. Painful necessities are still necessities and a king must not stop when he is faced with them. Not even when they hurt him. We have never been afraid to be harsh: It's the king knows what is best for the people, the people themselves don't know it, as regards punishment, for instance. We must apply what Our conscience dictates, nothing more. And We never suffer when We inflict punishment because

We believe in that punishment, We trust Our judgment completely. So it must be and so it is.

ORIANA FALLACI: Your Majesty, you frequently mention punishment and rebuke. Is it then true that you are as religious and devoted to Christian teachings as is believed?

HAILE SELASSIE: We have always been religious, ever since childhood, ever since the day Our father Ras Makonnen taught Us the commandments of Our Lord the Creator. We devote a great deal of time to prayer and attend church as often as possible: every morning when We can. We receive the sacraments every Sunday regularly. But We don't consider Our religion alone valid and have granted Our people the freedom to observe any religion they please . . .

ORIANA FALLACI: During your visit to Italy, Your Majesty, the Italians did their utmost to demonstrate how sorry they were for having waged war against you. In one word: With the welcome they gave you they told you that in 1935 it was Mussolini's war. Are you not convinced of this?

HAILE SELASSIE: It is not for Us to say whether there existed a distinction between Italians and Fascists. It is for your conscience to say so. When a whole nation accepts and maintains a government in existence, it means that the nation recognizes that government. We, however, must make it clear that We have always distinguished in our judgment Mussolini's war from Mussolini's government. They were two different things. At the same time, We do not feel able to judge Mussolini's government as regards the aggression against Ethiopia. It is the government itself that judges what may be useful to its people, and Mussolini's government obviously attacked us in the belief that such a war would be useful to the Italian people.

ORIANA FALLACI: Your Majesty, maybe I didn't quite grasp your meaning. May I ask how you judge Mussolini today?

HAILE SELASSIE: We refrain from judging him. He is dead and what purpose is served by passing judgment on the dead? Death changes everything, sweeps everything away. Even mistakes. We dislike mentioning hatred or scorn in connection with a man who is no longer able to answer Us. The same applies to the other invaders of Our country: Graziani, Badoglio. All dead. Silence is fitting. We met Mussolini in 1924, when We were not yet emperor and went to Italy on an official visit. He received Us very warmly, like a real friend. He was kind. We took a liking to him. We talked with him frankly, discussing the past and the future. He inspired Us with trust: After that talk all Our misgivings vanished. Later, he broke his word to Us. That is something We were never able to understand. But it is no longer important.

ORIANA FALLACI: In that case, Your Majesty, how do you see now those painful years? The war we waged against you?

HAILE SELASSIE: . . . it is impossible to forget what the Italians did to us: We suffered so much on your account. On the other hand, what can we say? To wage an unjust war and win it can happen to anyone. As soon as We returned to Our country in 1941, We declared: We must be friends with the Italians. Today we are truly so. You have changed in many ways and we have changed in many others. And . . . let's put it this way: History doesn't forget but man can. He can also forgive, if he is kind-hearted. And We try to be kind. Yes, We have forgiven. But not forgotten. No, not forgotten. We remember everything, everything!

ORIANA FALLACI: Your speech at the League of Nations, too, Your Majesty? And the day of your flight, too?

HAILE SELASSIE: Yes, indeed. Well do We remember that speech, the eve of that speech, the Fascist newsmen insulting Us, the words We uttered to claim justice: "Today it is happening to us, tomorrow it will happen to you." That's exactly what did happen. . . . We also remember the day We departed into exile because it was the most painful day in Our life. Maybe the least understood, too. Because it took a lot of courage: Sometimes things that do not appear inspired by courage demand great courage. The fact is We had nothing left except the hope of returning to govern Our people. But that hope was great and as We roamed farther it became a certainty. Oh, We would never have left if We had feared We might have to stay in Europe for good! . . .

ORIANA FALLACI: Your Majesty, in the 31 years since it regained its independence Ethiopia has certainly not known much peace. Widespread rebellion still prevails today and there have been attempts to overthrow the government. The most serious took place 12 years ago, the one the Crown Prince was involved in. What can you tell me of this, Your Majesty?

HAILE SELASSIE: That We are not worried, or not more than necessary. Such episodes occur constantly in a country's history. There's always something moving, brewing. There are ambitious people everywhere. Wicked people. The only thing to do is deal with them with courage and decision. One must beware of uncertainty, weakness, or conflicting emotions: They lead to defeat. We have never allowed Ourselves to fall as prey to them. Force must be used against force, and that is how We reacted in that circumstance. Certainly, the episode caused Us pain: We never expected some, any. . . . But the real culprits were only a handful. Thus, We punished them and forgave the others. That's all.

ORIANA FALLACI: Not quite all, Your Majesty. I was referring to the episode that . . .

HAILE SELASSIE: *Ça suffit, ça suffit!* Enough, enough!

ORIANA FALLACI: Your Majesty, if you are unwilling to discuss certain things, tell me more about yourself. They say you are very fond of animals and children. May I ask if you are equally fond of human beings?

HAILE SELASSIE: Human beings. . . . Well: It's hard to feel indulgent to human beings. It's much easier to show indulgence to animals and children. When one has led such a difficult life as Ours, one feels more at ease with animals and children. They are never wicked, or never deliberately so at least. Human beings on the other hand. . . . Well, there are good men and wicked. The former should be made use of and the latter punished, without attempting to understand why the ones are good and the others wicked. Life is like the theater: One mustn't try to understand it all at once and immediately. It is no longer amusing. Besides, We demand too much of men to be able to respect them.

ORIANA FALLACI: What do you demand of them, Your Majesty?

HAILE SELASSIE: Dignity, courage.

ORIANA FALLACI: The two leaders of that coup showed dignity, Your Majesty. They showed courage, too.

HAILE SELASSIE: *Ça suffit, ça suffit!* That's enough!

ORIANA FALLACI: As you will, Your Majesty. But what do you demand of a king, of yourself, Your Majesty?

HAILE SELASSIE: In this case, too, courage. And a balanced outlook. A king must be able to maneuver, be capable of oscillating between friends and enemies, old and new. A king must know how to take his time and bend everything to his predetermined air. We learned this in Our youth, when We read your books and imbibed your Western culture in accordance with the wishes of Emperor Menelik and Our Father. For indeed, We began very early to appreciate the new things you mention. We have traveled a great deal. We don't like traveling. It tires Us. Frequently, it doesn't even amuse Us. But We go just the same because We consider it useful to travel in search of friends, and this is a king's function.

ORIANA FALLACI: Your Majesty, you are Ethiopia. It's you that keeps it in hand, that keeps it united. What will happen when you are no longer there?

HAILE SELASSIE: What do you mean? We don't understand this question.

ORIANA FALLACI: When you die, Your Majesty.

HAILE SELASSIE: Ethiopia has existed for 3,000 years. In fact, it exists ever since man first appeared on earth. My dynasty has ruled ever since the Queen of Sheba met King Solomon and a son was born of their union. It is a dynasty that has gone on through the centuries and will go on for centuries more. A king is not and, besides, my succession is already ensured. There is a Crown Prince and he will rule the country when We are no longer there. That is what We have decided and so it must be.

ORIANA FALLACI: On the whole, Your Majesty, yours has not been a very happy life. Those you loved have all died: your wife, two of your sons, and two daughters. You have lost many of your illusions and many of your dreams. But you must, I imagine, have accumulated great wisdom, and of this I ask: How does Haile Selassie view death?

HAILE SELASSIE: What? View what?

ORIANA FALLACI: Death, Your Majesty.

HAILE SELASSIE: Death, Death? Who's this woman? Where does she come from? What does she want? Enough, go away, *ça suffit!*

Notes

1. Ecclesiastes 11:8.
2. Amos 3:8.
3. The following paragraphs are based on Erlich, *Alliance and Alienation,* pp. 111–173.
4. Israel State Archives [ISA], HZ 440/13, Ambassador to Africa Department, 4.6.1967.
5. ISA, HZ 440/13, Ambassador to Africa Department, 31.5.1967.
6. ISA, HZ 3/439, Haim Ben David to Africa Department, 6.6.1967.
7. ISA, HZ 3/439, Bitan to Africa Department, 4.3.1968.
8. FRUS, 1969–1976, Vol. E-5, Part 1, Memorandum from the President's Assistant for National Security Affairs (Kissinger) to President Nixon, July 6, 1969.
9. 1 Kings 3:12.
10. http://www.presidency.ucsb.edu, "President Richard Nixon Toasts Emperor Haile Selassie I of Ethiopia," July 8, 1969.
11. ISA, HZ, Lubrani to Africa Department 6.4.1971.
12. ISA, HZ, Shelef to Africa Department, 28.10.1971.
13. FRUS, 1969–1976, Volume E-5, Part 1, Documents on Sub-Saharan Africa, 1969–1972, Memorandum from the Assistant Secretary of State for African Affairs (Palmer) to Secretary of State Rogers, June 28, 1969; Emperor Haile Selassie laying a wreath at Martin Luther King Jr.'s grave site, Atlanta, GA, 1969, https://www.pinterest.com/pin/332140541251163062/.
14. ISA, HZ, Africa Department to Rupin, 29.1.1971, Following David Holden Article in Sunday *Times,* 20.12.1970.
15. ISA, HZ 11/4564, Embassy to FM, 13, 21 May 1970.
16. ISA, HZ 11/4564 Embassy to FM, 26 May 1970, 14 June 1970; "Ethiopian-Israeli Developments," by director of the foreign ministry, 18.6.1970.
17. Ibid.
18. See his 1962 conversation with the Israeli president of Technion University, in Erlich, *Alliance and Alienation*, pp. 152–154.
19. Randi Balsvik, *Haile Selassie's Students: The Intellectual and Social Background to Revolution, 1952–1977* (East Lansing: African Studies Center,

Michigan State University, 1985); Ghelawdewos Araia, "Ethiopian Students: Heroic, but Unfortunate Class in History," http://www.eastafricanforum.com/Articles /EthioStudents.htm.

20. Annual Address, November 3, 1971, www.jah-rastafari.com/selassie-words.

21. FCO 31/1689, P. Hall to FCO, 23.6.1972, "O. Wood's Interview with the Emperor."

22. Conversation with Prince Asfa-Wossen Asserate.

23. ISA, HZ 11/4564, Ambassador to Africa Department, A Meeting with Ras Asrate, 12.6.1970.

24. Erlich, *The Struggle Over Eritrea*, p. 41.

25. FRUS, 1969–1976, Vol. E-5, Part 1, 287; National Intelligence Estimate, May 21, 1970.

26. See a colorful description in Kapuscinski, *The Emperor*, pp. 7–12.

27. Annual Address, November 3, 1971, www.jah-rastafari.com/selassie-words.

28. See Hanna Rubinkowska, "Tananna Wark Hayla Selasse", *EAE*, Vol. 4, pp. 858–859.

29. FCO 31/1134, P. B. Hall, "Ethiopia: The Succession," 7.6.1972.

30. Hanan S. Aynor, *Africa in Crisis: His Imperial Majesty Haile Selassie's Ethiopia* (Jerusalem: S.S.Aynor, 1999), pp. 32–33.

31. Del Boca, *The Negus*, p. 315, quoting Jean Marie Damblain, *La Tragedie du negus* (Paris: Presses de la Cite, 1977), p. 31.

32. See the file FCO 31/557 (1970); FCO 31/802. Also in the file: Stanley Meisler, "Haile Selassie at 79," *International Herald Tribune*, n.d.

33. FCO 57/433, Alan Campbell to FCO, 24.4.1972.

34. Kapuscinski, *The Emperor*, p. 6.

35. Asfa-Wossen, *King of Kings*, p. 274.

36. Oriana Fallaci, *Interview with History* (Boston: Houghton Mifflin, 1977), includes interviews with Henry Kissinger, Golda Meir, Yasser Arafat, King Hussein, Indira Gandhi, Willy Brandt, Muhammad Reza Pahlavi, and others. For some reason the interview with Haile Selassie was not included. She referred to it in a later Italian edition, and it was quoted fully in the *Chicago Tribune*, June 24, 1973, as noted below.

37. Del Boca, *The Negus*, pp. 314–315, quoting Fallaci, *Intervista con la storia*, p. 371.

38. FCO 31/1471, "Interview by Oriana Fallaci, Journey into the Private Universe of Haile Selassie," *Chicago Tribune*, 24.6.1973.

11
Revolution

~

In late July 1972 Addis Ababa was cleaned. Thousands of national flags were hoisted, and electric bulbs were hung between the main buildings. Everyone prepared for the emperor's eightieth birthday. New tin walls were erected to block the sight of clusters of shabby huts. Beggars were put on trucks and dumped in distant places. New stamps and Swiss-made coins were issued. On July 23, Haile Selassie's birthday, tens of thousands of people crammed the streets, dressed in white and chanting praise for the king of kings. Limousines drove foreign representatives. In the main cathedral the abuna led the prayers. He blessed Haile Selassie, the defender of the faith. Journalists from all over the globe covered the event. But this time, unlike the 1930 coronation or the 1955 jubilee, there was significantly less joy. The world press reported more on poverty than on biblical authenticity. Haile Selassie still radiated dignity, still represented ancient glory. Yet something was clearly missing. The son of Ras Asrate described that morning in his biography of Haile Selassie. His father once again pleaded at the emperor's feet to exploit the opportunity and declare some reforms: "The emperor was visibly moved and said nothing for a while. Then he told my father to get up and answered him: "Tell me, did King David abdicate? . . . We shall reign as long as the Almighty allows Us to. And when the time has come for Us to depart, He will know what is best for Ethiopia."[1]

None of Ethiopia's modern rulers had managed to transfer power to his designated heir. Haile Selassie did not even consider it. He had no liking or respect for his older son Asfa-Wossen, who in any case suffered a stroke in January 1973 and was rushed to London. Ras Asrate accompanied the emperor's son and would not return before 1974. Ethiopia remained a one-man show. But the old emperor could no longer control the country, which was deteriorating rapidly. The year 1973 was far worse than the previous year. Armed by the Soviets, the Somalis gained a clear military advantage and prepared to invade Ogaden. The Eritrean Liberation Front scored victories even in the Christian-inhabited area. Ethiopia's leadership of the OAU came under heavier attacks. And, more acutely, the economy reached a disastrous low. The cumulative effect of the closure of the Suez Canal since 1967 and the drought inflicted on the northern regions as of late 1972 created a humanitarian crisis. Annual gross national product (GNP) per capita dropped to 83 USD, and life expectancy to age thirty. Sixty percent of children died in their first year of life. The ruling elite, lacking modern political frameworks, remained torn by old personal rivalries. The whole system revolved around an absolute monarch detached from reality. Many of the elite members simply ignored the simmering bitterness among the army's intermediate officers and the urban intelligentsia. Those who knew better felt that their very lives were at stake, but they remained paralyzed. Nobody dared confront Haile Selassie.

Golda Would Not Enable a Nobel Prize

The death of Nasser in September 1970 and Sadat's rise to power in Egypt changed the Egyptian-Ethiopian-Israeli equation. Sadat adopted a policy that aimed for political agreement with Israel—a ray of hope for Haile Selassie. He was convinced that such an arrangement between the two most important foreign states in his immediate international arena was vital for Ethiopia, and that it was possible. Haile Selassie believed that Sadat was no Nasser, that he had no revolutionary designs for pan-Arab unity at the expense of Egypt's neighbors. He also believed Sadat was just the moderate to restrain his Arab and Muslim enemies. Indeed, Sadat supported a new agreement between Ethiopia and Sudan in 1972 as well as rapprochement with Saudi Arabia. In February 1971 Sadat declared he was ready to work with UN mediators toward interim agreements with Israel leading toward peace, on the condition of Israel's full withdrawal from the areas occupied in 1967. Israel insisted on direct negotiations over the UN resolutions.

Although Haile Selassie repeatedly told the Israelis he understood their insistence on direct negotiations with Egypt, he also asked them to work differently. For him, the diplomatic arena had been always a game of indirect moves and complicated tricks—hardly a place for principles. True to form, Haile Selassie played such a game with Israel. He developed a full strategic treaty with Israel, but only under the table. He saw himself as the Lion of Judah but would not visit Jerusalem under an Israeli flag. He invited and hosted even his sworn enemies but avoided public appearances with Israeli leaders in Addis Ababa. With Sadat it was a different story. The two men understood each other. As of June 1971, the OAU supported the Egyptian position that by occupying Sinai, Israel had occupied an African territory. Haile Selassie's men scolded the Israelis time and again: "You are stubborn, inflexible, unwise. The Arabs play it smarter than you, and on all courts. . . . You attach too much importance to words and resolutions. Try to be compromising, do not rule out other options. Today's world is moving forward not on principles but on compromises."[2] Haile Selassie himself summarized this philosophy for the Israeli ambassador by quoting the Ethiopian adage: "Man invented stairs because God did not give him wings."[3] The message was clear: Israel would do well to begin climbing the staircase opened by Sadat, instead of insisting on flying together on the wings of peace. Israel had better adopt the art of patient manipulation.

Haile Selassie, it appears, had three objectives in mind: to avoid Egyptian-Israeli war, to enhance his reputation as a mediator, and—so it was whispered by many—to win the Nobel Peace Prize.[4] The Nobel would have been for him, no doubt, the apex of his long career. But the road to the award had to go through Jerusalem, and his chance ultimately relied upon Israeli acceptance of his mediation. In June 1971 the OAU announced the establishment of a special committee for the Middle East composed of ten African heads of state. The committee was nicknamed "the ten wise men." At first, Haile Selassie avoided the committee. But in August 1971 his foreign minister, Katama Yifru, offered the Israeli ambassador a deal. Haile Selassie would come to Jerusalem in person and open an Ethiopian embassy there, and, in return, he would be accepted as the leading mediator.[5] But Golda Meir, the Israeli prime minister, opposed the offer. She was already furious with Haile Selassie and his game, at his acceptance of the vital and costly aid Israel offered him while standing alongside Israel's enemies at the UN and OAU, at times even leading the charge. Ambassador Aynor was instructed to meet with the emperor and tell him that Israel would not like to see him heading the "the wise men."[6] Haile Selassie and the ten committee members each received personal letters form Golda Meir. She thanked the Africans for their goodwill and involvement but reiterated that only direct negotiations would bear fruit. And, that any one-sided interpretation of UN resolutions [like those the OAU adopted] would only damage chances for peace. In her personal letter to Haile Selassie, Golda Meir avoided repeating the long-standing Israeli invitation for Haile Selassie to visit Jerusalem.[7] A Nobel Prize would not be within Haile Selassie's grasp.

Nixon Refuses to Rearm

Israel went on supporting Ethiopia, but the United States remained indifferent, at least in Ethiopian eyes. In mid-March 1972, Washington reduced military aid to Ethiopia from $12.5 million per year to $9 million in the framework of general cuts. Haile Selassie responded angrily. He summoned the US ambassador and told him it was a boost for the enemies of his country. He sent word to Nixon expressing his disappointment, and in return he received a very nice letter from the president. The Americans found $1.5 million dollars more for Ethiopia.[8]

But America apparently was losing patience with Haile Selassie. The Suez Canal remained closed, and Washington found no reason to collide now with the Soviets in that corner. On top of that, there was growing concern that Haile Selassie's age and fragility, as well as his regime's fragility, put American assets and arms in danger. The US ambassador had already conveyed to Haile Selassie the president's message that he must "ensure an orderly and beneficial succession"[9] back in June 1971. The fondness held for Ethiopia in the days of Roosevelt and Kennedy eroded because of the country's worsening human rights record. In February 1972 the United States, following new interest with China, reversed its policy and abandoned Taiwan. Haile Selassie and his advisers were clearly alarmed. In September 1972 the emperor turned again to the Israelis to help save Ethiopian relations with Washington. Foreign Minister Abba Eban and the Israeli embassy in the American capital managed to organize a meeting for Haile Selassie with Nixon on May 15, 1973. The emperor came with a list of arms he'd prepared with the help of the Israelis in Addis Ababa. The meeting was less cordial than its predecessors. This time Nixon merely said that Haile Selassie met more presidents in the White House than any other head of a foreign state. Haile Selassie responded with a long lecture on the situation in the Horn of Africa and Ethiopia's acute need for better equipment. He also added that his friend President Sadat of Egypt authentically wanted peace (perhaps a hint that he, the emperor, was there to mediate in the Middle East). He then presented the list of arms, to which Nixon responded politely that he would certainly look into it, adding that all is subject to congressional approval. He also promised to have a word with the Soviet leader Leonid Brezhnev. The meeting ended with a promise to continue over dinner.[10]

Haile Selassie's request for upgraded arms went unanswered. "The list he presented to us," a State Department official told the Israelis, "is exaggerated, incompatible with Ethiopia's needs, their ability to absorb, and our ability to supply."[11] At the end of July an American mission met the top command of the Ethiopian army. The Ethiopians asked for Phantom fighters and M-60 tanks, and the Americans agreed to supply some more F-5 fighters and Sherman M-48s.[12] Shortly thereafter, in August, the Americans announced they would close the Kagenew Station by the end of 1974 (they had long estimated that the base would fall to unfriendly hands upon the emperor's death[13]). They did not bother informing the emperor of the announcement beforehand. Haile Selassie still thought he could outmaneuver the powers. At the end of October he invited himself to Moscow, where he was received routinely. John Spencer, his old American adviser, was hastily summoned to Addis Ababa. In his memoirs Spencer wrote that the whole issue was a clear sign of Haile Selassie's growing senility and his belief that he had a magic personal touch. Spencer added, "The disappointment with America left the Emperor with only one true friend, Israel."[14]

The Expulsion of the Israelis

When he returned from Washington, the emperor had to delve into his other front—Africa.[15] Ten years had passed since his greatest moment: the establishment of the OAU. It was arguably his highest diplomatic achievement, the pride of his life, and a renewed foundation for international prestige. The Ethiopian government prepared a special anniversary event reminiscent of the glory days of May 1963 in Africa Hall, a salute to the father figure of the continent. However, there was no such festival. The Ethiopians wanted to discuss the Somali issue in the hope that the countries of Africa would unite behind their host. But Siyad Barre, the Somali president, did not attend, and Arab pressure prevailed: Israel was put on top of the agenda. The deliberation lasted from May 27 to May 29, 1973, and Libya's Qaddafi stole the show. In bold language he blamed Ethiopia, and its emperor, for collaborating with colonialism by hosting imperialist Americans and Israelis, whose only aim was to destroy liberation movements and support racist regimes in South Africa and Rhodesia. Addis Ababa, said Qaddafi, was full of Zionist and American spies, and therefore the headquarters of the OAU should move elsewhere.

Qaddafi's speech was broadcast live on Ethiopian TV. No one in Ethiopia had ever heard anyone talk to Haile Selassie like that. The emperor appeared stunned, looking strangely at Aklilu, who sat frightened. Qaddafi's motion to take the OAU away from Haile Selassie was not approved, but the possibility was raised. Haile Selassie declared in his speech that Israeli withdrawal from Sinai was a precondition to peace, but he emphasized that Ethiopia's relations with Israel were based on ancient tradition. Israel was then denounced by nearly all the participants, but no operative resolution was officially adopted. The Egyptians and the Saudis did not give up. In September King Faysal and President Sadat met with Haile Selassie in Algeria. According to an Ethiopian source, the Saudi king promised Haile Selassie the equivalent of $200 million—half for military equipment, half for general development—if he broke ties with Israel and sent the Israelis away.

During the 1973 October War and in its immediate aftermath, twenty African states broke their relations with Israel. As the war began, Haile Selassie established a committee to consider the matter. General Asefa Ayene passionately argued that expelling the Israeli advisers would create a crisis in the army, especially among the already resentful intermediate and junior officers. The abuna supported him, adding religious arguments for maintaining relations with Israel. Former foreign minister Katama Yifru said he trusted the Israelis and not the Arabs. But the prime minister, Aklilu, recommended joining the other Africans. On October 19 Sadat cabled Haile Selassie for the fourth time: "This is the time to act. Enough of talking."

On October 23, just as the battles in the Middle East ended, the Israeli ambassador was told that he and all other Israelis had one week to evacuate Ethiopia. It did not take long to prove that General Asefa Ayene had been correct. In November the army's young officers began a protest movement from within the military's ranks. This time there was nobody in the field camps to care for the soldiers' basic needs, nor anybody to report about what was simmering around the bonfires. The protest movement began unnoticed.

The expulsion of the Israelis and the break with Jerusalem, far from being one of the main causes for the 1974 fall of Haile Selassie, was neither a minor factor. A few weeks after the expulsion, Ambassador Aynor, who knew Ethiopia and its elite's Christian culture well, penned a long report. In retrospect it reads like a prophecy:

> The Ethiopian public was taken by surprise and reacted with amazement upon hearing this unexpected news. The roots of the historical, religious and emotional ties between Christian Ethiopia and Israel are so deep and rich that they occasionally verge on the irrational. Cutting off relations while Israel is struggling for survival had a stunning effect on many, for beyond everything else, it smacked of betrayal and a stab in the back. . . . Among the members of the establishment as well as the masses, there was first disbelief, then grief. The issue was soon added to growing resentment by the masses against the regime. Ethiopian political humor resorted to rhymes with double meanings and the following line was heard all over: —I, Haile Selassie the first, Ethiopia's Emperor, the Lion of Judas Iscariot. There is no doubt that the overwhelming majority of Christian Ethiopians, from the royal family, to the nobility, and down to the peasants in the remotest provinces, conceived the severing of relations as a matter of great shame and little benefit. The basic [Christian] Ethiopian concept is fundamentally anti-Islamic. What was done is seen as an act of betrayal and of surrender to Arab blackmail, an act for which Ethiopia is soon to pay dearly. In the eyes of the [Christian] Ethiopians, Israel has a special status with Providence. Hurting Israel cannot but yield the worst of evils.[16]

In January 1974 Haile Selassie went to Riyadh to collect the fee from King Faysal. But the Saudi king—whose newly declared oil embargo further impoverished Ethiopia—had forgotten about the $200 million. He rather remembered $35 million, of which half should go to the establishment of an Islamic Center in Addis Ababa.[17] According to a credible source, Haile Selassie returned so humiliated that for a full week he did not leave his room.[18]

Protest Meets Vacuum

While Haile Selassie was busying himself with world affairs, his home was burning. The Revolution of 1974—its development and consequences—had not been foreseen by anyone.[19] The participants in the 1974 drama were themselves acting in total uncertainty. The political rules of old Ethiopia quickly evaporated, and new ones were still unimagined. Haile Selassie, the greatest maestro, walked blindfolded in an uncharted territory. He was too old to realize that he was no longer a magician in a court of kings.

The history of Ethiopia can be traced by its cycles of famines.[20] With such an underdeveloped infrastructure, the country was often treated cruelly by nature. This time, Ethiopia's horrible famine was on display to the rest of the world. Approximately three hundred thousand people had died in northern Ethiopia prior to October 18, 1973, when the BBC broadcast "The Hidden Famine," a story that brought images of walking skeletons to viewers around the globe. The imperial government of Ethiopia was exposed as incapable, corrupt, and indifferent—it went on exporting grains while Haile Selassie fed his dogs on silver plates. In November 1973 the old emperor went to the north and announced a reduction of taxes. The oil embargo initiated by the Saudis after the Yom Kippur War brought misery even to the taxi drivers of Addis Ababa. They could not afford fueling their ancient cabs and went on strike. The Ethiopian masses did not need the foreign media to learn of the catastrophe; it was experienced by all. Public rage gradually became directed toward the emperor. On January 12, 1974, the soldiers in the army camp at Negele, in the Sidama region, arrested their commanders. Haile Selassie ordered General Deresae Dubale to fly there as his special envoy. The soldiers forced the general to eat the soldier's rotten food and drink the smelly water from their canteens. This was perhaps the moment of no return.

We cannot describe here or analyze the 1974 events in full. It began as a protest movement and met no response from a paralyzed system. Many key actors were murdered in the process and took their story to their graves. We shall focus here singularly upon our weary old hero during the last winter of the Lion of Judah.

Throughout February 1974, the young officers arrested their superiors across many camps. Strikes and demonstrations by students and other hungry town dwellers shook the capital. The chief of security, Solomon Qadir, advised Haile Selassie to send loyal forces and put the mutineers in jail, but the emperor ignored him. Haile Selassie probably realized that something was changing, but he was apparently confident that he could control the new energy and manipulate it as always. On February 24 he declared a raise in army salaries and canceled the tax on fuel. He also canceled a controversial plan to reform education, which had ignited some of the disturbances.

Finally, he made changes at the top. By March 1, 1974, Haile Selassie had removed Aklilu (who remained in the palace for his safety) and promoted those whom he had sidelined for years—those who dared to suggest reforms going back to the early 1960s. Endalkatchaw Makonnen was declared prime minister, Abiy Abebe was appointed minister of defense, and Ras Asrate returned as a close adviser. Moreover, Ras Imru Haile Selassie was now summoned daily to the palace. The "red ras," who had been suggesting comprehensive change for decades, and who was summarily sent abroad to represent Ethiopia in India, the United States, and the USSR, was back at Haile Selassie's side. They had been like twin brothers in their youth. Now, aged eighty-two, they brought the circle to a close, devoting hours to intimate talks.[21]

On March 5, 1974, Haile Selassie canceled the 1955 constitution and announced the preparation of a new one in which the prime minister would be answerable to the Parliament. Prime Minister Endalkatchaw announced the initiation of land reform. It was not enough. On March 7 a general strike began. Students continued rioting, and on April 26 the university was closed. Earlier, on April 20, tens of thousands of Muslims demonstrated in Addis Ababa for the first time in modern Ethiopian history. They demanded equality and the separation of church and state. Nearly all army camps across the country had come under control of committees of junior officers—company commanders and lower. The establishment no longer had authority, and the imperial system was completely out of work. Endalkatchaw, Abiy, Asrate, and Imru still tried to save it, but no words could extinguish the fire.

One hope remained within the armed forces. A paratroop battalion commanded by Colonel Alam-Zawd Tessama was stationed in Debra Zeit, not far from Addis Ababa. On March 23 the colonel established a "Coordination Committee of the Armed Forces" that was joined by some rebelling officers from other camps. Two days later the committee—*Derg* in Amharic—arrested officers considered overly radical. Endalkatchaw relied on the loyalty of this committee and the paratroops. Their collaboration remained effective until late June.

While Alam-Zawd's committee, remembered as "the first Derg," continued to arrest high officials as well as radical officers, Ras Asrate tried to save the system. He flew to London, where he visited the Israeli embassy and petitioned for Mossad agents to return to Ethiopia (Alam-Zawd and his paratroops had been trained in Israel). He said the emperor was in control and regretted breaking off relations. Israel, shaken by the Yom Kippur War, was neither ready nor able to turn back the clock. On May 1, 1974, Asrate was back in Addis Ababa. He advised Haile Selassie to fly to a distant province in Ethiopia and rally the people like in the old days. The emperor said he had once run away (1936) and would do so no more, that there was no need to panic, and that he knew what to do. Back home, Asrate confided in his diary:

> When I left the Jubilee Palace, I felt great sadness and I understood that the era of Haile Selassie was coming to its end, and that [there] was nothing any of us could do to prevent that. How different things could have been if we had only had today the Haile Selassie that we knew in 1941. The fox who came up with the stratagem to win back the Ethiopian sovereignty that our British "allies" were trying to take away from us would certainly have sensed all the gravity of our situation and would certainly have found the way out of this hopeless tragedy.[22]

But the Haile Selassie of 1941 was no longer. The half-senile old man still had the illusion that the people were behind him and that he could outfox everybody. On May 5, 1974, the thirty-third anniversary of his return to Addis Ababa as Ethiopia's savior, Haile Selassie spoke an embarrassing collection of clichés over the radio. Ethiopia was in anarchy.

On June 22 Colonel Alam-Zawd lost control over his Derg and fled to Gojjam. Committee member Major Atnafu Abate and his associates had been in contact with battalion committees around the country. They now called on each battalion to send representatives to the capital. By June 28 three to four representatives from each of the army's thirty-six battalions had gathered at the headquarters of the Fourth Division. These representatives were majors, captains, lieutenants, and sergeants. The first plenary was held in complete uncertainty. Most of the young officers hardly knew each other. The fearless Major Mangistu Haile Mariam of the Third Division grabbed a megaphone. Waving his pistol, he made a long, intimidating speech that inspired his counterparts to vote him chairman of the new Central Coordinating Committee, the new Derg, on the spot. As of that moment, the roughly one hundred members of the committee ruled Ethiopia, though they were not entirely aware of it. The new Derg quickened the pace of arrests, aiming for ever-higher echelons of Ethiopia's elite. Top army commanders, ministers, and prominent members of the nobility and of the royal family were rounded up. On July 1 they arrested Ras Asrate. The prisoners were put in the cellars of the Fourth Division. On July 22 Derg officers forced the emperor to remove Prime Minister Endalkatchaw. They dictated that Dr. Michael Imru, son of Ras Imru, would become prime minister and Dr. Zewde Gabra-Selassie foreign minister. Both were members of the nobility and keen advocates of liberal reforms. The next day, July 23, was Haile Selassie's birthday. Only a few prominent figures like the abuna and Ras Imru gathered in the old palace. Together with veterans of the Gideon Force and some bodyguard officers, they listened to Haile Selassie's speech:

> This army is our creation . . . it has the right to all our support. . . . The Ethiopian army must remain that same tranquil and disciplined force that has allowed it to gain so many victories in the past. . . . I would like to thank God who has given me the strength to perform my duty for all those years. When my grandson Zar'a Yaeqob succeeds me, I am sure that the people will give him the same support that they have never ceased offering me.[23]

Haile Selassie's Deposition

The young officers of the Derg did not remain "tranquil and disciplined." They had internal conflicts in the Fourth Division's headquarters but were able to work out a temporary compromise: General Aman Andom, one of the few retired army generals whom the public respected and the soldiers admired, would be their chairman. For years he had clandestinely been in touch with university professors and army officers who resented the imperial autocracy. Aman also had been occasionally in touch with some of the young officers who now led the movement.

Haile Selassie realized that Ras Imru was the only one who could negotiate with the Derg, and he asked him to do so on his behalf. The young officers agreed to speak with Imru alone. In his memoirs, Imru describes a fateful meeting in late July with Aman Andom and some Derg officers. He managed to make them promise that they would not constitute a military dictatorship but rather a constitutional monarchy, and that Haile Selassie would remain the monarch. When he reported their promise to Haile Selassie, the emperor remained suspicious.[24]

Inside the Derg, tension was building. Aman saw himself as a responsible father figure, but many defied his authority. Some called him mockingly "Nagib," after the Egyptian general who thought he was leading the 1952 revolution headed by Nasser and the "Free Officers" before being deposed by Nasser and his followers in 1954. Overly ambitious, Aman wanted to reduce the Derg's numbers, to conduct proper judicial procedure against those arrested, and to come to an agreement with the Eritreans (Aman was himself a native of Eritrea). On August 25, Aman flew to Asmara and stayed there twelve days, leaving the field open for Mangistu and his men to seize power.

While Aman was in Eritrea, the winds in the Derg turned more violently against Haile Selassie. On television he had been exposed as a coward and corrupt, as the man who ran away from facing the Fascists, and as the indifferent ruler who ignored his hungry, dying subjects. To this a new matter was raised: where was the money the emperor must have surely accumulated? The young officers began to speak of overblown figures, even billions of dollars.[25] Aman returned on September 6 and was asked to raise the matter with Imru. The emperor was horrified at Imru's report of the Derg's accusation. He denied hiding any money, but he likely realized that the very allegation signaled the forthcoming end to his rule. It was then that Haile Selassie's granddaughter Seble Desta (daughter of Tananya-Warq) told the British ambassador that the emperor understood that the radicals in the Derg had gained the upper hand, and that he was doomed.[26]

Upon leaving the emperor's room, Imru witnessed the young officers of the Derg having an argument with Aman in the palace yard. On September 11 Ethiopian television broadcast the BBC film *The Hidden Hunger*, edited by the Derg's men to magnify the image of Haile Selassie as cruelly indifferent. A group of officers forced the emperor to watch it with them in the library. The abuna's greeting for the new Ethiopian year was also broadcast, but this time it made no mention of the emperor, "the defender of the faith."[27] The abuna must have done so out of fear for his life.

Ras Imru described the events of September 12, 1974:

September 11 was Ethiopia's New Year's Eve. But this time, it was not joyous. Aman Andom called me at home and told me to meet him the next day in Jubilee Palace. He told me it was an important matter,

without elaborating. . . . I went there at nine in the morning, but Aman
was not there. When I entered the waiting room the emperor was in
the upper floor. He heard me and sent someone to call for me. I saw
him seated in his chamber. With him were his grandchildren, the children of Tananya-Warq, Admiral Eskander and Princess Seble. Someone was sent to find if General Aman had arrived. He returned with
the answer, no, he would not come. . . . Around the yard there were
many soldiers . . . about fifteen of them entered, their machine guns on
them. . . . One of them approached me and said they intended to read
aloud to the emperor from a document he was holding. . . . I asked to
see it, but he [the soldier] refused. . . . I went up and told the emperor
what they had said. He was somewhat terrified. I advised him to go
down and hear them. He put on his coat and went down and sat with
me at his side. . . . One of the armed soldiers, the officer who held the
document . . . approached Haile Selassie and read to his face: "From
this moment your rule is over. It caused only damage. It was a corrupt
government, with no justice, only robbery and bribery. The misery you
inflicted on the masses is unforgivable. Therefore, as of this moment,
the power is in the hands of the army." He then asked the emperor if
he had anything to say and opened a tape recorder. Haile Selassie said:
"You took all, you have it all in your hands. What shall I say? Do as
you will." The photographers moved around for new angles. Then, the
emperor was told to get up and start walking. I asked one of them:
"Where are you taking him? Can he change his clothes?" The soldier
said: "There is no need, we are going now ... we have already prepared a place for him. He can take a servant if he wishes." I asked
again: "Where are you taking him?" but no one answered. . . . We
went outside. In the yard there were only soldiers. Many soldiers. A
Volkswagen Beetle was waiting at the stairs. I said: "If you do not
have a better car, I can drive him in my Jaguar." The officer said: "No,
no, he will go with this one, we know why." When they squeezed him
to the back of the car I wanted to follow them, but they ordered: "Go
home!" I drove home immersed in sorrow.[28]

The officers of the Derg knew the reason for the Volkswagen
Beetle; it was the car of the army's intermediate officers, up to the
rank of major. Colonels had much finer cars, and generals were
driven in Mercedes. They would not dirty their shiny cars by visiting
the battalions' field camps. The Beetle was now not only an act of
defiance against the imperial fleet of Rolls-Royces and Cadillacs but
also a symbol of the revolution in the army. Most of the generals and
other high officers were already behind bars, and majors and captains ruled Ethiopia. They themselves were overwhelmed by their
new power. They were surprised by the helplessness of the old elite
and the speedy evaporation of the mighty Church's political presence. They were even struck by the pitiable state of Haile Selassie,
who until his last days believed he could ride the young, loose tiger.

The deposition: pushed into a Volkswagen Beetle in front of the Jubilee Palace.

Asfa-Wossen Asserate interviewed one of the first members of the Derg in the 1990s and was told that the Derg had been sure that the imperial establishment was far stronger and that the transition of power would take a long time, "but in the event we pushed at the very first door and walked into an empty room. So we opened the next door, and again the room was empty. And so we continued until we came to the Crown. We found an empty house that was just waiting to be occupied by someone else."[29]

A major pushed Haile Selassie unceremoniously into the Volkswagen's rear seat. After some hesitation, they allowed Eskander to join him in the car. Accompanied by two security vehicles, they drove to the Fourth Division headquarters. There, the emperor was paraded in front of the other prisoners and led to a hastily furnished room, watched over by four guards.[30] Haile Selassie was then interrogated for many days about the money he'd allegedly hidden. The interrogation led to nowhere. After a few weeks, in late October 1974, Haile Selassie was taken to a room in Menelik Palace. They allowed him to have a servant, read newspapers, listen to the radio, and watch television. The arrangement would not last long.

Notes

1. Asfa-Wossen, *King of Kings*, pp. 275–276.
2. HZ 4564/6, Ambassador to Africa Department on Conversation with Dr. Tesfaye, 27.1.1971.
3. HZ 439/3, Aynor to Shimoni, 14.12.1972.
4. HZ 4564/13, Ambassador to Africa Department, "Conversation with Katama Yifru,"13.7.1971. On the emperor's yearning for a Nobel Prize see FO 371/190145, "Ethiopia—an Introduction," by J. Russel, 6.12.1965. Haile Selassie was a candidate for the prize in 1964, which was awarded to Dr. Martin Luther King Jr.
5. HZ 4564/6, Aynor to Africa Department, 18, 19.8,1971; 4564/13, Aynor to Africa Department, 14.9.1971.
6. Aynor, *Africa in Crisis*, pp. 43–46.
7. HZ 4564/7, Aynor to Africa Department, 17.8.1971; Africa Department to Aynor, 1.10.1971; *Ethiopian Herald,* 25.8.1971.
8. FRUS, 1969–1976, Vol. E-5, Part 1, Memorandum from the President's Assistant for National Security Affairs (Kissinger) to President Nixon, Washington, April 25, 1972, 20, 1972, 25.9.1972; Asfa-Wossen, *King of Kings*, p. 272.
9. Asfa-Wossen, *King of Kings*, p. 272.
10. Memoranda of Conversation: May 15, 1973—Nixon, Emperor Haile Selassie of Ethiopia, https://www.fordlibrarymuseum.gov/library/document/0314/1552582.pdf.
11. Israeli State Archive, A 372/7, Washington to FM, 18.5.1973.
12. HZ 6804/4, Embassy to Africa Department, 25.7.1973.
13. FRUS, 1964–1968, Vol. 24, Africa, Special National Intelligence Estimate, "The Outlook for Internal Security in Ethiopia," April 11, 1968; FRUS, 1969–1976, Volume E-5, Part 1, Memorandum to the President's Assistant for National Security Affairs (Kissinger), January 21, 1971, FRUS, 1969–1976, Vol. E–6, National Security Decision Memorandum, August 14, 1973.
14. Spencer, *Ethiopia at Bay,* pp. 322–325.
15. The following is a short summary of chapter 7 in *Alliance and Alienation*, pp. 207–257.
16. Hanan Aynor's papers (now in the Israeli State Archives), "The Disconnection," 26.11.1973.
17. See the chapter "The Saudis and the End of the Christian Kingdom" in Erlich, *Ethiopia and Saudi Arabia*, pp. 97–132. This information is from Dr. Asfa-Wossen, the son of Ras Asrate who went to Riyadh with Haile Selassie.
18. Interview with Dajjazmach Zewde Gabra-Selassie.
19. See, for example John M. Cohen, "Ethiopia After Haile Selassie: The Government Land Factor," *African Affairs*, Vol. 72 (October 1973), pp. 365–382.
20. Richard Pankhurst, *The History of Famine and Epidemics in Ethiopia, Prior to the Twentieth Century* (Addis Ababa: Relief and Rehabilitation Commission, 1985).
21. In 2010 Addis Ababa University Press issued the Amharic memoirs of Ras Imru, containing firsthand evidence on the last year of the emperor's life. Ras Imru Haile Selassie, *Kayahut mastawsau* (Addis Ababa: Addis Ababa University Press, 2010).
22. Del Boca, *The Negus,* p. 323, quoting the diary of Asrate Kassa, which was kept with his son Asfa-Wossen Asserate.
23. Ibid., pp. 327–328.
24. Imru Haile Selassie, *Kayahut mastawsau*, pp. 317–320.
25. FCO 31/1861, Morris to FCO, 2.9.1975.
26. FCO 31/1689, Morris to FCO, "Contacts with the Imperial Family," 24.9.1974.
27. Asfa-Wossen, *King of Kings,* p. 299.

28. Imru Haile Selassie, *Kayahut mastawsau*, pp. 324–327. See a similar description by Princess Seble in FCO 31/1689, Morris to FCO, "Contacts with the Imperial Family," 24.9.1974.

29. Asfa-Wossen, *King of Kings*. p. 301.

30. FO 31/1689, Memorandum by the British Ambassador Based on Conversations with Princess Desta, 24.9.1974.

12

The Burial of a Donkey

~

He will have the burial of a donkey—dragged away and thrown
outside the gates of Jerusalem.
                                        —*Jeremiah 22:19*

While around 150 senior members of the imperial elite and the
armed forces languished in jail, the internal struggle in the Derg intensified. General Aman demonstrated self-confidence. On the day
the emperor was deposed, he promised the British ambassador and
the Americans that Haile Selassie would not be harmed.[1] Three days
later the Derg redefined itself as the Provisional Military Administrative Council and declared Aman its chairman. He was now the
acting head of state. Older, senior, and widely admired, Aman was
sure he could lead the revolution. But most younger officers thought
otherwise. The majority of the Derg were graduates of the Holeta
Military School, a less prestigious institution than the Harar Military
Academy, whose graduates they mostly disliked. Major Mangistu
soon became the leader of the Holeta graduates and knew how to
manipulate their sensitivities. He sent his men to liquidate senior officers in various army units and intimidate other members of the
Derg. Aman did not hesitate to confront them, and Mangistu determined to kill him as well.

On November 15, Aman sent clandestine messages to some army
commanders to hurry to the capital, but the messages were intercepted

by Mangistu's men. Aman's followers pleaded with him to fly to Harar, where they believed the Third Division would rally around its old commander. But Aman arrogantly refused. Instead of flying to Harar he went home, threatening to resign, confident that the young officers would come to beg him to return. When the latter did come to Aman's home on November 23, they brought a tank with them. They destroyed his house and killed him and five of his associates. That same night, Mangistu's men led fifty-four of the prisoners out of their cells and put them against the wall. They executed them in groups of ten and threw their bodies into a mass grave. This is how nearly all of Haile Selassie's contemporaries were murdered: Aklilu Habte-Wold, Endalkatchaw Makonnen, Ras Asrate Kassa, General Abiy Abebe, Prince Eskander Desta, and General Asefa Ayene. Mangistu led General Haile Baykedanye, who had been his commander in the Third Division and whom Mangistu hated personally, to the wall himself. The head of imperial security, Colonel Solomon Qadir, and Colonel Alam-Zawd Tessama, commander of the paratroops and leader of the first Derg, were also among the slaughtered. In his memoirs Mangistu wrote that at first they intended to kill all 150 prisoners, but they made do with those fifty-four only.[2] Members of the Derg who refused to participate in the massacre were shot themselves. From that moment they all shared the collective responsibility for the massacre, and they all dreaded the cold-blooded assassin, Mangistu Haile Mariam.

The Final Year in the Old Palace

Haile Selassie's life was spared for a while. Mangistu's men hoped he would lead them to the money they thought he had stolen.[3] They may have also feared that murdering the emperor would ignite the masses. Haile Selassie was given a room in Menelik Palace and spent his last year there.

On December 13, 1974, a Red Cross doctor saw Haile Selassie in his room and reported that his health was good. He was forbidden to communicate with the outside world and was allowed only one daily stroll. He knew that compound well. Here, he had made his way to the throne; here, he prepared to face Mussolini; here, he celebrated the establishment of the OAU. Menelik Palace was the site of his greatest moments of glory and his greatest moments of agony. The old man tried to keep a daily routine: morning prayers, a modest breakfast, a walk to the nearby high ground from where he could see the view of Addis Ababa. His guards respected him, and some even fell on their knees. He treated them with his usual paternalism, ordering them to walk straight, like good soldiers.[4] The deposed monarch was allowed to read Ethiopian newspapers in his room, listen to the radio, and watch the local television. If he deluded himself that he was still a king, the facts could not be ignored: the radio reported the mass murder of his men. The television demonized him with pictures from hunger-stricken areas alongside pictures of him feeding his dogs and with accusations of stealing the people's money. In nearby streets, students were ordered by the army officers to shout "Hang him!" loud enough for the emperor to hear it.[5]

On March 21, 1975, the monarchy was abolished. For those who ascribe to the legend of Solomon and the Queen of Sheba, it meant the end of the oldest royal institution in the world. According to that tradition, Haile Selassie was the 225th king in the Solomonic dynasty. For Mangistu, the time had come to finish the deposed emperor.

Haile Selassie's health remained strong. In mid-May, British surgeon and dean of the Faculty of Medicine at Haile Selassie I University, Dr. Charles Leithead, along with Professor Asrat Woldeyes checked the emperor and reported that "his blood pressure was that of eighteen-year-old boy" and that his mind was crystal clear. They also reported that he spent his time reading Psalms, and, as was typical for his age, he had a prostate problem, but initially refused the operation that would treat his condition. When they told him that the Pope had undergone prostate surgery two years earlier, he told them he knew, "for the Pope told him all about it." A few days later, he admitted he was in pain. The officers of the Derg wanted him to undergo the operation in his room, but the two doctors warned them they were taking a huge risk. On May 28, under heavy guard, Haile Selassie was driven to the clinic of the imperial bodyguard and was successfully operated upon three days later. The two doctors purposely slowed his recovery so he could enjoy better living conditions. On June 10 he was returned to house arrest despite their protests. They visited Haile Selassie the day after his return. His medical condition was good, they reported, but after two weeks of diligent care in the clinic, he had become depressed with his isolated conditions. When Professor Asrat saw him again in late July, he reported that the former emperor was physically well.[6]

The Murder

Rumors that the Derg had decided to eliminate Haile Selassie spread after his return from the clinic.[7] The committee voted on the matter in early August 1975. Mangistu's rage at Haile Selassie had probably outgrown the hope of finding the money the emperor had supposedly hidden. The Austrian cook, Lore Trenkler, who had prepared Haile Selassie's meals since 1960, still cooked for him but was only allowed to do so in Jubilee Palace, and not deliver the food to Menelik Palace herself.[8] This arrangement was apparently designed as a means to slowly drug Haile Selassie to death.

On August 23, Princess Tananya-Warq was told that her father's condition was deteriorating. She and her daughter, Princess Aida, were rushed from their prison cells in Akaki and were driven to Addis Ababa to say their good-byes.[9] No one knew what was behind this gesture, but it was the final curtain for Haile Selassie. Tananya-Warq told the British ambassador that he was quite well.[10] In 1991 historian Asfa-Wossen Asserate interviewed the emperor's butler, Eshetu Tekle-Mariam. On the evening of August 27, 1975, he saw Mangistu and another man walking near the emperor's room, and recalled that in the morning, "as I [Eshetu] entered the bedroom, the first thing that struck me was a powerful smell of ether. Then I noticed the emperor lying motionless on his bed. His face had turned a dark blue color. His pillow was not beneath his head, but immediately next to it. Everything pointed to his having been drugged in his sleep and then suffocated."[11]

More details were discovered later. According to historian Angelo Del Boca,[12] Atnafu Abate was in the bedroom with Mangistu, along with a military physician and two soldiers. They suffocated the old man, either with his pillow or with a mattress. Then they returned to the Derg headquarters. Other officers were charged with hiding the body. They dug three deep holes beneath the bathroom in Mangistu's office, threw the body into one of them, and covered the holes with cement. At seven o'clock in the morning, the radio announced that the deposed *negus* (the Derg officers had avoided calling him an emperor and instead called him a king) was found dead by his servant, and that the cause of death was respiratory complications connected to the prostate operation, a possibility ruled out by the brave Professor Asrat. On August 28 the *Ethiopian Herald* reported Haile Selassie's death in six dry lines.

From that moment, and throughout his seventeen years in power, Mangistu Haile Mariam and his Derg did their best to wipe out the memory of Haile Selassie. No one knew where he was buried. Haile Selassie I University was renamed Addis Ababa University. The emperor's image—on banknotes, coins, stamps, and monuments—was systematically erased. Ethiopians were afraid to even mention his name. On August 9, 1980, Mangistu said that the negus had died broken-hearted at having witnessed the success of the revolution. The military dictator was later deposed in 1991, found asylum in Zimbabwe, and published his memoirs in 2011.[13] In exile, Mangistu was interviewed on television. Smiling nervously, Mangistu denied he had killed Haile Selassie.[14] In the same breath, he denied ever killing anyone, though the story of his regime of terror tells otherwise.

A Late Funeral

Mangistu tried to impose an overambitious Stalinist revolution, and in the process he brought about endless internal wars, misery, hunger, and famine. He tried (disastrously) to import ideologies and political structures, disconnecting Ethiopia from its ancient cultures and rich traditions, and decimated the urban intelligentsia. It was liberation fronts from the periphery that finally defeated the Derg regime. They were headed by the Tigray People's Liberation Front (TPLF), which also benefited from the Eritreans' victories over Mangistu's army. In 1989 the Tigrayans united with other regional fronts to establish the Ethiopian People's Revolutionary Democratic Forces (EPRDF); the organization liberated the country from Mangistu in May 1991, and it still leads Ethiopia today (2018). Its leader, Meles Zenawi, was prime minister until his death in 2012. The new regime rebuilt Ethiopia as a federation of nine states that represent Ethiopia's different ethnic groups.

In February 1992 Meles gave orders to find the burial place of Haile Selassie. Staff members of the old Menelik Palace were summoned and indicated the site. The bones of Haile Selassie were exhumed, put in a box in the cellar of the nearby Saint Mary Church, and then transferred to the nearby Menelik mausoleum. First, it was rumored that on July 23, 1992, the 100th birthday of Haile Selassie, he would be buried in the Trinity Cathedral. But soon, a controversy emerged. The emperor's family, in Ethiopia and in exile, demanded an official state funeral, but Meles was firmly opposed. Meles had been a student in Addis Ababa during Haile Selassie's final years and was unwilling to forget the legacy of the emperor's leadership (or lack thereof) in that time. When the Derg captured power, Meles fled back to his homeland in Tigray, where he witnessed the horrors of the famine that Haile Selassie had failed to prevent. He never forgave Haile Selassie for the misery of the poor and considered him a reactionary who kept Ethiopia backward. Meles was also resentful of what Tigrayans called "Amhara domination." The fighters of the TPLF had adopted the name "Woyane" after the 1943 rebellion of Tigray, which Haile Selassie suppressed (see Chapter 7). From the view of the young Tigrayans who were now in government, Haile Selassie had purposely impoverished their region and left it in the hands of the local feudal aristocrats, who cared little for the peasants. Even after seventeen years of Mangistu's regime, Meles was unable to be graceful to Haile Selassie. Only in the year 2000 did he become more flexible. Following pressure from leaders and scholars beyond Ethiopia's borders, he agreed to a compromise: Haile Selassie would have a Christian funeral but not a state one.

The chosen date was symbolic: November 5, 2000, the seventieth anniversary of Haile Selassie's 1930 coronation. Sixty members of the family attended, including the emperor's aging daughter, Tananya-Warq, and his grandchildren, Aida, Sophia, Sebele, Zara-Yaqob Asfa-Wossen, Irmayas Sahla-Selassie, and Ba'da-Mariam. Other relatives and prominent nobles also came, including Dajjaz-mach Zawde Gebre-Selassie and Dr. Asfa-Wossen Asserate. The Church, headed by Abuna Paulos, organized the event. The funeral procession marched from the Menelik mausoleum through the main squares of the capital to Trinity Cathedral. Representatives of the UN, the OAU, and foreign diplomats also attended, and the media reported on emotional speeches. It was a solemn, quiet salute. The leaders of Ethiopia did not come. Four days earlier, the government released an announcement detaching itself from the man and the event. The young generation of Ethiopia hardly knew who Haile Selassie was, for by that time he was already a distant memory. The widow of the legendary singer Bob Marley, Rita Marley, came, but the other Rastafarians who attended were somewhat confused—for them, Haile Selassie was the living son of God, not bones in a coffin.[15]

The Greatest Ethiopian

Every human being has a story, but those worthy of a biography are those whose lives influenced their people and the times in which they lived, and sometimes even beyond. Haile Selassie was one such individual. His story is the story of Ethiopia in the twentieth century. He was indeed an icon, a person who inspired black people everywhere, who was the pride of an oppressed continent. He was a man who stared down racists, was respected by all, and even worshipped by many—a biblical lion and a leader striving to build the future. And yet, he was also a dictator, harsh to himself and to others. His story ended with a shameful tragedy, a surreptitious murder that followed a humiliating year on the sidelines and preceded a cruel effort to erase his name.

Haile Selassie's doctors reported that he spent his final months reading Psalms. He must surely have had bitter thoughts reading chapter 103:15: "As for man, his days are as grass." Haile Selassie's life ended the way of all flesh.[16]

The eastern wing of the Trinity Cathedral in Addis Ababa is dedicated to Haile Selassie. A big twin tombstone, in honor of the emperor and his wife, dominates the space. His imperial throne is also there, and there are wall paintings commemorating major historical events. Ethiopians and tourists frequent the site. The spacious yard of the cathedral is a cemetery for *abuna*s, *arbanyoch*, *ras*es, for other members of the royal family, and for the fifty-four men murdered on

Photo of young Tafari taken by Father Louis-Antoine d'Orgueil at Harar; photo of Haile Selassie reprinted from Ethiopia Today, prepared by Atnafu Makonnen, Addis Ababa, 1960.

Tafari at age four.   *Haile Selassie at age sixty-eight.*

November 23, 1974. A tour in the cathedral is like visiting a museum for twentieth-century Ethiopia and a mausoleum for Haile Selassie. Arguably the greatest Ethiopian in history, Haile Selassie lived long enough to be nearly everything. He was the last traditional emperor of the country as well as Ethiopia's first modern king.

Ethiopia's history in many ways has been determined by the strength or by the weakness of its rulers. This is true of every human community, but perhaps more so in a society so deeply influenced by religious-political legacies, and which was never really defeated and occupied by others. Ethiopia knew centuries of anarchies but also golden periods of powerful kings and emperors: Kaleb of the sixth century, Amda-Tsion and Zara-Yaqob of the Solomonic dynasty (1270–1529), and Tewodros II (1855–1868) and Yohannes IV (1872–1889) of the early modern period. And, of course, Menelik II, who built the Ethiopia into which Tafari/Haile Selassie was born and in which he made his early steps. The great Menelik defeated Italian imperialism; expanded Ethiopia, doubling its size; and was recognized by the European powers as the head of a sovereign African empire. Haile Selassie was as great as Menelik in these terms but far greater as a modernizer. He opened his people to the world, saved the country's independence, regained Eritrea, led Africa—and, above all, built a new generation of schooled Ethiopians, officers, and bureaucrats. He was the last Christian king of Ethiopia and a pioneer of meaningful transformations. Where he failed was to change emphasis from the old to the new, and to do so without losing both. Even in old age he persisted in treating the modernly educated as if they were still subjects of an elect of God. For this he paid with his life, and for this he betrayed Ethiopia into the hands of the worse and the immature. Mangistu and his officers worked to uproot Ethiopia from its traditions and rebuild it on imported crude communism. Mangistu was the last ruler of Ethiopia; Meles Zenawi was its first leader.

A few dozen steps from Haile Selassie's grave, in the courtyard of the Trinity Cathedral, there stands a monument for Meles Zenawi, who died in 2012, aged fifty-seven. Some pictures on the wall tell his story. He was a guerrilla fighter, a man of learning, and a devout reader. One cannot escape the difference between the young leader's grave and that of Haile Selassie. The contradiction reflects today's Ethiopia. Addis Ababa is no longer the sleepy town of its imperial days. It is a busy urban center, full of high-rise buildings, malls, and traffic jams. Millions of people move at the city's new pace. Dozens of mosques testify to a new dimension of speedy change: Muslims are now an integral part of Ethiopia, in every aspect. The country's economic growth is amazing, complete with relevant pains, including an expanding middle class that is experiencing energies and frustrations. Ethiopia moves forward, but it also looks back to its past, inspiring its modern sons and daughters. Churches and mosques are full, and holidays are celebrated as if in biblical days. Recall Nelson Mandela's prescient words from 1962: "Meeting the Emperor himself would be like shaking hands with history."[17] Ethiopia, we dare say, will ever continue to shake hands with and be guided by its past.

Notes

1. FCO 31/1689, Morris to FCO, 24.9.1974.
2. See ethiomedia.com/broad/3473.html, book review of *Tiglachin* (Our Struggle) by Colonel Mengistu Hailemariam, February 6, 2012.
3. The Derg officers exerted pressure on the Swiss government to investigate the matter. The Swiss responded they could do so only by order of Haile Selassie and only if it was clear it was his free will—namely, if he was released. FCO 31/1861, Morris to FCO, 2.9.1975.
4. FCO 31/1860, Morris to FCO, 26.5.1975.
5. See Del Boca, *The Negus*, pp. 25–35.
6. FCO 31/1860, Morris to FCO, 19.5.1975, 25.5.1975, and 17/6/1975; FCO 31/1861, Morris to FCO, 2.9.1975.
7. FCO 31/1860, Morris to FCO, 17/6/1975.
8. See the memoires of the emperor's Austrian cook, "Life and Work at the Court of Haile Selassie I: Memoirs of Lore Trenkler," https://anglo-ethiopian.org/publications/articles.php?type=L&reference.
9. FCO 31/1860, Morris to FCO, 25.8.1975.
10. FCO 31/1861, Morris to FCO, 2.9.1975 and 11.9.75.
11. Asfa-Wossen, *King of Kings*, pp. 307–308.
12. Del Boca, *The Negus*, pp. 2–35.
13. See ethiomedia.com/broad/3473.html, *Tiglachin* book review.
14. See https://www.youtube.com/watch?v=-yPoTQiZ1Xc, Mengistu Hailemariam denied killing Imperial Haile Selassie.
15. See www.haileselassie.net/pictures-and-stories-on-the-imperial-funeral-events-part-1, 2; Christina Lamb, "Haile Selassie to Get Funeral 25 Years Late," *Telegraph,* https://www.telegraph.co.uk/news/worldnews/africaandindianocean/ethiopia/1372352/Haile-Selassie-to-get-funeral-25-years-late.html, October 29, 2000; "Haile Selassie laid to rest," *BBC News,* news.bbc.co.uk/2/hi/africa/1007736.stm, November 5, 2000.
16. Indeed, most of the twenty-five "Political Icons" mentioned in the introduction (note 5) ended miserably: Mohandas Gandhi was murdered; Alexander the Great died at thirty-three from a mysterious disease; Mao Zedong lived to eighty-three, but in his last years he was ill and begged to die; Winston Churchill lived to celebrate ninety but had his share of humiliations and mental let-downs; Genghis Khan died at sixty-five; Nelson Mandela lived to ninety-five but had spent twenty-seven years in jail; Abraham Lincoln was assassinated at fifty-six; Adolf Hitler met his violent death at the same age; Ernesto "Che" Guevara was executed at thirty-nine; Ronald Reagan lived

to ninety-three but suffered from Alzheimer's disease for his last decade of life; Cleopatra committed suicide at forty-nine; Franklin Roosevelt suffered from his paralyzed legs and died at sixty-three; the current Dalai Lama, born 1935, is still alive but in exile; Queen Victoria lived eighty-two years but spent her last forty mourning her beloved husband; Benito Mussolini ended at age sixty-two, his body mutilated by his angry countrymen; Akbar the Great died at the same age from natural causes; Lenin died at fifty-four, half-paralyzed toward his end; Margaret Thatcher lived to eighty-seven but became a mockery in old age; Simón Bolívar died frustrated at forty-seven; Qin Shi Huang died a painful death by poisoning; Kim Il-Sung died of a heart attack; Charles de Gaulle had to retire in frustration before dying at eighty; Louis XIV lived to seventy-seven; Richard the Lionheart died at forty-two from infection caused by an arrow wound; Saladin died in his bed at fifty-six.

17. Mandela, *A Long Walk to Freedom*, p. 255.

Bibliography

~

Archival Material
British Archives, London
Foreign Relations of the United States (FRUS)
Institute of Ethiopian Studies, Addis Ababa University
Israel State Archives (ISA), Jerusalem
Ministero Degli Affari Esteri, Archivio Storico, Rome

Books and Articles
Abraham, Emanuel. *Reminiscences of My Life*. Oslo: Lunde Forlag, 1995.
Ahmed, Hussein. "The Historiography of Islam in Ethiopia." *Journal of Islamic Studies,* Vol. 3, No. 1 (1992), pp. 15–46.
Akavia, Avraham. *Orde Wingate: His Life and Activity*. Tel Aviv: Ma'arachot, 1993 (in Hebrew).
———. *With Wingate in Abyssinia*. Tel Aviv: Am Oved, 1944 (in Hebrew).
Allain, Jean. "Slavery and the League of Nations: Ethiopia as a Civilized Nation." *Journal of the History of International Law*, Vol. 8 (2006), pp. 213–244.
Asfa Yilma (Princess). *Haile Selassie: Emperor of Ethiopia*. London: S. Low, Marston, 1936.
Asserate, Asfa-Wossen. *King of Kings: The Triumph and Tragedy of Emperor Haile Selassie I of Ethiopia*. London: Haus Publishing, 2015. Originally published as *Der Letzte Kaiser Von Afrika: Triumph und Tragödie des Haile-Selassie*. Frankfort: Ullstein Taschenbuchverlag, 2014.
Aynor, Hanan S. *Africa in Crisis: His Imperial Majesty Haile Selassie's Ethiopia*. Jerusalem: S. S. Aynor, 1999.
Baer, George W. *The Coming of the Italo-Ethiopian War*. Cambridge, MA: Harvard University Press, 1967.

191

Balsvik, Randi. *Haile Selassie's Students: The Intellectual and Social Background to Revolution, 1952–1977.* East Lansing: African Studies Center, Michigan State University Press, 1985.

———. "Student Movement, Ethiopian." *Encyclopaedia Aethiopica*, Vol. 4, p. 752. 2010.

Barrett, Leonard E. *The Rastafarians.* Boston: Beacon Press, 1997.

Berhanou, Abbebe. *Histoire de l'Éthiopie: d'Axoum à la Révolution.* Addis Ababa: Centre Francais de Etudes Ethiopiennes, 1998.

Bonacci, Giulia. "Rastafari/Rastafarianism." *Encyclopaedia Aethiopica,* Vol. 4, pp. 339–340. 2010.

Borruso, Paolo. *L'Ultimo Impero Cristiano: Politica e Religione nell'Etiopia Contemporanea, 1916–1974.* Milan: Guerini e Associati, 2002.

Bowers, Keith. *Imperial Exile: Emperor Haile Selassie in Britain, 1936–40.* London: Brown Dog Books, 2016.

Buckner-El, Brian. *Haile Selassie the Conquering Lion of the Tribe of Judah.* iBooks, Lulu.com, 2011.

Carmichael, Tim. "The Lion of Judah's Pen." *International Journal of Ethiopian Studies*, Vol. 4, No. 1 (2009), pp. 55–83.

Cerulli, Enrico. *Etiopi in Palestina.* Rome: Libreria de Lo Stato, 1943–1947.

———. *L'Islam di Ieri e di Oggi.* Rome: Istituto per l'Oriente, 1971.

———. *Storia della letteratura Etiopica.* Milan: Nuova accademia editrice, 1956.

Clapham, Christopher. "The Ethiopian Coup d'Etat of December 1960." *Journal of Modern African Studies*, Vol. 6 (1968), pp. 495–507.

———. *Haile Selassie's Government.* London: Longman's, 1969.

Clarke, J. Calvitt. *Alliance of the Colored Peoples: Ethiopia and Japan Before World War II.* Woodbridge, UK: James Currey, 2011.

Cohen, John M. "Ethiopia After Haile Selassie: The Government Land Factor." *African Affairs*, Vol. 72 (October 1973), pp. 365–382.

Conti Rossini, Carlo. *Storia d'Etiopia.* Milan: A. Lucini, 1928.

Cuoq, Joseph. *L'Islam en Ethiopie: des origines au XVIe siècle.* Paris: Nouvelles Editions Latines, 1981.

Damblain, Marie. *La tragedie du negus.* Paris: Presses de la Cite, 1977.

De Bono, Emilio. *Anno XIII: The Conquest of an Empire.* London: Cresset Press, 1937.

De Waal, Alexander. *Evil Days: Thirty Years of War and Famine in Ethiopia.* New York: Human Rights Watch, 1991.

dei Sabelli, Luca. *Storia di Abissinia.* 4 vols. Rome: Edizioni Roma, 1936–1948.

Del Boca, Angelo. *Gli Italiani in Africa Orientale.* 2 vols. Roma-Bari: A. Mondadori, 1979.

———. *The Negus: The Life and Death of the Last King of Kings* Addis Ababa: Arada Books, 2012. Originally published as *Il negus: Vita e morte dell'ultimo re dei re* (Rome: Laterza, 1995).

Dombrowski, Franz A. *Ethiopia's Access to the Red Sea.* Leiden: Brill, 1985.

Ellingson, Lloyd. "The Emergence of Political Parties in Eritrea." *Journal of African History* 1977, pp. 261–281.

Erlich, Haggai. *Alliance and Alienation: Ethiopia and Israel During Haile Selassie's Time.* Trenton, NJ: Red Sea Press, 2014.

———. *The Cross and the River: Ethiopia, Egypt, and the Nile.* Boulder: Lynne Rienner Publishers, 2002.

———. "The Egyptian Teachers of Ethiopia." In *Athiopien zwichen Orient und Okzident,* by Walter Raunig and Asfa-Wossen Asserate, eds. Pp. 117–138. Munster: LIT Verlag, 2004.

———. *Ethiopia and the Challenge of Independence.* Boulder: Lynne Rienner Publishers, 1986.

———. "Ethiopia and Egypt: Ras Tafari in Cairo, 1924." *Aethiopica*, Vol. 1 (1998), pp. 64–84.

———. *Ethiopia and Eritrea: Ras Alula, 1875–1897.* East Lansing: Michigan State University Press, 1982.

———. *Ethiopia and the Middle East.* Boulder: Lynne Rienner Publishers, 1994.

———. "Identity and Church: Ethiopian-Egyptian Dialogue, 1924–1959." *International Journal of Middle Eastern Studies*, Vol. 32 (2000), pp. 23–46.

———. *Islam and Christianity in the Horn of Africa, Somalia, Ethiopia, Sudan.* Boulder: Lynne Rienner Publishers, 2010.

———. "Mussolini and the Middle East in the 1920s: The Restrained Imperialist." In *The Great Powers in the Middle East, 1919–1939,* edited by Uriel Dann, pp. 213–221. New York: Holmes and Meier, 1988.

———. *Saudi Arabia and Ethiopia: Islam, Christianity, and Politics Entwined.* Boulder: Lynne Rienner Publishers, 2007.

———. *The Struggle Over Eritrea, 1962–1978.* Stanford, CA: Hoover Institution, 1983.

Erlich, Haggai, Steven Kaplan, and Hagar Salamon. *Ethiopia: Christianity, Islam, Judaism.* Tel Aviv: Open University Press, 2003 (in Hebrew).

Ermias Sable Selassie. *The Wise Mind of Emperor Haile Selassie.* Barnsley, UK: Frontline Books, 2004.

Eshcoli, A. Z. *Abyssinia: People, Country, Culture, History, and Politics.* Jerusalem: Skira 1935 (in Hebrew).

Eshete, Tibebe. *Growing Through the Storms: The History of the Evangelical Movement in Ethiopia 1941–1991.* East Lansing: Michigan State University Press, 2005; digital 2017.

Fallaci, Oriana. *Interview with History.* Boston: Houghton Mifflin, 1977.

———. *Intervista con la storia.* Milan: Rizzoli, 1981.

Ficquet, Eloi, and Wolbert Smidt, eds. *The Life and Times of Lij Iyasu of Ethiopia: New Insights.* Munster: LIT Verlag, 2014.

Fuller, J. F. C. (John Frederick Charles). *The First of the League's Wars.* London: Eyre and Spottiswoode, 1936.

Gaitachew, Bekele. *The Emperor's Clothes: A Personal Viewpoint on Politics and Administration in the Imperial Ethiopian Government.* East Lansing: Michigan State University Press, 1993.

Getachew, Indrias. *Beyond the Throne: The Enduring Legacy of Emperor Haile Selassie I.* Addis Ababa: Shama Books, 2001.

Ghith, Fathi. *Al-Islam wal-habasha `ibra al-ta'rikh.* Cairo, 1967.

Gilkes, Patrick. *The Dying Lion: Feudalism and Modernization in Ethiopia.* London: J. Friedmann, 1975.

Greenfield, Richard. *Ethiopia: A New Political History.* London: Pall Mall Press, 1965. Jerusalem: Haberman Institute, 2011 (in Hebrew).

Habashi, Sadiq, al-. *Ithyubya fi 'asriha al-dhahabi, fi 'asr Hayla Silasi al-Awwal.* Cairo: 1954.

Haber, Lutz. "The Emperor Haile Selassie I in Bath 1936–1940" In *Bath History,* Vol. 3, edited by Trevor Fawcett. London: 1990.

Habte Selassie, Bereket. *Conflict and Intervention in the Horn of Africa.* New York: Monthly Review Press, 1980.

Habte-Wold, Aklilu. *Aklilu Remembers.* Addis Ababa: Addis Ababa University Press, 2010.

Haile Selassie. *Selected Speeches of Haile Selassie.* New York: CreateSpace Independent Publishing Platform, 2000.

Haile Selassie. *Selected Speeches of His Imperial Majesty Haile Selassie First, 1918 to 1967.* Addis Ababa: One Drop Books, 1967.

Haregot, Seyoum A. *The Bureaucratic Empire: Serving Emperor Haile Selassie.* Trenton, NJ: Red Sea Press, 2013.

Hayla-Giorgis, Gra-geta. *Zenahu Lele'ul Ras Mekwennin.* Addis Ababa: Addis Ababa University Press, 1965.

Henze, Paul B. *Layers of Time: A History of Ethiopia.* London: Hurst, 2000.

Heruy Walda-Selassie. *Dastana Kibr.* Addis Ababa: Berhanena Selam, 1924.

————. *Experiencing and Seeing It All.* Addis Ababa: Berhanena Selam, 1934 (in Amharic).

Hess, Robert L. *Ethiopia: The Modernization of Autocracy.* Ithaca, NY: Cornell University Press, 1970.

————. *Italian Colonialism in Somalia.* Chicago: University of Chicago Press, 1966.

Huss, Mahmud, al-. *Ithyubya fi 'ahd Hayla Silasi al-awwal.* Beirut, 1960.

Iadarola, Antoinette. "Ethiopia's Admission into the League of Nations: An Assessment of Motives." *International Journal of African Historical Studies,* Vol. 8 (1975), pp. 601–622.

Imru Haile Selassie. *Kayahut mastawsau.* Addis Ababa: Addis Ababa University Press, 2010.

Ithyubi, Abu Ahmad al-. *Al-Islam al-jarih fi al-Habasha.* Addis Ababa: 1960.

Iyob, Ruth. *The Eritrean Struggle for Independence: Domination, Resistance, Nationalism, 1941–1993.* Cambridge: Cambridge University Press, 1995.

Jalata, Asafa. *Oromia and Ethiopia: State Formation and Ethnonational Conflict, 1868–1992.* Boulder: Lynne Rienner Publishers, 1993.

Jardine, Douglas. *Mad Mullah of Somaliland.* London: H. Jenkins, 1923.

Jembere, Aberra. "Aklilu Habtawald." *Encyclopaedia Aethiopica,* Vol. 1, 2003, pp. 170–172.

————. "Balay Zallaka." *Encyclopaedia Aethiopica,* Vol. 1, 2003, p. 456.

————. "Katama Yifru." *Encyclopaedia Aethiopica,* Vol. 3, 2007, pp. 359–360.

Kabha, Mustafa, and Haggai Erlich. "Al-Ahbash and Wahhabiyya: Interpretations of Islam." *International Journal of Middle East Studies,* Vol. 38 (2006), pp. 519–538.

Kaplan, Steven. "Christianity: Imperial Religion Between Hegemony and Diversity." In *Ethiopia: Christianity, Islam, Judaism,* edited by Haggai Erlich, pp. 17–138. Tel Aviv: Open University Press, 2003 (in Hebrew).

Kapuscinski, Ryszard. *The Emperor: Downfall of an Autocrat.* New York: Vingate Books, 1978.

Konovaloff, T. *Con le armate del negus: Diarie e memoria,* Bologna: Zanichelli, 1938.

Lefebvre, Jeffrey Allan. *Arms for the Horn: U.S. Security Policy in Ethiopia and Somalia, 1953–1991.* PA: University of Pittsburgh Press, 1991.

Legum, Colin, ed. *Africa Contemporary Record: Annual Survey and Documents.* Various volumes. London.

Levine, Donald. "Haile Selassie's Ethiopia: Myth or Reality?" *Africa Today,* May 1961, pp. 11–14.

Lockot, Hans Wilhelm. *The Mission: The Life, Reign, and Character of Haile Selassie I.* London: Hurst, 1989.

Mack, Douglas R. A. *From Babylon to Rastafari: Origin and History of the Rastafarian Movement.* Chicago: Research Associates, School Times Publications, 1999.

Maki, Momoka. "Wayyana." *Encyclopaedia Aethiopica,* Vol. 4 (2010), pp. 1164–1166.

————. "The Wayyane in Tigray and the Reconstruction of the Ethiopia Government in the 1940s." *Proceedings of the 16th International Conference of Ethiopian Studies,* Vol. 2, edited by Svein Ege, Harald Aspen, Birhanu Teferra, and Shiferaw Bekele, pp 665–664. Trondheim: Norwegian University of Science and Technology, 2009.

Makuriya, Takla-Sadiq. *Yaityupya tarik ka'atse Tewodros eska qadmawi Hayla Se-lase.* Addis Ababa: Berhanena Selam, 1967–1968.

Mandela, Nelson. *A Long Walk to Freedom: The Autobiography of Nelson Mandela.* Boston,: Little, Brown, 1994.

Marcus, Harold. *Ethiopia, Great Britain, and the United States, 1941–1974.* Berkeley: University of California Press, 1983.

———. *Haile Selassie I: The Formative Years, 1892–1936.* Berkeley: University of California Press, 1987.

———. *A History of Ethiopia.* Berkeley: University of California Press 1994.

———. *Life and Times of Menelik II, Ethiopia 1844–1913.* New York: Oxford University Press, 1975.

———. The *Politics of Empire: Ethiopia, Great Britain, and the United States, 1941–1974.* Lawrenceville, NJ: Red Sea Press, 1995.

———. "Prejudice and Ignorance in Reviewing Books About Africa: The Strange Case of Ryszard Kapuscinski's *The Emperor.*" *History of Africa,* Vol. 17 (1990), pp. 373–378.

———, ed. *My Life and Ethiopia's Progress: Haile Sellassie I, King of Ethiopia.* East Lansing: Michigan State University Press, 1994.

Marein, Nathan. *The Ethiopian Empire Federation and Laws.* Rotterdam: Royal Netherlands Print and Lithographing, 1955.

Markakis, John. *Ethiopia: Anatomy of a Traditional Polity.* Oxford: Clarendon Press, 1974.

———. *Ethiopia: The Last Two Frontiers.* Woodbridge, UK: James Currey, 2011.

McCann, James. "Ethiopia, Britain and the Negotiations for the Lake Tana Dam, 1922–1935." *International Journal of African Historical Studies,* Vol. 14 (1981), pp. 667–699.

McPherson, Ras E.S.P. *From Rastaology to Pan Ethiopianization.* Bloomington, IN: Authorhouse, 2008.

Ministry of Information. *Important Utterances of H.I.M. Emperor Haile Selassie I, 1963–1972.* Addis Ababa: Ministry of Information, 1972.

Miran, Jonathan. "A Historical Overview of Islam in Eritrea." *Die Welt des Islams,* Vol. 2 (2005), pp. 177–215.

Mockler, Anthony. *Haile Selassie's War: The Italian-Ethiopian Campaign 1935–1941.* New York: Random House, 1984.

Mosley, Leonard. *Haile Selassie: The Conquering Lion.* London: Weidenfeld and Nicolson, 1964.

Negash, Tekeste. *Eritrea and Ethiopia: The Federal Experience.* Piscataway, NJ: Transaction, 1997.

Oded, Arye. *Africa and Israel: A Unique Case of Radical Changes in Israel's Foreign Relations.* Jerusalem: Magnes Press, 2011 (in Hebrew).

Omar, Mohamed. *History of Somalia, 1827–1977.* New Delhi: Somali Publications, 2001.

Pankhurst, Richard. *Economic History of Ethiopia 1800–1935.* Addis Ababa: Haile Selassie I University Press, 1968.

———. *The Ethiopians: A History.* Oxford: Blackwell, 2001.

———. *The History of Famine and Epidemics in Ethiopia, Prior to the Twentieth Century.* Addis Ababa: Relief and Rehabilitation Commission, 1985.

———. "Lions as Royal Symbol." *Encyclopaedia Aethiopica,* Vol. 3, 2007, pp. 573–575.

Pankhurst, Richard, and Rita Pankhurst. *Ethiopian Reminiscences.* Addis Ababa: Tsehai Publishers, 2013.

Parnell, Anjahli. *The Biography of Empress Mennen Asfaw: The Mother of the Ethiopian Nation.* Kealakekua, HI: Roots Publishing, 2011.

Perham, Margery. *The Government of Ethiopia.* London: Faber and Faber, 1969.

Petrides, Pierre. *Le Heros d'Adoua: Ras Makonnen, Prince d'Ethiopie.* Paris: E. Plon, 1963.

Ras Nathaniel. *50th Anniversary of His Imperial Majesty Haile Selassie I First Visit to the United States.* Victoria, Canada: Trafford Publishing, 2004.

Reta, Zewde. *Tafari Makonnen razmu yasultan guzu.* Addis Ababa: Shama Books, 2005.

———. *Yaqadamawi Haile Selassie Mengest.* Addis Ababa: Shama Books, 2012.

Rubinkowska, Hanna. *Ethiopia on the Verge of Modernity: The Transfer of Power During Zewditu's Reign, 1916–1930.* Warsaw: Agade Publishing, 2010.

———. "History That Never Was: Historiography by Haile Selassie." In *Studia Ethiopia: Essays in Honor of Siegbert Uhlig,* edited by Verena Boll, pp. 221–231. Wiesbaden: Harrassowitz Verlag, 2004.

———. "New Structure of Power: The Message Revealed by the Coronation of Zawditu (1917)." *Annales d'Éthiopie,* Vol. 28 (2013), pp. 19–44.

———. "Tananna Wark Hayla Selasse." *Encyclopaedia Aethiopica,* Vol. 4, 2010, pp. 858–859.

Sabbe, Osman Saleh. *Ta'rikh irtirya.* Beirut: 1974.

Samnoy, Ashlid. "Organization of African Unity." *Encyclopaedia Aethiopica,* Vol. 4, pp. 50–52. 2010.

Sandford, Christine. *Ethiopia Under Haile Selassie.* London: J. M. Dent, 1946.

———. *The Lion of Judah Hath Prevailed: Being the Biography of His Imperial Majesty Haile Selassie I.* London: J. M. Dent, 1955.

Sbacchi, Alberto. *Ethiopia Under Mussolini: Fascism and Colonial Experience.* London: Zed Books, 1985.

———. "Italy and the Treatment of the Ethiopian Aristocracy, 1937–1940." *International Journal of African Historical Studies,* Vol. 10 (1977), pp. 209–241.

Scholler, Heinrich. "Constitutions." *Encyclopaedia Aethiopica,* Vol. 1, 2003, pp. 788–791.

Segre, Claudio. "Liberal and Fascist Italy in the Middle East, 1919–1939." In *The Great Powers in the Middle East, 1919–1939,* edited by Uriel Dann, pp. 199–212. New York: Holmes and Meier, 1988.

Shinn, David Hamilton, and Thomas P. Ofcansky. *Historical Dictionary of Ethiopia.* Lanham, MD: Scarecrow Press, 2004.

Smith, M. G., Roy Augier, and Rex Nettleford. *The Rastafari Movement in Kingston, Jamaica.* Kingston: University College of the West Indies, 1960.

Spencer, John H. *Ethiopia at Bay: A Personal Account of the Haile Sellassie Years.* Algonac, MI: Reference Publications, 1984.

Steer, George. *Caesar in Abyssinia.* London: Hodder and Stoughton, 1936.

Talbot, David. *Haile Selassie I, Silver Jubilee.* The Hague: Van Stockum and Zomm, 1955.

Tareke, Gebru. *Ethiopia: Power and Protest—Peasant Revolts in the Twentieth Century.* Cambridge: Cambridge University Press, 1991.

Trenkler, Lore. "Life and Work at the Court of Haile Selassie I: Memoirs of Lore Trenkler." https://anglo-ethiopian.org/publications/articles.php?type=L&reference.

Trimingham, John Spencer. *Islam in Ethiopia.* London: F. Cass, 1965.

Tzadua, Paulos. "Fetha Nagast." *Encyclopaedia Aethiopica,* Vol. 2, 2005, pp. 534–535.

Uhlig, Siegbert, et al., eds. *Encyclopaedia Aethiopica,* Vol. 1: A–C. Wiesbaden: Harrassowitz Verlag, 2003.

———. *Encyclopaedia Aethiopica,* Vol. 2: D–Ha. Wiesbaden: Harrassowitz Verlag, 2005.

———. *Encyclopaedia Aethiopica,* Vol. 3: He–N. Wiesbaden: Harrassowitz Verlag, 2007.

Uhlig, Siegbert, and Alessandro Bausi, et al., eds. *Encyclopaedia Aethiopica,* Vol. 4: O–X. Wiesbaden: Harrassowitz Verlag, 2010.

————. *Encyclopaedia Aethiopica*, Vol. 5: Y–Z, Supplementa, Addenda et Corrigenda, Maps, Index. Wiesbaden: Harrassowitz Verlag, 2014.

Ullendorff, Edward, ed. *The Autobiography of Emperor Haile Sellassie, 1892–1937*. New York: Oxford University Press, 1976.

————. *Ethiopia and the Bible*. London: Oxford University Press, 1968.

————. "Haile Selassie at Seventy." *Times* (London), July 23, 1962.

Vestal, Theodore M. *The Lion of Judah in the New World*. Santa Barbara, CA: Praeger, 2011.

————. "Peace Corps." *Encyclopaedia Aethiopica*, Vol. 4, 2010, pp. 127–128.

Zabiyan, Muhammad. *Al-habasha al-muslima*. Damascus: 1937.

Zabolotskikh, M. "Takla Hawaryat Takla Mariam." *Encyclopaedia Aethiopica*, Vol. 4 (2010), pp. 829–830.

Zewde, Bahru. "A Century of Ethiopian Historiography." *Journal of Ethiopian Studies*, Vol. 2 (2000), pp. 1–26.

————. *A History of Modern Ethiopia, 1855–1991*. Athens: Ohio University Press, 2001.

————. *Pioneers of Change in Ethiopia: The Reformist Intellectuals of the Early Twentieth Century*. Oxford: J. Currey, 2002.

Zoli, Corrado. *Cronache Ethiopiche*. Rome: Sindacato Italiano, 19. 1930.

————. *Etiopia d'Oggi*, Rome: Societa Anonoma Italiana Arti Grafiche, 1935.

Dissertations and Theses

Carmichael, Tim. *Approaching Ethiopian History: Addis Ababa and Local Governance in Harar, c. 1910 to 1950*. PhD dissertation, Michigan State University, 2001.

Kendie, Daniel. *The External and Internal Dimensions of the Eritrean Conflict*. PhD dissertation, Michigan State University, 1994.

Teshome, Fasil. *The History of Menelik II School, 1907–1962*. BA thesis, Addis Ababa University, College of Social Sciences, June 1986.

YouTube Guide

~

For YouTube documentaries, Google the following:

Chapter 1: A Political Icon
HIM. Haile Selassie, the Lion of Judah (full documentary)
Man of the Millennium—History of his imperial majesty Haile Selassie, parts
   1–8
Billy Graham presents HIM Emperor Haile Selassie I of Ethiopia, World
   Congress on Evangelism, Berlin, October 26, 1966
Christmas in Ethiopia, Children of the Emperor
Bob Marley—Selassie Is the Chapel
Faces Of Africa—Haile Selassie: The pillar of Ethiopia, 2 parts

Chapter 2: In Father's Shadow
First Italo-Ethiopian War, 3 Minute History
The First Italo-Ethiopian War (1894–1896): Every Fortnight
The Biography of Ras Mekonnen Wolde Mikael (1852–1906), chapters 1–6

Chapter 3: The Road to Power
Zewditu, Empress of Ethiopia
Empress Mennen Asfaw, b. March 25
Her Imperial Majesty Empress Mennen Asfaw

Chapter 4: The Crown
1930 Addis Ababa celebrates the coronation of H.I.M. Emperor Haile Selassie I
Ethiopia coronation 1930 Haile Selassie

HIM Haile Selassie I coronation 1930, Addis Abeba St. George Church
Remembering Belaten Geta Hiruy Woldeselassie
The King of Kings and His army, 1934, historical, by Walter Mittelholzer
Walter Mittelholzer arriving in Addis Ababa to deliver air crafts for Emperor
   Haile Selassie 1934

Chapter 5: Facing Mussolini
Abyssinia Crisis, 1935–1936
Haile Selassie I Ethiopia's war preparation service 1934–1935
Addis Ababa (1935)
Ethiopia prepares for war against Italy/war hist ethnic
Ethiopia 1935—Ethiopians preparing for war against Italian invaders
[Wars] The Second Italo-Ethiopian War (1935–1936): Every day
Lion of Judah War with Ethiopia 1935 1936, parts 1–8
Italian invasion of Ethiopia (1935–1936)
Italian Ethiopian War footage 1935–1936
Ras Gugsa joins in march on Makale
Haile Selassie Gugsa & Bandas of Tigrai 1930s

Chapter 6: From Refugee to Liberator
Jerusalem Emperor attends Abyssinian Church mass 1936
Emperor Haile Selassie I of Ethiopia and Princess in Jerusalem
Haile Selassie in London after sea trip via Gibraltar
Footsteps of the Emperor Haile Selassie 1st's exile to Bath (FULL)
Stock footage, 1936 news: Emperor Haile Selassie of Ethiopia addresses League
   of Nations
Historic appeal to the League of Nations: Read by Dan Tafari
World War 2 in East Africa: Every day
The Ethiopian patriots, Ras Abebe Aregai, Ark of the Covenant & the emperor
   returns
Haile Selassie enters Addis Ababa (1941)
The Truth about May 5th, the day that changed the world forever!
Haile Selassie returns and death of Mussolini

Chapter 7: Absolutism
Haile Selassie's new army
US President Franklin Roosevelt and Ethiopian Emperor Haile Selassie aboard
   USS Q...HD stock footage
Haile Selassie at military academy, no sound
Haile Selassie accepts Eritrea (1952)
Haile Selassie state visit to Eritrea (1952)

Chapter 8: The Road to Loneliness
Abyssinians off to Korea (1951)
Ethiopia in the world—Korean War and United States relations
Haile Selassie visits America (1954)
Haile Selassie sightseeing in New York (1954)

Ethiopian Emperor Haile Selassie the First visits UK (1954)
Queen greets Haile Selassie (1954)
Ethiopia's New Deal (1955)
25th anniversary of the coronation of Haile Selassie.mp4
Ethiopia, Africa's ancient kingdom, 1961
General Mengistu Neway caught and hanged (no sound)

Chapter 9: We Are Not God
Dr. Nkrumah and Emperor Haile Selassie, 1958
Episodes in the life and times of Emperor Haile Selassie
Conference towards African unity (1963)
CAN 24 4-11-63 Emperor Haile Selassie visits President Nasser
Haile Selassie's second state visit to the United States, October 1963
Bob Marley and Haile Selassie speech
The visit of Emperor Haile Selassie to Jamaica
Haile Selassie April 21, 1966, state visit to Jamaica
Bob Marley about reggae, Haile Selassie, Marcus Garvey, Ethiopia, Rasta, Africa
Bob Marley, "Lion of Judah" live
Bob Marley & The Wailers, "Iron Lion Zion" (RE-AFT remix)

Chapter 10: Nothing New Under the Sun
SYND 06/06/70 Haile Selassie greeted by Nasser
Rare speech of King Haile Selassie the responsibility of African youth
Ethiopia in the early 70s, Parts 1–2: Student movement, the Monarchy
Neftegna Amhara dictator for life (50+years), Haile Selassie 1973
SELASSIE I Tempted by devil & Ms. Oriana Fallaci?! Asks #RasTafari Disciple
    #LionOfJudah @LOJSociety

Chapter 11: Revolution
SYND 6/3/1973 President Numeiri and Haile Selassie at Unity Day
SYND 12 5 73 Haile Selassie one-day visit to Cairo
SYND 18 5 73 Emperor Haile Selassie opens OAU session
September 12, 1974, Last public words of Emperor Haile Selassie I
The truth about Haile Selassie I stolen money exposed by the head of the
    Ethiopian National Bank

Chapter 12: The Burial of a Donkey
SYND 19 9 74 Students demos against Haile Selassie continue
SYND 21 9 74 Acting head of state Aman Andom press conference
Ethiopia: On the evening of November 23, 1974, 60 senior officials were
    summarily executed
Mengistu Hailemariam denied killing Imperial Haileselassie
Ethiopia: former emperor Haile Selassie reburied

Index

~

About the Book

~

With scholars far from agreement in their opinions of Ethiopia's Haile Selassie, the questions remain: Who was Haile Selassie? What was the secret of his survival across half a century—and how did he come to be a virtual exile in his own country, then murdered, the last emperor in a centuries-old dynasty?

Haggai Erlich's *Haile Selassie*, full of fresh perspectives and insights, adds much to our understanding of the emperor. Drawing on new archival sources, as well as decades of research on Ethiopia, Erlich tells the multifaceted, sometimes tragic, story not only of a single individual but also of modern Ethiopia both domestically and in world affairs.

Haggai Erlich is professor emeritus of Middle East and African history at Tel Aviv University. His numerous publications on Ethiopia include *Saudi Arabia and Ethiopia: Islam, Christianity, and Politics Entwined* and *The Cross and the River: Ethiopia, Egypt, and the Nile*.